Zenith

A Postcard Perspective of Historic Duluth

Tony Dierckins

Duluth, Minnesota

X-communication
The Garfield News Building
1604 West Superior Street
Duluth, Minnesota 55806
218-722-7565
www.x-communication.org

Zenith: A Postcard Perspective of Historic Duluth

Text, research, cover design, and interior design and layout by Tony Dierckins.
Further research by Maryanne Norton with assistance from Melissa Estlow.
Copy editing and editorial guidance by Scott Pearson.
Proofreading by Kerry Elliott and Chris Godsey.

Hardcover edition front endpapers: *Duluth, Minn. 1883* bird's-eye etching by Henry Wellge.
Hardcover edition back endpapers: *Superior, Wis. 1883* bird's-eye etching by Henry Wellge.

Nearly all of the postcard images in this book come from the private collection of Jerry Paulson.
A complete list of image credits appears on page 197.

First Edition, 2006
06 07 08 09 10 • 5 4 3 2 1

Library of Congress Control Number: 2005939217

Softcover ISBNs: 1-887317-30-9, 978-1-887317-30-6
Hardcover ISBNs: 1-887317-29-5, 978-1-887317-29-0

Printed in Singapore by Tien Wah Press.

The hardcover version of this book is from a limited press run of 350 slipcovered editions available exclusively through the publisher.

For L.A.H., my very favorite thing about Duluth (and everywhere else, for that matter).
— T. J. D.

➤

Without the generosity of postcard collectors Jerry Paulson, Bob Swanfeld,
Tom Kasper, and others, there wouldn't be much in these pages to look at;
and lacking the help of researcher Maryanne Norton and those who
assisted her, well, the text of this volume wouldn't be much worth reading.
This book is as much a reflection of their passions as it is of the author's efforts.

➤

The author would like to thank…

Laura Jacobs of the Lake Superior Maritime Collection;
Pat Maus of the Northeast Minnesota Historical Center;
Kris Aho and all her colleagues at the Duluth Public Library;
Teddie Meronek and all her colleagues at the Superior Public Library;
Grace Goh, Martha Oresman, and their colleagues at TWP America;
Carol Bock, Marty Sozansky, and UMD's English and Composition Departments;
Emily Aldrich, Kent Aldrich, Kerry Elliott, Melissa Estlow, Chris Godsey,
Adam Guggemos, Tod Hilde, Tom Kasper, Mildred Nimmo, Maryanne Norton,
Joel Ness, Jerry Paulson, Scott Pearson, and Bob Swanfeld.

Contents

Opposite page: A rare oversized linen postcard of Gooseberry Falls, printed some time between 1930 and 1945.

DELIVERING MAIL ON MINNESOTA POINT IN WINTER,
DULUTH, MINN.

No. 667.   V. O. Hammon Pub. Co., Minneapolis and Chicago

While one can't be sure about rain, heat, or gloom of night, it's obvious that snow did not stay this courier from the swift completion of his appointed rounds—in this case delivering mail (including, no doubt, some postcards) to snowed-in Park Point residents on Duluth's Minnesota Point some time between 1907 and 1915.

Preface: A Short Chronology of the Postcard

As its title suggests, this book is a look at the bygone days of Duluth (and its surrounding communities) through the imagery of vintage postcards. Obviously a book driven by postcard images cannot cover Duluth's entire history, because of course not every aspect of the region's past has been documented on a postcard. (Several of the volumes listed in this book's "References" section provide more detailed, academic accounts of the events that shaped the region.) But this book is as much a look at historic postcards from a Duluth perspective as it is a postcard perspective of historic Duluth and the western Lake Superior region—and the history of postcards, much like the area's history, is not as simple as one might think.

Some say postcards got their start in Germany, when, at the Austro-German Postal Conference of 1865, German postal Official Heinrich von Stephan introduced the "open post sheet." But according to postcard historian Stefano Neis, the earliest patent for a postal card belonged to John P. Charlton of Philadelphia in 1861 and was later transferred to H. P. Lipman. Lipman's "postal cards" were hardly postcards as we think of them today: they had no pictures, just a decorative border. But Neis also points out that the earliest-known postcard is postmarked "Dec. 1848"—apparently historians still have a large gap to fill. Whatever the case, in 1869 Austria began allowing privately produced "postcards," and the following year picture postcards slowly became popular all across Europe. By 1873 governments across Europe began issuing their own "postals," cards pre-printed with postage.

The postcard's **Pioneer Era** includes cards printed prior to 1898. The first of these cards in the U.S. were sold at Chicago's Columbia Exposition of 1893 and featured many of the expo's buildings. Outside of the Chicago

The back of a Private Mailing Card, in use between 1898 and 1901—no message was allowed on the back of the card.

expo, most Pioneer Era postcards featured large eastern cities. Only the federal government was allowed to use the word "postcard" on the card's back; privately published cards had to use terms such as "souvenir card" or "correspondence card." The government preprinted its cards with one-cent stamps featuring Thomas Jefferson or Ulysses S. Grant; private cards required a two-cent stamp.

Congress ushered in the **Private Mailing Card Era** (1898–December 24, 1901) when it granted private printers the right to print their own cards with the inscription "Private Mailing Card." You can recognize a PMC by the fact that its back is not divided into message and address sections. In fact, until 1907 regulations would not allow senders to write anything more than an address on the back of the postcard; messages appeared only on the front (so when you see a card in this book with space for writing on the front, you will know it was printed before 1907).

Christmas Eve 1901 saw the first card of the **Undivided Back Era**, which lasted until March 1, 1907. Since earlier cards already used the undivided back, the significant change was that the government now allowed private printers to use "postcard" or "post card" (one or two words) on the cards. During this time post-

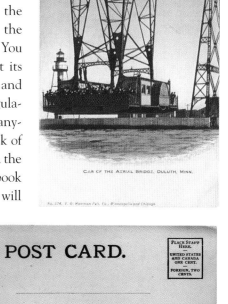

CAR OF THE AERIAL BRIDGE, DULUTH, MINN.

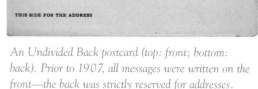

An Undivided Back postcard (top: front; bottom: back). Prior to 1907, all messages were written on the front—the back was strictly reserved for addresses.

A Divided Back postcard, distinguished by borderless printing on the card's front (top); starting in March 1907, changes in federal regulations allowed senders to write both message and address on the card's back.

Duluth's Carnegie Library, actually made of Lake Superior Brownstone, mistakenly portrayed as a marble structure in this miscolored Undivided Back card.

card popularity exploded, with sales doubling almost every six months. Kodak's "postcard" camera made it easy for anyone to make black-and-white postcards—the negatives were postcard size, and each camera came with a stylus that allowed the user to inscribe descriptions directly on the negative. (Many of the cards featured in the "Unfortunate Events" section were no doubt made using these cameras.)

The **Divided Back Era** (March 1, 1907–1915) is known as the golden age of postcards and featured the format we still see today: an image on the front, with the left side of the back reserved for a message and the right side for the recipient's address. Most of the cards from this era were printed in Germany because its lithographic printing technology was by far the most advanced on the planet. The lithography process made it possible to colorize black-and-white photos. Because many of the artists coloring the images had never seen the original subject, they relied on photographers' notes to determine colors.

Nevertheless, they often got the colors wrong, as in the image of Duluth's Carnegie Library on this page. Colorists also sometimes took liberties to make a card more vibrant, such as including stunning sunrises or sunsets on cards of views facing north or south. Even the photographers themselves used artistic license—note Hugh McKenzie's 1910 photo, allegedly of Halley's Comet passing over Duluth (see page 127), and an anonymous photographer's doctored image of "a winter residence on Minnesota Point" (see page 97).

It took a war to diminish the postcard's popularity. World War I ended the supply of cards from Germany, and U.S. and English printers began providing cards made using printing techniques inferior to those used by the Germans. At the same time the telephone became affordable to more people, decreasing the practical need for postcards. Postcard collecting as a hobby also declined rapidly. By killing the German publishing industry, World War I also gave birth to the **White Border Era** (1915– 1930). To save ink, a white border was left around "view" cards, giving the era its name. Cards from this era are marked not only by their white border, but also by the often poor image quality, for which increased costs and

A White Border postcard, produced some time between 1915 and 1930.

A "Real Photo" postcard of the Interstate Bridge, produced not through the lithographic printing process but with a rotary drum imprinter.

A Linen postcard, distinguished by the card's "rag" content and vibrant colors.

inexperienced labor were blamed. This time also saw the advent of the "Real Photo" postcard, produced not by lithography but by rotary drum imprinters. Produced in great volume, these cards gave traditional lithographic card publishers more competition than they could handle.

New printing processes in America revived postcards by allowing them to be printed on paper containing high "rag" (cotton) content—and so began the **Linen Era** (1930–1945). The new paper gave the cards a textured feel and also allowed the use of vibrant inks, making them the most colorful lithographic cards produced in America. With the advent of photochrome postcards in 1939, however, lithographic postcard publishers began to fade away, and most were gone or had converted to photochrome by 1945 (a few in the South hung on through the 1950s). The fading of vintage postcard lithography happened to correspond with major changes in Duluth's economy: after World War II, with the lumber and commercial fishing industries long dead, shipbuilding would once again be mothballed and mining on the Iron Range would begin its slow descent.

The Union Oil Company introduced the **Photochrome Era** in 1939, when it started selling the new cards at its western service stations. These cards looked like actual photographs, and today's postcards are produced using essentially the same method. Except for the example of the *Edmund Fitzgerald* on this page, this book contains no photochrome cards. Indeed, outside of the rare white-bordered linen postcard of the ore boat *Wilfred Sykes* (built in 1949), all of the cards in this book were printed before 1940.

The most recent postcard of Duluth itself features Enger Tower, which was built in 1939—the same year the Incline Railway was torn down—the end of an era for Duluth as well as vintage postcards, and a fitting year to end the historic scope of this book.

So by noting whether a card includes a border, looks

This postcard of the infamous Edmund Fitzgerald *is an example of Photochrome cards, which were first made in 1939 and closed the book on lithographic postcards.*

fairly realistic, or includes vibrant colors and a textured background, you can tell which era it represents—but this does not identify the year the image was first captured. Many cards carry a postmark, but that only indicates the year they were mailed. Few cards include a copyright date, and those that do often give the year a card was first printed, not necessarily the year the picture was taken—a caption on one of the scenes of Duluth in 1871 (page 110) indicates that it wasn't published until 1908. And many of the same images were printed by different publishers over the years, so it is not uncommon to find an identical image first appearing in Germany in the early part of the century then reproduced as a linen card in the 1930s.

Because of these reasons, this book does not attempt to list the year each card represents unless it was clearly indicated on the card itself. The cards are also intentionally reproduced "as is"—that is, in the condition they came to me from their collectors, no matter if a card looked like it just came off the press or had been roughed up from years of handling or a tough trip through the postal system. Rather than worry about details such as those, I hope you simply enjoy, as I did, each postcard's unique perspective as it brings to life the region's colorful history.

This painting by Clarence Rozenkranz depicts Daniel Greysolon Sieur du Lhut and his French and Ojibwe companions greeting a party of Dakota at Little Portage, where today the Duluth Ship Canal slices through Minnesota Point, in June of 1679. In 1856 city founders would name their fledgling township after the French soldier and explorer.

An Extremely Brief History of Duluth from the Last Ice Age to 1939

Back in the day, those who wanted to take in the postcard view from Duluth's Skyline Parkway would have found themselves standing on the beach of what geologists now call Glacial Lake Duluth, five hundred feet above the surface of today's Lake Superior. Of course, that was at the end of the last Great Ice Age, roughly ten thousand years before postcards and parkways, when the runoff from melting glaciers, filling the huge gouges the glaciers had carved on their frozen journey south, became the Great Lakes. Over a thousand years or so, Glacial Lake Duluth drained down to the level of Lake Superior as the glacial dam to the northeast melted away. There were other big changes, too. By the end of this period the giant mammals that once roamed the region would be extinct, robbing contemporary Duluthians of the chance to live with woolly mammoths and mastodons, giant camels and ground sloths, short-faced bears and saber-toothed cats, and at least one rodent of unusual size: the giant beaver. This prehistoric lumberjack grew to nine feet in length and weighed over five hundred pounds; its smaller, modern cousin would prove pivotal to the region's history (and would be much easier to trap).

Early Residents

Few sightseers lived in the region when the glaciers receded. From the end of the Great Ice Age until about 5,000 B.C., the region's human population consisted of small bands of Paleo-Indian cultures that hunted deer, elk, and caribou—and likely some leftover oversized mammals—with stone projectile points. Those hunters gave way to Eastern Archaic peoples, who thrived in the Great Lakes area until about 1,000 B.C. This group developed into a variety of cultures, including the Old Copper peoples who mined for copper on Michigan's Upper Peninsula and Isle Royale and refined the stone-working methods of their predecessors. The Eastern Archaic peoples gave way to the Woodland cultures, who made pottery and buried their dead in mounds and populated the area until roughly A.D. 1600. While these folks still hunted for bison and the like, they also found stable food sources such as wild rice, which allowed them to form permanent villages.

As the Woodland cultures died out, the area became populated with the Dakota, meaning "friend" or "alliance of friends." French explorer Jean Nicollet called the Dakota *Naudowasewug*, "the snake," which pluralized in French is *Nadouessioux*, from which the term "Sioux" derives. (Descendants of these people today prefer Dakota.) It is unknown if the Dakota migrated to the area or descended from the Woodland Indians or even tribes from the Old Copper culture, but by the time folks like Nicollet showed up, they populated Minnesota's Arrowhead Region.

The Dakota made tools of stone, bone, antler, and wood; hunted bear, buffalo, elk, and deer; fished with spears and hooks; and gathered roots, berries, and wild rice. Historian Theodore Blegen describes the Dakota as "gregarious lovers of feasts and councils and games and jokes and betting. Eloquence

Described by a historian as "gregarious lovers of feasts and councils and games and jokes and betting," the Dakota were also a spiritual people who regarded highly those with oratory skills. Seth Eastman painted this 1857 depiction of Dakota engaged in a takapsicapi or lacrosse match.

The Ojibwe, who migrated to the Lake Superior region from the "shores of the Great Salt Water in the east," not only hunted and gathered food, but processed it from nature, as shown in this anonymous nineteenth-century watercolor painting of an Ojibwe maple syrup camp.

among them was an art and its exercise by men of wisdom singled them out for leadership in their pipe-smoking councils." Blegen also points out that the Dakota had a "pervading sense of the supernatural." Indeed, mysteries of nature were, to the Dakota, a spirit or *wakan*. They most often directed their worship to *Wakan Tanka*, the Great Spirit that created earth and man.

The Dakota eventually found life at the western edge of Lake Superior too crowded for comfort, as the eastern migration of the Ojibwe brought competition and conflict. The Ojibwe, the largest tribe of the Algonkian peoples (a language group that includes the Potawatomi, Cheyenne, Fox, and Cree), stood fifty thousand strong when Columbus stumbled upon the islands of the Caribbean and opened the door for the coming of Europeans to the Americas. Europeans often called the Ojibwe "Chippewa," which may have occurred from a misunderstanding or mispronunciation. (Ojibwe today also call themselves "Anishanabe," the "real" or "genuine people," which derives from *Anishinaubag*.) A particularly spiritual people, the Ojibwe practiced *Medawe* or *Midewiwin* ("Grand Medicine") religion. According to legend recorded by William W. Warren in the 1850s, the Ojibwe once lived "on the shores of the

Great Salt Water in the east." At one point, as they experienced a period of great suffering, sickness, and death, the Great Spirit sent word through *Manaosho*, a hero figure in Ojibwe culture, to tear down the *Medawe* lodge and head west and north. This set off a migration that lasted centuries, but they had guidance along the way—guidance that came in the form of a sea shell.

Ojibwe oral history recorded by Warren explains that a prophecy told Ojibwe leaders to keep following images of the mengis shell, sacred to their *Medawe* beliefs, until they reached their final destination, a place where "food grows on water." So they would travel until an elder had a vision of the mengis shell, at which point they would stop and rebuild the *Medawe* lodge. Eventually a vision of *Manaosho* would tell them to move on, and they'd tear down the lodge again and head west. They first journeyed to *Moneuang*, today's Montreal, and eventually headed for Lake Huron, then to *Boweting* (Sault Ste. Marie), where Huron meets Lake Superior. After a time they pulled up stakes once more and finally gave the *Medawe* a permanent home on *Moningwunakauning* or "home of the golden-breasted woodpecker," known to Europeans as the island of La Pointe. From their base on *Moningwunakauning* the Ojibwe ventured out and indeed found food growing on the water: *manomin*, better known today as wild rice.

Although revered in society, Ojibwe women led hard lives. Colonel Thomas McKenney described an Ojibwe woman's life as one of "continual labor and unmitigated hardships." Much of that labor was done while caring for small children. The cradle shown could be strapped to the mother's back, allowing her hands to remain free while she carried a child; a hoop around the child's head protected it should the cradle tip over when set on the ground. Eastman Johnson painted Ojibwe Women *(and many others) when he visited Western Lake Superior in 1857.*

(*Moningwunakauning* became Madeline Island after Equaysayway, daughter of Chief White Crane, married Michel Cadotte, a Frenchman, who in 1793 established a trading post at La Pointe; she was baptized a Christian and adopted the name Madeleine, and her father renamed the island in her honor—it is unclear how the spelling changed.)

The Ojibwe separated into four major groups midway through the seventeenth century and began expanding further west. The northern Ojibwe migrated to Lake Superior's north shore; the southwestern Ojibwe populated *Moningwunakauning* and the south shore and, later, Fond du Lac (French for "bottom of the lake") and the interiors of what would become Minnesota and Wisconsin. This westward movement encroached on Dakota territory, and the two great peoples soon found themselves uncomfortable neighbors and, eventually, bitter enemies. The Ojibwe would later replace the Dakota on Lake Superior's western shores and most of Minnesota. While some say the Dakota happily began moving west to the plains, "where the buffalo was plenty," others claim they were pushed west by the superior fighting power of the Ojibwe, who had the advantage of steel-bladed knives, muskets, and gun powder. Why did the Ojibwe have access to European weaponry? Because of the beaver, of course.

Enter the Ever Fashion-Conscious French

From about 1550 until 1850, dandies throughout Europe wouldn't consider stepping outdoors without donning felt hats made from beaver underfur. This fashion trend became so popular that by the end of the sixteenth century,

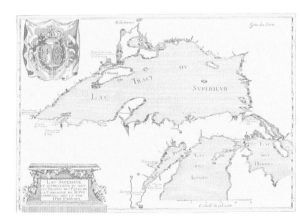

A 1671 Jesuit map (probably by Father Claude Jean Allouez) of Lac Tracy, the name the French gave Lake Superior when they claimed the area as New France (governed by the Marquis Prouville de Tracy). Daniel Greysolon Sieur du Lhut undoubtedly used a similar map when he journeyed to the head of the lakes in 1679 to secure peace between the Dakota and Ojibwe.

trappers had hunted the beaver to extinction in western Europe and nearly wiped the animal out in Scandinavia and Russia as well. So Europeans, particularly the French, looked to the "new world" for fur. Explorers such as Robert de La Salle, Jean Nicollet, Jacques Marquette, Louis Joliet, Pierre Esprit Radisson, and Sieur des Groseilliers—along with Jesuit missionaries including Jacques Marquette, Claude Jean Allouez, and Louis Hennepin—traveled with French soldiers and native guides throughout the Great Lakes area, mapping the region (which they claimed as New France) and opening trade with the various tribes they encountered. Well established at Sault Ste. Marie and La Pointe, the Ojibwe became natural trading partners with the French, providing the much-sought-after beaver pelts in exchange for food, clothing, guns, and ammunition. But the Dakota got in the way. The bitter conflicts between the Dakota and Ojibwe hampered the fur trade, which inconvenienced the French. Europe needed beaver pelts. Something had to be done.

It took a brokenhearted Frenchman to bring the two warring peoples together—for a while, at least. Daniel Greysolon Sieur du Lhut, a lower French nobleman from Saint-Germain-Laval (near Lyons), had first sought to make a name for himself fighting in wars for Louis XIV, but by his early thirties found himself in Quebec, where his brother had gone before him. There he led a relatively quiet life until France called him back to serve in the King's Guard in the Battle of Seneff in Holland, after which he returned to Quebec and seemed prepared to settle down as a gentleman soldier. He apparently found himself romantically involved with the daughter of an important local family, but this affair would not last. Some accounts say du Lhut became "disillusioned" with the relationship. Whatever the case, in 1678, as he approached his fortieth birthday, du Lhut decided to venture into the wilderness of New France with two very lofty goals: bring peace to the warring native peoples living on the shores of Lake Superior (or *Lac Tracy* to the French) and find passage to the Vermilion Sea, a "great lake whose water

The Paris Beau, an example of a hat made from beaver underfur worn in France about 1813. The popularity of beaver hats, more than empire expansion, brought the French to the Lake Superior region in the seventeenth century.

Daniel Greysolon Sieur du Lhut, shown in his hometown of Saint-Germain-Laval, France, when he served as a member of the Royal Guard of Louis XIV, as depicted in this detail of a painting by renowned Duluth artist David Ericson.

is unfit to drink," which du Lhut assumed was the Pacific Ocean. So du Lhut headed west on September 1 with seven of his countrymen and three native guides on a historic quest—perhaps to impress a certain young lady—and in violation of a 1676 decree by the governor of New France prohibiting inland travel and trade.

In June the following year the party landed at Little Portage, where today the Duluth Ship Canal cuts through Minnesota Point. They headed west to Minnesota's Lake Mille Lacs and explored along the Mississippi, and then headed back to Fond du Lac for a meeting of Ojibwe, Dakota, Cree, and Assiniboin peoples on September 15, 1679. The gathering had been arranged by du Lhut, no small logistical task in those days. To secure peace, he also arranged marriages between the peoples and stayed on throughout the winter, encouraging the nations to hunt and feast together, as du Lhut himself put it, "to establish closer bonds of friendship." In the end the Dakota promised to befriend the Ojibwe and the French, and the Ojibwe agreed to facilitate trade between the French and the Dakota. Within three years the Ojibwe and Dakota were conducting trades as far as 150 miles from Lake Superior's shores.

While du Lhut never did continue toward the Vermilion Sea (which turned out to be Utah's Great Salt Lake), and, in fact, never ventured beyond Mille Lacs, he did seek other adventures during his time in Minnesota. He found a water route from Lake Superior to the Mississippi: along the Brule River off Superior's south shore, a mile portage to Lake St. Croix, and then down the St. Croix River to the Mississippi. He took time from his own work to "rescue" Father Louis Hennepin from a group of Dakota—the only problem was that Hennepin had been enjoying his stay. Later, de La Salle, jealous and petty (like many of his compatriots), used the incident to sully du Lhut's reputation, painting him as an adventurer lacking scruples.

Even after his achievements, which also included meting out justice among natives on the frontier, du Lhut made his way back to Montreal in 1681 only to find his reputation marred not only by de La Salle's claims but also by those of others, who said that du Lhut had conducted affairs with the Dakota and Ojibwe solely for personal gain and that he may have even traded with the hated English. Charged with violating the 1676 decree, local authorities had him briefly imprisoned. After his release the king declared a royal amnesty for those who had violated the decree, clearing du Lhut's name in Montreal. He returned to France the following year, cleared up any questions as to his reputation, and headed back to Canada to serve once again as a soldier. He remained a bachelor and on March 17, 1710, succumbed to the gout. The governor of New France sent a brief but poignant message to the king that du Lhut would surely have approved of: "Captain du Lhut died last winter. He was an honest man."

Wars and Treaties

The peace du Lhut established would not last. Ojibwe conflicts with the Dakota beginning in 1736 lasted beyond the French and Indian War, in which the British ultimately defeated the French and their native allies in 1760 (the war officially ended in 1763 with the Treaty of Paris). By 1770 the Ojibwe had all but left La Pointe for the Fond du Lac area and had taken over northern Minnesota. The French and British also continued to clash after their war ended, a battle now fought over beaver pelts as the French-controlled North West Company and the British-run Hudson's Bay Company competed to see who could send home the most hat-making material.

Not long after the Ojibwe took control of the region a bunch of upstart colonists back east held a revolution, kicking out the British and creating the United States of America. In the 1780s the North West Company established Fort St. Louis at the mouth of the St. Louis River; the post became the region's center of trade and remained so until it burned in 1800. In 1809 John Jacob Astor formed the American Fur Company and set up a post at Fond du Lac, only to discover that the Ojibwe preferred to trade with the French and British. The War of 1812 put an end to all that, as the post-war American Congress barred foreigners from trading in American territory. And so in 1816 Astor took over the North West Company's interests and built a new fort at Fond du Lac, handing the reins over to William Morrison.

Astor's outpost became a center of trade and a natural spot for gatherings. In 1826 Michigan territorial governor William Cass and Colonel Thomas L. McKenney, the head of the newly formed U.S. Indian Department (which would later become the Bureau of Indian Affairs), gathered native leaders from throughout the region at Fond du Lac to ratify a treaty designed to both stop fighting among the Ojibwe, Dakota, and other tribes and to establish U.S. dominance in the region. While the treaty established peace and gave the Ojibwe land guarantees, a little money, and a school at Sault Ste. Marie, it also took from them the mineral rights to their lands—an aspect of the treaty that would prove very important years later, when European fashion sense changed and trapping beaver no longer supported the local economy.

Unfortunately for Astor, the fur trade declined steeply just five years after the signing of the 1826 treaty. The 1830s saw the fur post turn to commercial fishing to bolster its profits, and then Astor's charter expired in 1833, leaving trader Ramsay Crooks in charge of the post. At this same time protestant missionaries like Edmund Ely came to the region. Ely helped establish a mission and taught grammar and arithmetic to native and mixed-race children who lived near the fort. Ely also worked on converting locals to Christianity and set to work on a Chippewa language dictionary. But economic realities continued to hinder population growth: A financial panic in 1837 coincided with the increasing popularity of silk hats in Europe, and the fur trade came to a screeching halt. The fisheries operated by the fur company saw bountiful harvests, but had few people to sell fish to. The company failed in 1842, the fur post ceased operating by 1847, and the mission closed its doors in 1849.

The American Fur Company's Fond du Lac trading post painted by James Otto Lewis in 1826 during the signing of the Fond du Lac Treaty; Lewis accompanied Colonel Thomas McKenney, head of the U.S. Indian Department, to Fond du Lac, painting examples of Indian life.

Despite the death of the fur trade and failure of commercial fishing, the head of the lakes looked poised for something big in 1852. Many speculated that copper mining would fill the void left by the abandoned fur trade; Isle Royale was thought to be made entirely of copper, and the Ontonagon Boulder found on the south shore of Michigan's Upper Peninsula was a 3,700 pound hunk of pure copper. Construction had begun on locks and channels at Sault Ste. Marie; when finished, they would allow for larger sailing craft to navigate into Lake Superior, which is twenty-one feet higher than the lower lakes. These factors led many to flock to the obvious place of destiny, the head of the lakes where the St. Louis River fed into Lake Superior—a marshy area that would eventually become Superior, Wisconsin.

That year George Stuntz started surveying the area, establishing borders between Wisconsin and Minnesota, which set off a land rush the following year; by early 1854, new landowners established Superior . Its new residents thought it would eclipse Chicago in importance as a trading center. Indeed, when congress decided to build a military road between St. Paul and the head of the lakes, Wisconsin lobbyists successfully fought to have the road terminate in Superior rather than Fond du Lac, restricting the Minnesota side of the line to native inhabitants only.

But that changed after the signing of another treaty involving the Ojibwe. In 1854, representatives of the U.S. government met on the island of La Pointe with over five thousand Ojibwe who had lost their livelihood with the

Negotiating the 1854 Treaty of La Pointe. The U.S. was represented by Agent Henry C. Gilbert and David S. Harriman; Kechewaishke (Chief Buffalo) of La Pointe was one of many chiefs from the Lake Superior region representing the Ojibwe. Detail of a painting by an unknown artist.

fur trade's demise. They negotiated a treaty that gave native lands north and west of Lake Superior to the United States. The agreement also created the Fond du Lac and Grand Portage reservations, and the Ojibwe received some cash and goods—such as furniture, kitchen utensils, household furniture, clothes, and hunting and trapping gear—and were provided with a blacksmith. (In subsequent years even more Ojibwe land would be claimed by both private sales and the General Allotment Act of 1887, which reduced Ojibwe property in some areas by nearly sixty percent.) The Arrowhead region had become U.S. territory and therefore open to settlement and exploitation.

Boom, Bust, Boom

Two years before the Treaty of 1854, George Stuntz had pulled up stakes in Superior, made his way to Minnesota Point, and driven them back down, becoming Duluth's unofficial first resident of European descent. He wasn't alone for long. With the treaty in place, mining speculators hoping to make it rich pulling copper from the ground swarmed to the Minnesota side of the head of the lakes, and by 1859 had platted no less than eleven townships: Fond du Lac, Oneota (much of West Duluth or "Spirit Valley"), Rice's Point, Fremont (near the present-day site of the Duluth Entertainment and Convention Center and Union Depot), Duluth (Minnesota Point and downtown), North Duluth (roughly Central Hillside), Portland (roughly East Hillside), Endion (roughly the eastern edge of East Hillside to the Congdon neighborhood), and Belville (Lakeside).

Legend muddies the truth behind the naming of Duluth Township, which then included Minnesota Point. Early settlers George and William Nettleton allegedly organized a picnic on Minnesota Point on a lovely summer's day in 1856, inviting those Superiorites making claims on the newly platted township to propose a name for the fledgling city. After many names were suggested and rejected, the Reverend J. G. Wilson of Pittsburgh regaled the audience with the tale of Daniel Greysolon Sieur du Lhut, and his listeners enthusiastically received the name "Duluth," anointing the choice with the popping of champagne corks just as the sun set; the crowd toasted Duluth, surely to be the "Queen of the West."

A wonderful tale, and indeed Wilson proposed the name, but the picnic itself probably never occurred (and the reverend may have hailed from Massachusetts or Logansport, Indiana). He had been promised a deed to two lots if he came up with a moniker for the town, and after researching books borrowed from George Nettleton, Wilson came up with a list, "Duluth" among the choices. He got his land.

Those first Duluthians—and residents of other fledgling townships—included mostly transplanted Superiorites such as the families of the Nettleton brothers, Colonel J. B. Culver, Orrin Rice, Reverend Ely, and Sidney Luce as well as the Lewis Merritt family of Oneota and others whose names remain prominent in Duluth. Still more came from throughout the country to stake their claims on what they hoped would become, as General George B. Sargent had predicted, the "center of trade of twenty American states yet unborn, and the British trade of the Red River settlements, and of Hudson's Bay." The local population grew to about 1,500. As in Superior, many speculated that Duluth would surpass Chicago as a center of trade and a destination for immigrants, and that its population would grow to 300,000 by the end of the century.

The Panic of 1857 put an end to such thoughts, triggering an exodus of fortune seekers away from Lake Superior's shores. By 1860 just 353 persons populated the three largest townships of Fond du Lac, Oneota, and Duluth. According to early resident and amateur historian Jerome Eugene Cooley, those who stayed on would become known as the "Ancient and Honorable Order of the Fish Eaters," for when times were tough they had little to eat but "fish or snowballs." The Civil War also took a toll on the local population, as the unemployed left the region to find work fighting for the Union. Those who toughed it out scrabbled to find ways to make a living, including four young men—one with brewing skills—who opened a brewery along a waterway they named Brewery Creek, about two blocks from the site where the Fitger's Brewery would later stand.

The coming of the Lake Superior & Mississippi Railroad from St. Paul to Duluth, backed by a dandy from Philadelphia, would change all that. Financier Jay Cooke arrived in Duluth in 1866, sporting a silk hat and handing out coins to Ojibwe on Minnesota Point (they called him "Great White

Philadelphia financier Jay Cooke, whose fortune saw the United States through the Civil War. Cooke invested heavily in Duluth in the 1860s, pulling it out of the Panic of 1857, until he too went bust in 1873.

Father"). Anticipation that Cooke's rail line would put easy money in the pockets of landowners spawned another land rush in 1869, and the population soared. James J. Egan, a state representative, would say that "the lifeless corpse of Duluth…touched by the wand of Jay Cooke, sprang full-armed from the tomb." Soon they were calling Duluth "Jay Cooke's Town" and "Philadelphia's western suburb."

Rumors of gold also brought a crush of speculators to the townships on the Minnesota side of the St. Louis. An 1865 geological survey claimed the shores of Lake Vermilion, north of Duluth, were rife with gold deposits. Prospectors swarmed to the region and even built a rough road, staked out by George Stuntz, along an old trail used for centuries by Dakota and Ojibwe (it ran roughly along what is today Seventh Avenue East in Duluth, County Road 4, and State Highway 135). Mining began in earnest in 1866, but prospectors uncovered very little gold. When Lewis Merritt visited the region, blacksmith North Albert Posey showed him something he had found that would prove much more valuable: a chunk of iron ore, evidence of a vast deposit that would later change the face of the entire Arrowhead region.

Despite the lack of gold in the Lake Vermilion area, the summer of 1866 found Duluthians feeling pretty confident about the region's future. At an Independence Day picnic on Minnesota Point, newspaper publisher Dr. Thomas Foster (who produced Duluth's first paper, the *Minnesotian*) gave a grand oration, during which he called Duluth the "Zenith City of the Unsalted Seas." It was a speech filled with optimism; by January 1869 just fourteen families lived at the base of Minnesota Point.

Duluthians elected their first mayor, J. B. Culver, the next year. If you believe Jerome Eugene Cooley, some Ojibwe men contributed to the voting roles. They had come to town, they thought, to attend a great celebration. Instead some unethical townspeople plied their "guests" with drink then forced them to put on borrowed pants and cast votes under the name "Joe LePorte" in exchange for another drink. Election officials counted 448 ballots that day, "without troubling to get out the woman vote," as Cooley says. By the middle of 1870, the population of Duluth had grown to 3,130

This color woodcut titled Duluth at the Head of Lake Superior, *most likely made in 1870 since it does not show the ship canal, appeared in the April 29, 1871, supplement of* Harper's Weekly.

people—a mix of "Fish Eaters," "Sixty-Niners" (who had arrived the year before for the land and gold rush), and the European immigrants who would build Jay Cooke's railroad and log the hillsides for timber that would be milled and become Duluth's first houses. The once-dying township was becoming a thriving city.

Again with the Booming and the Busting and the Booming

While Duluth floundered to find its feet, life in the late 1850s and throughout the 1860s had been more stable across the bay in Superior, Wisconsin, then considered the only town of note in the entire region. But the Lake Superior & Mississippi Railroad's terminus in Duluth threatened Superior's position as the region's premier city. Superiorites had campaigned aggressively to get the railroad to come to their city—even suggesting that Cooke drop

the word "Lake" from the railroad's name—and felt Cooke had snubbed them.

So Cooke's railroad and his other projects brought prosperity to Duluth rather than to Superior. Loggers felled virgin timber throughout the region, and lumber mills sprung up on Rice's Point and along Lake Avenue, where Roger Munger set up his mill. Cooke became the mills' biggest customer, as they provided timber for his railroads and Union Improvement and Elevator Company, which built the huge grain terminal Elevator A along the shore on the outer harbor. The railroads built docks to reach Elevator A, connecting the waterfront to the railway. Elevator Q went up along the shore and more were built on Rice's Point; a breakwater rose to protect ships anchored at Duluth outside the bay. The shipbuilding industry blossomed, and commercial fishing thrived. The Northern Pacific began working its way to Duluth as well. When the first telegraph reached the region, it would connect St. Paul to Duluth, not Superior. On March 6, 1870, the Minnesota State Legislature officially declared Duluth a city.

The fledgling city got off to a shaky start. Superior Street was little more than a trail of mud, boulders, and stumps. Camille Poirer, who would start Duluth Tent & Awning and create the Duluth Pack, hired a man to act as the city's water department, transporting unfiltered Lake Superior water in "a large hogshead put on a cart." As the fire department attempted to respond to its first call—a fire on Minnesota Point—the steam engine itself caught fire; flames spread to the fire hall, destroying it. On April 21 the city appointed Robert Bruce police chief, whose duties included lighting lamps on moonless nights; by June he had disappeared—along with the breakwater construction crew's payroll, with which he had been entrusted. Despite these early setbacks, the city continued to move forward.

On the other side of the St. Louis Bay, snubbed Superior still had one great advantage over Duluth: the Superior entry. This natural divide between Minnesota Point and Wisconsin Point allowed ships to easily sail into the harbor where the St. Louis River feeds into Lake Superior. This kept a great deal of industry on the Wisconsin side of the bay, and the towns became rivals. In 1869 Duluth leaders had revived an idea first discussed in 1857, the building of a ship canal through Minnesota Point. Instead the Army Corps of Engineers had built piers at Superior's natural entry and dredged seven miles of channels from Superior Bay to Duluth. Still, Minnesota lobbied hard for its own ship canal—Lake Superior had turned the breakwater built on the lakeside of the point to rubble, and docking ships outside of the harbor would never be safe. In March 1870 the Minnesota Legislature created the Minnesota Canal and Harbor Improvement Commission, contracting with W. W. Williams & Co. to dig a canal. In autumn of that year, the steam dredge *Ishpeming* took its first bite out of Minnesota Point.

Superior businessmen viewed the canal as a great threat to their city's future and filed suit in federal courts to stop the dredging. This legal action and a particularly tough winter put a stop to the digging, but when the spring thaw came, nothing had been resolved. So the *Ishpeming* went back to work. In June, Superior got the answer it wanted, and the U.S. Supreme Court ordered the Minnesotans in Duluth to "absolutely desist and abstain from digging, excavating and constructing…said canal." Unfortunately for those on the Wisconsin side, a telegram tipped off Duluthians of the pending order three days before it would officially arrive. By the time the courier, none other than surveyor George Stuntz, arrived in Duluth—well, let's have the legend first.

As author Dora May McDonald tells the story, many claim that as the *Ishpeming* went to work on a Saturday morning in April 1871, it struck frozen gravel. Soon after this, word came that Stuntz had left St. Paul bound for Duluth with the injunction in hand, destined to arrive Monday morning. Resilient Duluthians sent out a call for every able-bodied man, woman, and child in Duluth "who could handle a spade or shovel, or beg, borrow, or steal a bucket or a bushel basket." Citizens rushed to the work site and "dug, scratched, and burrowed till it was finished." They toiled

Albert Beirstadt painted this view of Duluth in 1871, after the town had seen its hopes of becoming a great city rise, flounder, and rise again through the 1850s and 1860s.

throughout the day Saturday and long into the night, the women tending fires and providing food and coffee, then all day Sunday and Sunday night. Sunday also brought rowboats filled with angry Superiorites who watched and heckled the efforts of the Duluthians. At the break of dawn on Monday morning, they had cleared the canal.

Truth be told, the *Ishpeming* did all the work, working around the clock to finish the canal before George Stuntz arrived—a task worthy of a legend all its own. And the bay itself helped: because the lake was a few inches lower than the inner harbor, water pressure helped widen and cut through the canal. By the time Stuntz arrived, he was just in time to watch the steam tug *Frank C. Fero* become the first vessel to pass through the new waterway—an act that would give Duluth the leverage it needed. Though it would take some time, the courts eventually allowed Duluth to keep its canal.

Unfortunately for some, more than just watercraft began passing through the canal. Early settlers had platted the township of Fremont between Minnesota Point and Rice's Point, a marshy area that included many floating islands experts speculate were "probably caused by driftwood and accumulating vegetable matter." New currents caused by dredging the ship canal swept a great many of these floating islands against

In 1871, Gilbert Munger painted Duluth from the Hillside; today the painting hangs in the Duluth Public Library.

filled timber cribs stood on both sides of the canal's entire 2,470-foot length. The canal opened Duluth to another population burst. By 1873 more than five thousand souls called Duluth home. Schools and churches popped up all over town; logging, rail, shipping (chiefly grain), and fishing industries flourished; and retail shops began selling not only necessities, but luxury goods as well. Michael Fink had bought the fledg-

the shore of Minnesota Point or through the canal and out to the big lake; in either case, the islands broke up, and Fremont essentially floated way, along with the hopes of those who originally settled the town site.

Fremont residents weren't the only ones damaged by the canal's creation. Superiorites were up in arms—literally. One firm advertised a sale of surplus muskets leftover from the Civil War to arm Superiorites against those cliff dwellers across the bay, but no real threat ever developed. In order to pacify their angry neighbors, Duluth issued $100,000 in bonds to build a dike from Rice's Point to Superior to separate shipping traffic between the two towns, but currents of the St. Louis River destroyed it. An 1872 effort by the Northern Pacific Railroad created a mile-long dike to again divide Superior Bay, but the following winter's ice and wind helped currents destroy that as well. Nature wouldn't allow man to divide the harbor, so the towns had to learn to share it.

The Northern Pacific Railroad helped complete the canal in 1872. Dredgers had cut the canal sixteen feet deep, and piers made of 24-foot rock-

ling brewery that the Fish Eaters had started during the lean years of the 1850s and would in turn sell it to brewmaster August Fitger and his partner Percy Anneke just a year later, creating Fitger's Brewery. The Duluth Iron and Steel Company fired up a blast furnace on Rice's Point. It all looked pretty promising, but the old timers had seen it boom—and bust—before.

And they would see it bust again: in September 1873, Jay Cooke ran out of money. This not only impacted Duluth particularly hard, it also sent the national economy spiraling first into panic and then into depression. Duluth businesses had gambled their future on Duluth becoming the railroad's easternmost supply point, but work on the Northern Pacific halted. Within two months nearly half of Duluth's business owners closed up shop, many of them going bankrupt along the way. Duluth's population sank to below 1,500 people. In 1877 state officials allowed Duluth's charter to expire, reducing it to village status.

But the very depression that shut down Duluth would in the end redeem it. The faltering economy caused many to take their chances farming the great plains, and the fruits of their labor were shipped back east—through Duluth's and Superior's docks. Grain elevators rose on Rice's Point and Conner's Point across the bay. By 1881 so much grain made its way through the Twin Ports that officials formed the Duluth Board of Trade; five years later elevators dotting the harbor docks held twenty-two million bushels.

The first half of the 1880s saw a renewed interest in industry. As the decade began, the Northern Pacific found competition in the St. Paul & Duluth, which had replaced Jay Cooke's failed Lake Superior & Mississippi; by 1889 sixteen thousand miles of track served ten railroads that carried goods to and from Duluth's docks and warehouses. During this same time Charlemagne Tower, Jr. and his capitalist friends from the east began investing in the iron fields near Lake Vermilion, opening the Vermilion Iron Range and forming the Minnesota Iron Company and the Duluth & Iron Range Railway. But Duluth missed out at first, as Tower directed his railroad to Agate Bay (now Two Harbors) and erected massive ore docks on its shores.

The first shipment of iron ore from the town of Tower headed for Agate Bay on July 3, 1884, where it was loaded onto the steamer *Hecla* destined for Philadelphia. The Arrowhead Region's iron mining industry had begun in earnest. The lumber industry had also picked up steam. Many of the sawmills that failed with Jay Cooke fired up again, more were built, and by the midpoint of the decade they dotted the St. Louis Bay from Rice's Point to Oneota, annually cutting about ten million board feet of lumber.

As industry grew in the 1880s, so did the town's population. Neighborhoods sprang up in all directions from downtown. By 1887 streetcars operated by the Duluth Street Railway Company, organized in 1881, ran fifty-five blocks, from Twenty-third Avenue West to Twenty-second Avenue East. Public and parochial schools rose along with more churches and St. Luke's and St. Mary's hospitals. The 1885 state census placed the city's population at 18,036. The village continued to pay off the defunct city's debts, clearing the books in early 1887, which allowed the state legislature to

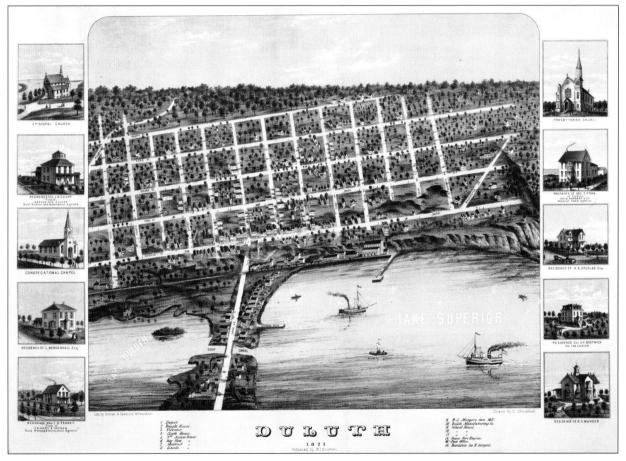

A highly idealized bird's-eye map of Duluth in 1871 by artist E. Chrisman. In actuality, Duluth in 1871 had very few trees—most had been cleared to provide lumber for housing—so those beautiful green spaces were more likely mud and stumps. A few of the homes depicted at the side belonged to Duluth's "Ancient and Honorable Order of the Fish Eaters," pioneers like Colonel J. B. Culver (elected the city's first mayor) who rode out Duluth's lean years to see it prosper—fail again—and prosper once more.

The history of Duluth relies on its inextricable connection to the history of Superior, its rival across the bay seen here in a bird's-eye view drawn by Henry Wellge in 1883.

sanction the incorporation of the city. Nearly 33,000 people lived in the Zenith City that year, and they elected village president John B. Sulphin mayor in March. The township was once again a city.

The Zenith City Prospers

As the decade came to an end, the view from the Zenith City was framed in promise. Duluth stretched eastward from roughly Fortieth Avenue West to the outskirts of Endion and included many of the townships that once hoped to become grand cities all their own: Endion, Portland, North Duluth, and Rice's Point (Fremont, of course, had floated away with the birth of the canal). It did not include Minnesota Point, which had incorporated itself as the village of Park Point after Duluth failed in 1877. The village refused to rejoin the newly sanctioned city until a bridge was built connecting the

point to the rest of the city—the digging of the ship canal had cut off its residents in 1871. Duluth promised a bridge, and Park Point became part of Duluth in 1889.

The expansion continued into the 1890s. In 1891 Duluth acquired Duluth Heights, Glen Avon, Hunter's Park, Kenwood, Morley Heights, Piedmont Heights, and Woodland. Two years later saw the eastward annexation of Belville, Lakeside Village, New London, and Lester Park. Duluth still did not include anything from Fond du Lac to Oneota, but it was only a matter of time. West Duluth, including Oneota as a neighborhood, had incorporated in 1888. Its founders widely believed it deserved to become the "new Pittsburgh" after gaining a blast furnace and tolling mill from the Duluth Iron and Steel Company—but that vision didn't materialize, and it became a part of Duluth in 1894, along with Bay View Heights and

This bird's-eye view of Duluth in 1883 by Henry Wellge is more realistic than Chrisman's 1871 map, but it is not without whimsy—note the size of the rowing skiffs alongside the cargo vessels.

Riverside. A year later Gary and New Duluth joined the rolls. The city also finally annexed Fond du Lac, where the Dakota and Ojibwe had been brought together for the first time by that heartsick Frenchman from whom Duluth derived its name.

The years between its rebirth through the 1890s and into the next century bore witness to a building explosion. In 1888 the city council had established four parks—Cascade Park, Lincoln Park, Portland Square, and Garfield Park (later Chester Park)—the first of more than one hundred green spaces that would eventually grace the city. They also approved an idea proposed by park board president William K. Rogers: a roadway along a remarkably level stretch of gravel at the top of Duluth's hillside—the prehistoric shoreline of Glacial Lake Duluth. The roadway would eventually connect most of Duluth's major parks, seven of which would be platted along the creeks that ran

through the city on their way to the lake. Initially its design covered just four miles, from Chester Park along Chester Creek in the east to Garfield Park on Miller Creek. Rogers also proposed a name for the roadway: "Carriage Drive," a name that gave way to "Terrace Parkway" before any street signs went up.

Parks made up only a portion of Duluth's grand expansion from the late 1880s through the end of the century. Many of Duluth's great brownstone buildings, constructed from sandstone quarried in the Apostle Islands and at Fond du Lac and elsewhere along the South Shore, began to give shape to the city's streets. The Spalding Hotel, the Federal Building, Duluth's original City Hall and Police Station, the Carnegie Library, Central High School, the Temple Opera Building, the Lyceum Theatre, the Torrey Building, the Duluth Union Depot, and many, many others went up at this time. Executives and attorneys who had made a fortune in the lumber, iron, and shipping enterprises donated generously to the construction of grand churches their families attended. The laborers who built those buildings—European immigrants, for the most part—took up residence in homes and row houses along the hillside and further uphill, in the Heights. The Incline Railway went up in 1891 to bring workers from their homes in the Heights to work downtown and along the waterfront. A pump house went up in Lakewood, east of Lester Park to bring fresh water to a growing population and a sewer system went underground to carry wastewater away.

The new growth created new demand: the increasing population needed to eat. This spurred the rebirth of the commercial fishing industry, which had shut down fifty years earlier with the demise of the American Fur Company. Firms such as the Lake Superior Fish Company and A. Booth and Sons employed thousands from Duluth to Isle Royale and Superior to Ashland on the Wisconsin side, their harvest of lake trout, siskiwit, herring, and pike feeding populations throughout the entire Midwest. During the winter fishing companies shipped fresh fish ("frozen with the wiggle in its tail," as one Duluth firm advertised) as far away as Montana.

At Sault Ste. Marie on the other end of the big lake, the federal government expanded the locks between Lake Huron and Lake Superior, allowing much larger ships with greater cargo capacity to make

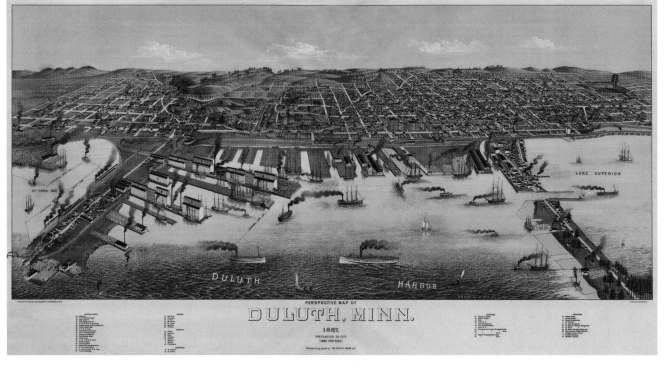

Another bird's-eye view of Duluth by Henry Wellge, this one produced in 1887, when Duluth once again regained status as a city.

their way to and from the Zenith City. Back in Duluth, Captain Alexander McDougall saw this development as an opportunity to get into the shipbuilding business, another industry that would intermittently fuel Duluth's and Superior's economies. McDougall came up with a radical design: a barge-like ship with a flat bottom, a rounded top, and a spoon-shaped bow. He called the ships "whalebacks." Others called them "pig boats" because their blunted bows looked like a hog's snout. McDougall found immediate success: his boats made great ore carriers, and with the financial backing of John D. Rockefeller, he started the American Steel Barge Company. Unfortunately for Duluth, some local businessmen made a stink about the noise a shipbuilding operation would create, and so McDougall moved his operations across the bay to West Superior.

Investing in McDougall's funny-looking boats wouldn't be Rockefeller's last interest in the region; the industrialist later became part of iron mining lore as well. When Lewis Merritt first returned from Lake Vermilion in 1866, he had told his seven sons that the Arrowhead country would one day be covered with mines "worth more than all the gold in California." So the Merritt boys had gone looking, and eventually, on the western end of a region the Ojibwe called "Mesaba," found ore rich enough in iron to bring to market. In 1890 the Merritt brothers drilled a mine at a site they called Mountain Iron. The next year they built the Duluth, Missabe & Northern Railway to transport the ore to Duluth, giving birth to the Mesabi Iron Range. The Merritts had performed all this work on speculation, and before they could generate profit to pay for it, their creditors came calling, demanding payment. That's when Rockefeller stepped in, trading the cash the Merritts needed for a significant interest in their mining and railroad operations. By 1894 the mines still failed to produce a profit, and stock values fell, forcing the brothers to sell their shares to Rockefeller. They later tried to sue the industrialist for fraud, but only managed to get back just under a million dollars—barely enough to pay off their debt. After toiling ceaselessly for five years, the Merritts had created and lost a fortune. Their efforts did little for them, but they had created the Mesabi Range, which, along with Charlemagne Tower's Vermilion Range and, eventually, the Cuyuna Range, made up the Minnesota Iron Range in the heart of Minnesota's Arrowhead Region. The Range would be a major contributor to the region's economy for nearly one hundred years to follow.

As the century ended, commercial fishing and lumber industries reached their peak, the Army Corps of Engineers completed improvements on the ship canal, and Duluth's population had reached nearly fifty-three thousand. Attorney and real estate investor Samuel Frisbee Snively had begun a labor of love, a roadway that would wind from his farm near Hawk Ridge to the Lake Superior shore near the mouth of the Lester River, crossing the western arm of the Lester and Amity Creek over several stone bridges along the way. (It would later be known as Seven Bridges Road.) Duluth's other great parkway continued to grow and change, and in 1899 the Park Board renamed Terrace Parkway—now extended by an additional mile—"Rogers Boulevard" in honor of the man who had first envisioned it.

In 1905 Duluth would enjoy a banner year. The Great Northern Power Company constructed the Thomson Dam, bringing electricity to town. That same year Duluth fulfilled a promise to Park Point residents made sixteen years earlier as the Aerial Transfer Bridge rose up and reached over the canal. Shipping, iron, and lumber magnates had been building stately homes in Duluth's eastern environs and along London Road, and that year construction reached its symbolic peak when work began on Duluth's most famous mansion, Glensheen, the Congdon Estate. Lakeside blossomed with grand

Captain Alexander McDougall's passenger whaleback the Christopher Columbus *depicted in an 1893 etching; designed to haul ore, most whalebacks were barge-like, without the upper decks.*

Victorian homes built by lawyers, merchants, and other professionals as well as the more modest houses of the servant class who had found employment tending to the estates and families of the rich. That same year city fathers would first make the oft-repeated claim that Duluth had "more millionaires per capita than anywhere else in the U.S." Just two years later the 1907 shipping season saw Duluth overcome New York in tonnage that moved through the harbor—Duluth, in the middle of the continent, had become the biggest port in the U.S. By 1910 more than seventy-eight thousand people lived within its borders.

The same year Duluth surpassed New York, the United States Steel Corporation announced plans to build a "monster" plant in Duluth as part of a compromise between the Steel Trust and political leaders throughout the state to kill a bill that would have essentially doubled taxes for steel producers and ore exporters alike. But it would take eight years to get the plant up and running—it didn't produce steel until 1915. By then U.S. Steel had invested twenty million dollars into the project and had built an entire town along the way. Named for U.S. Steel founder J. P. Morgan, Morgan Park sprang up on the banks of the St. Louis between Gary and Riverside. The company town (only U.S. Steel employees and their families could live there) was built with concrete manufactured on site at the Universal Portland Cement Company, a U.S. Steel subsidiary: the homes, buildings, and churches (one each for Catholics and Protestants) were made of poured concrete and cinder block. Civic and business leaders optimistically thought that the U.S. Steel plant would be one of many that would dot the shoreline "from Fond du Lac to Two Harbors" and that the population would reach 300,000 by 1920, but that promise never materialized.

Between the Wars

In 1915 Duluth appeared to be firing on all cylinders. Commercial fishing on Lake Superior hit its all-time high; Duluth fishing interests alone hauled in ten thousand tons of fish. Other industries profited from the first world war: U.S. Steel, itself fed by ore from the Iron Range, cranked out steel to feed the war machine. The Mesabi Range alone produced twenty million tons of ore during the war years. Alexander McDougall, who had closed his shipbuilding operation in New Superior as the century turned, opened a new operation at Riverside along with some new partners—Chester Congdon,

A 1909 bird's-eye etching of Duluth and Superior, again by Henry Wellge, this time in full color.

Marshall Alworth, and Julius Barnes—and began making freighters eight at a time for the allied nations. McDougall-Duluth employed so many people that the company essentially turned Riverside into a company town much like Morgan Park. During the war and through to 1921, the McDougall-Duluth Company and other shipbuilders in Duluth built 103 vessels.

Prohibition, ratified in 1919, hit one of Duluth's first industries hard. The brewery operation that started with four men during the lean years of the Fish Eaters had grown into Fitger's Brewery, which by 1918 cranked out 150,000 barrels a year. Two other breweries, Duluth Brewing and Malting and People's Brewing, kept many a family fed in Duluth as well. During Prohibition all three had to shut down their kettles and bottling lines. In order to keep their employees working, they turned to a variety of non-alcoholic drinks and other products—including soft drinks, candy, and even cigars—but they did not operate at full capacity again until 1933, when Prohibition ended. The lumber industry also suffered. It was thought all but dead in Duluth by 1920 when the Alger-Smith mill closed, but many had already considered lumber pretty much done in 1912, when Canadian investors dismantled the Howard Mill and hauled it north, across the border.

Despite Prohibition and the demise of lumber, the Twenties were good to Duluth. In 1920 the city held 98,917 residents who enjoyed the use of fifty city parks, and over 17,000 students filled its forty-one public schools. Grain elevators and coal and ore docks operated at maximum capacity, and as went the docks, so went the shipping industry. In 1921 Duluthians elected Sam Snively to the first of four consecutive terms as mayor. A long-time fan of Duluth's park system and a road-builder in his own right, Snively made William Rogers' dream of connecting the parks by a parkway his pet project. By 1929 Rogers Boulevard stretched westward all the way to Jay Cooke Park and the town renamed it "Skyline Parkway." The Twin Ports continued to prosper throughout the decade, and Duluth's population hit an all-time high of 112,000 residents in 1928.

Samuel Frisbee Snively, Duluth's longest-sitting mayor, held that office from 1921–1937. Snively also created Seven Bridges Road and expanded and completed William Rogers' dream: Carriage Drive, known today as Skyline Parkway. Snively reportedly disliked this portrait because it made him look too stern.

But then in 1929 it hit the same wall that every other city in the nation would run smack into: the Great Depression. It affected every industry, and by 1930 one-third of all Duluthians had lost their jobs. Still, Duluth somehow managed to progress. The Williamson-Johnson Municipal Airport, Duluth's first foray into air travel, opened in 1930, the same year workers finished transforming the Aerial Bridge from a transfer bridge to a lift bridge. Throughout the Depression not a single Duluth bank failed, and the city took advantage of Franklin Roosevelt's W.P.A. program, with 450 area projects—from park improvements to storm sewers under downtown streets—keeping locals working.

But while most of Duluth weathered the Great Depression fairly well, the fishing industry again floundered. Already on the decline, it soon went the way of logging: its yield by the mid-1930s had dropped to less than four thousand tons and would soon fall to less than one thousand tons. World War II would briefly revive the shipbuilding industry and boost the demand for iron ore, but even that stalwart industry would slow to a crawl. While the Mesabi Range continued to produce impressive tonnage (and still does), the Vermilion shut down in 1963, and the Cuyuna, which never attained the level of the others, closed in the mid-1970s. Shipping would remain strong, but Duluth, Superior, and the smaller towns that dotted Lake Superior's north and south shores would have to look at new ways to bolster the local economy.

As the 1930s came to a close, one landmark went up as another came down: Enger Tower, a gift from local businessman Bert Enger, rose above the town in June, but the Incline Railway carried its last passengers on Labor Day. Sam Snively, though voted out of office in 1937, had completed his vision of William Rogers' plan; laborers had finally finished work on Skyline Parkway, which ran twenty-eight miles from Jay Cooke Park in the west to connect with Snively's Seven Bridges Road in the east, nearly the entire length of Duluth. Today anyone wanting to take in the postcard view from Skyline Parkway can walk, bike, or drive along the roadway without fear of getting wet in the freezing waters of a glacial lake, or of encountering beavers of any size.

Part I

Greetings from Duluth

The Duluth Ship Canal

As Duluth and Superior grew along with the Great Lakes shipping industry, Superior had a natural edge: the Superior Entry, a break between Minnesota Point and Wisconsin Point that allowed ships entry to the harbor close to Superior's docks, leaving the Wisconsin town poised to become the larger of the two cities. That all changed in 1871, when Duluthians dug a canal through Minnesota Point. Superior residents opposed to the canal succeeded in getting a federal injunction to prevent the Canal's digging. When they caught wind that a federal marshal was on his way with the injunction, Duluthians started digging. Legend has it that every able-bodied person in town grabbed a pick or shovel and started to dredge the canal by hand; in reality, while many may have helped with their hand tools, the dredging tug *Ishpeming* did nearly all of the work. For three days and nights it toiled. By the time the notice arrived, the steam tug *Frank C. Fero* had passed through the canal, thus making it a "navigable waterway" and rendering the injunction moot. In 1898 the Canal was widened to three hundred feet and the timber piers were replaced with concrete.

The canal as seen facing Lake Superior (top), facing the Duluth-Superior Harbor (left), and in rough weather (above).

LIGHTHOUSE, HARBOR ENTRANCE, DULUTH, MINN.   118625

The North Pierhead Lighthouse

Built in 1910, Duluth's North Pierhead Lighthouse is an iron tower enclosed by steel plates. It stands 37 feet tall, measures 10.5 feet in diameter at its base, and tapers to a diameter of 8 feet. An octagonal cast-iron lantern holds a Fifth Order Fresnel lens made in Paris in 1881. The lens was originally illuminated by a 210-candlepower incandescent electric lamp. In clear conditions light from the lens can be seen up to eleven miles away.

Keepers first displayed the light on the night of April 7, 1910. Since the Duluth ship canal was only three hundred feet wide, navigating between the two protective piers was extremely difficult at night or in the thick fog common to the Duluth waterfront—so difficult the Lighthouse Board Annual Report for 1908 called the Duluth Harbor the most dangerous in the Great Lakes. The report helped the Lake Carrier's Association procure $4,000 to build the lighthouse.

Wilhelm Boeing's Claim on the Canal

Years after the Duluth ship canal was dug, German immigrant and Michigan lumberman Wilhelm Boeing, who didn't even live in the town, claimed ownership to the land on either side of the canal. Boeing had apparently bought fourteen lots after the panic of 1873.

In 1888 Boeing's Duluth attorney, Marshall W. Alworth, stretched a string across the canal to establish Boeing's rights. In October of the following year Boeing launched a broadside stating he would deny passage to all who would use the canal, and that a rope would be placed across the waterway; anyone breaking that rope would also be breaking the law. Nothing ever happened: Boeing died a month later.

His son William would eventually move to the Pacific Northwest and start building airplanes. Today Bill Boeing's company is one of the world's largest.

LIGHTHOUSE, HARBOR ENTRANCE, DULUTH, MINN.—23

Duluth's Aerial Transfer Bridge

After the ship canal was dug in 1871, residents of Minnesota Point became isolated from the rest of Duluth. And after Duluth lost its charter as a city in 1877, they formed the township of Park Point. They relied upon ferries such as the *Ellen D.*, the *Annie L. Smith*, and the *Estelle* to cross the canal. During winter months, a temporary suspension bridge was used (or sometimes just planks set upon the ice), but the community remained separate from Duluth. In fact, while other small townships became part of Duluth, Park Point remained its own town until 1891, when the promise of a bridge across the canal convinced residents to join Duluth proper.

In 1892 the city held a contest for a bridge design. John Alexander Low Waddle won the contest with a radical idea: a vertical lift bridge. It would have been the first in the world. Unfortunately, the War Department rejected the design (the canal was owned by the federal government). Waddle's design did not go to waste: modified, it became Chicago's South Halstad Street Bridge.

The promise of a bridge would not be kept until 1905, when Duluth built one of only two transfer bridges ever constructed in the United States. Patterned after a suspended-car bridge in Rouen, France, and designed by city engineer Thomas McGilvray, the transfer bridge used a gondola to ferry passengers and goods (and, later, streetcars) across the canal.

Crossing the three-hundred-foot canal in the Aerial Transfer Bridge's gondola cost five cents and took about a minute for a one-way trip. Every five minutes the gondola carried up to sixty-two tons of horses, wagons, trolley cars, automobiles, and people—up to 350 of them. Two 40-horsepower electric motors pulled the gondola along cables. In the event of a power failure, the motorman could hand-power the gondola.

A sight worth seeing.

AERIAL BRIDGE, ENTRANCE TO DULUTH-SUPERIOR HARBOR.

SPAN 393 FEET 9 INCHES-135 FEET HIGH FROM WATER LINE-COST $100,000.

11711 AERIAL BRIDGE, DULUTH, MINN.   COPR. DETROIT PUBLISHING CO.

CAR OF THE AERIAL BRIDGE, DULUTH, MINN.

The postcard directly below was mailed on a Tuesday afternoon and sent to Sault Ste. Marie at the Michigan/Ontario border. The sender wrote that the trip should take "36 hours" and to "look for us"—apparently the mail made it to the Soo faster than passenger steamers of the day.

The sender of the bird's-eye view card (below, middle of page) had some tentative praise for the Aerial Bridge: "Quicker & safer, but not nearly as much fun as crossing on the old ferry."

The Aerial Lift Bridge

118-D—Passenger Steamer Leaving Duluth-Superior Harbor

139-D—Aerial Lift Bridge and Ship Canal, Entrance to Duluth-Superior Harbor

The Aerial Transfer Bridge served Duluth well, but by the latter half of the 1920s a growing population meant increased traffic of streetcars and automobiles, which forced the city to consider a more efficient system. C. P. A. Turner redesigned the bridge in 1929, turning it into the vertical lift bridge originally proposed in 1892.

The bridge was made forty-two feet taller and a lift span replaced the gondola. The plans called for a 386-foot center span that weighed 900 tons. The span was balanced by two giant counterweights made of concrete and weighing 450 tons each. In the end the span was made 17 tons heavier to provide stability in high winds and to allow gravity to help out when the span was on the way down. When it was working its way up, four 95-horsepower electric motors pulled cables nearly two inches thick that were in turn attached to the span and the counterweights.

The bridge first lifted for a ship on March 29, 1930, when the *Essayons*, a Corps of Engineers tug, passed through the canal as a test.

The Bridge raised over 5,300 times that year, and has gone up nearly 450,000 times since. Each season it

121-D   Great Lakes Packet Freighter Entering Duluth-Superior Harbor. Lift Bridge Raised

makes an average of 5,500 lifts, but in 1978 that average was shattered: it lifted 7,583 times. The year it raised the fewest times—2,764 lifts—was 1932, arguably the hardest year of the Great Depression

The lift bridge stands 227 feet tall. Its lift span, just 15 feet above the water when lowered, rises 123 feet above the water, allowing for 138 feet of clearance when raised. It takes about two and a half minutes for each lift (and another two and a half minutes to bring it down). Ten operators make sure the bridge is in top shape and ready to lift twenty-four hours a day, seven days a week during the shipping season (and on fairly short notice during mid-winter). It has been constantly maintained and renovated over the years, including a major overhaul in 1985–1986, when it received new motors and had its capacity increased, weight added to its counterweights, and a new control house installed with modern, computerized controls. Every twenty years its cables are replaced, and every fifteen years the bridge receives a fresh coat of paint. It takes so much paint that the additional weight actually affects the balance, and the counterweights must be adjusted.

While smaller boats have collided with the bridge from time to time, it has never been hit by a commercial ship or ore boat. Sadly, that is not to say

the bridge has remained immune from tragic accidents. In 1982, a nineteen-year-old man from Grand Rapids, Minnesota, grabbed onto the bottom of the bridge as it began its ascension; when the bridge was seventy feet in the air, he lost his grip and fell to his death. In 1990 a fifty-year-old Duluth woman panicked when the bridge's warning bells sounded as she walked across the bridge. She either leaned out to grab a vertical beam or tried to jump, but became caught in the bridge's superstructure. She died instantly.

Because the Lift Bridge was completed in 1929, most of the older postcards of the bridge are on linen, the most popular format between 1930 and 1945. The card at the lower left of page 24 is one of few postcards showing the lift span lowered; most of the cards feature a ship entering or leaving through the canal, so the lift span is raised. The card on the lower left of this page shows the lift span rather low considering the position of the ship. The ensuing pages include many more images of the Aerial Bridge—as both transfer and lift bridge—in postcards featuring some of the many ships that either called on the port of Duluth or called it home.

The Arrowhead Bridge

The Arrowhead Bridge, built in 1927 for a cost of $500,000, stretched eight hundred feet from Grassy Point in West Duluth to Superior's Belknap Street, extending U.S. Highway 2 across the state line. A rolling lift bridge, two spans of the bridge lifted like a draw bridge to let marine traffic through.

Its opening on July 16, 1927, was a gala event. Celebrations were held on both sides of the St. Louis, in Duluth at Memorial Park and along Superior's Tower Avenue. Each celebration led a parade onto the bridge, stopping at either side of the lift spans. While the crowd waited, the spans lifted and a replica Viking ship *Leif Erikson* (then owned by Captain Gerhard Folgero) was escorted between the spans by the fire tug *McGonagle*. After the watercraft cleared and as the spans lowered, Duluth Mayor Sam Snively and Fred Baxter, his counterpart in Superior, headed for the middle and clasped hands just as the spans closed.

Superior's Walter Buch claimed to be the first person to cross the bridge in a car—and the first to pay its toll. Tolling came to an end in March 1963. The bridge itself came to an end in 1985 after being rendered obsolete with the construction of the Richard I. Bong Bridge.

ARROWHEAD BRIDGE, DULUTH-SUPERIOR—9

106-D—Arrowhead Bridge over St. Louis River, between Duluth and Superior

ARROWHEAD BRIDGE OPEN FOR TUG AND FREIGHTER TO PASS THROUGH, ORE DOCKS BEYOND

The Interstate Bridge

When the Interstate Bridge opened on April 23, 1897, crossing from Duluth at Rice's Point to Connor's Point in Superior, Mayor C. S. Starkweather of Superior called the event the "marriage of Helen and Troy." Like the Trojan horse itself, the opening was a deception—in this case, to give the appearance of compliance to the bridge's charter. Work hadn't actually been completed on the Superior side, much to the chagrin of a farmer from Tower, Minnesota, who tried to cross in a wagon drawn by oxen.

A swing bridge, the Interstate's center span swivelled to allow boats and ships to pass, and all had to pay a toll to cross: a nickel for pedestrians and bicyclists, fifteen cents for a wagon, and cattle at a dime a head. It closed in 1961 with the opening of the Blatnik Bridge and was razed ten years later.

The images below appear to be made from photos taken from identical perspectives. So why is the foreground of one water and the other grass? The card on the bottom was probably colorized by someone provided with misinformation, more than likely a colorist in Germany who never saw the actual bridge.

INTER-STATE BRIDGE CONNECTING MINNESOTA & WISCONSIN, DULUTH, MINN.

Interstate

INTERSTATE BRIDGE, CONNECTING SUPERIOR, WIS., AND DULUTH, MINN.

A-9612

The Interstate Bridge was prone to accidents, its most infamous occurring at 1 A.M. on August 11, 1906. Postcards of the aftermath and repairs appear on page 132.

Steam Ships and Ore Boats that Called on the Twin Ports

The first steamboat on the Great Lakes was the passenger ship *Walk-In-The-Water*, built in 1818 to serve Lake Erie. In the 1850s, railroads established steamboat lines on the Great Lakes to join railheads at various ports. The Anchor Line (see page 31) was formed by the Pennsylvania Railroad in 1865 to connect their terminals at Buffalo, New York, to those of the Great Northern Railroad at Duluth, Minnesota. Many of the ships that navigated the Great Lakes had surprisingly long lives. Changing owners—and often names—throughout the years, they were often rerigged for tasks other than their original design. Most were eventually scrapped, others lost. Perhaps the first recorded shipwreck on Lake Superior was the American Fur Company's *Madeline*, a forty-five-foot fishing schooner that went down near Knife River in April 1838. The most recent—and most infamous—was the ore boat *Edmund Fitzgerald*, which went down with twenty-nine hands on November 10, 1975.

"THE WORLD'S FINEST VACATION ON YOUR OWN GREAT LAKES".

THE GREAT WHITE LINER "SOUTH AMERICAN". CHICAGO. DULUTH & GEORGIAN BAY TRANSIT CO., CHICAGO, ILL.

STEAMER NORTH AMERICAN (*top*). Built in 1913 in Ecorse, Michigan, the North American *had a history of running aground as she sailed the Great Lakes and St. Lawrence Seaway. She served in various ports throughout the Great Lakes. On tow for Piney Point, Maryland, for use as a training vessel, the ship suddenly sank about twenty-nine miles northeast of Nantucket Island on September 13, 1967, in about two hundred feet of water.*

STEAMER SOUTH AMERICAN (*left*). The North American's *sister ship was also built in Ecorse, Michigan, by the Chicago, Duluth & Georgian Bay Transit Company of Detroit. She served that fleet from 1914 until 1967, when ownership transferred to the Seafarers' International Union of Piney Point, Maryland, which converted it to a training ship at Newport News, Virginia. Its engine was removed and it served as a dormitory for the Lundberg School of Seamanship. It sold for scrap in 1974.*

Steamer America Leaving Dock. Duluth, Minn.

Popular Excursion Steamer Columbia. Duluth, Minn.

STEAMER AMERICA (left). The excursion boat America first hit the water in 1898, when it was built by the Detroit Dry Dock Company in Wyandotte, Michigan. Designed to make daily trips between Michigan City and Chicago, she could hold 277 passengers and 40 crew. The Booth Steamship Line purchased her in 1902 for the "Duluth, Port Arthur [Two Harbors], and Isle Royale route." She served the North Shore well, and in 1908 saved three hundred people fleeing a forest fire. On June 7, 1928, the America struck a reef near Isle Royale's Washington Harbor and slid off into deep water. Fortunately, no lives were lost.

EXCURSION STEAMER COLUMBIA (lower left). The Detroit Shipbuilding Company launched the Columbia in 1902 for the Detroit & Windsor Ferry Company—what it's doing in this Duluth postcard is a mystery. From its launch the Columbia and her sister ship, the St. Claire, ran the "Bob-Lo"—ferrying picnickers from Detroit eighteen miles up the Detroit River to Bob-Lo Island. During a Labor Day excursion in 1971, a gang fight broke out on board; several people were arrested. The Columbia retired as the oldest passenger steamer in the U.S., and since 1991 has been docked in Escorse, Michigan. Records indicate that during the 1990s she was owned by a company that operated night clubs. A plan to return her to the Detroit River has yet to come to fruition.

EXCURSION BOAT S.S. WAYNE (bottom right). Built in 1923 by the Great Lakes Engineering Works of River Rouge, Michigan, the Wayne didn't get to Duluth until 1946, spending her first twenty-three years serving the Walkerville & Detroit Ferry Company running the Detroit River. Once in the Zenith City she was fitted with a large dance floor and ran moonlight rides on St. Louis Bay. By 1950 she was operating out of Toledo, and found her way to Sturgeon Bay, Wisconsin, in 1952 for use as a yacht—but the deal fell through, and the Wayne was towed to Lockwood, Illinois, and partially dismantled. The last record of the Wayne is April 15, 1958— lying in the shipyards of New Orleans' Bisso Ferry Company, which used it as a storehouse.

D-148

PHOTO BY GALLAGHER

Steamer Huronic at Dock, Duluth, Minn.

18270

Steamer Hamonic at Duluth, Minn.

STEAMER NORONIC, DULUTH-SUPERIOR HARBOR.

CANADIAN STEAMSHIP LINES SISTER SHIPS

Originally built for the Northern navigation Company, which was later absorbed by the Canadian Steamship Lines, the Huronic, Hamonic, and Noronic sailed the Great Lakes for the first half of the twentieth century, serving as passenger ships and package freighters.

STEAMER HURONIC (upper left). *The oldest of the sisters, the Huronic's maiden voyage was in May of 1902. On November 21 of that same year she passed the Bannockburn, which sank later that night. In 1928 she beached on Lucille Island, southeast of Lake Superior's Pigeon Point. Late in the 1930s her cabins were removed from the upper deck, and passenger service ended. She was scrapped in Hamilton, Ontario in 1950.*

STEAMER HAMONIC (top). *In 1908 the Hamonic joined the Huronic. Considered the most beautiful passenger and freight ship to ever run the Great Lakes, she came to a fiery end July 17, 1945. All but one of four hundred aboard the Hamonic lived to tell tales of daring rescue, including the efforts of a coal crane operator who lifted fifty passengers from the bow of the burning ship to the shore. In 1946 she was scrapped in Hamilton, Ontario.*

STEAMER NORONIC (left). *The last and largest of the Canadian Steamship sisters, the Noronic hit the water in 1913. From 1914 to 1949 she ran from Detroit and Windsor, Ontario, to the "Lakehead"—the Twin Ports of Duluth and Superior. Docked in Toronto during a post-season cruise, a fire in the linen closet spread. Sadly, 139 passengers died and the gutted ship sank. The salvaged hull was later sold for scrap.*

STEAMER OCTORARA, DULUTH-SUPERIOR HARBOR

118623

STEAMER JUNIATA, DULUTH-SUPERIOR HARBOR

118624

THE ANCHOR LINE TRIPLETS

The Octorara, the Juniata, and the Tionesta were sister ships built in Cleveland, Ohio, by the American Shipbuilding Company for the Anchor Line, a subsidiary of the Pennsylvania Railroad. Each was a 346-foot-long propeller-driven steamship that carried 350 passengers and 3,500 tons of cargo at a top speed of eighteen knots. The ships made regular runs between Duluth, at the terminals of the great Northern Railroad, and their home port of Buffalo, New York, where the Pennsylvania Railroad terminated. Their names come from Pennsylvania rivers.

STEAMER OCTORARA (top). The last of the Anchor Line triplets, the Octorara was built in 1910. The Great Depression forced the Octorara to lay up in 1936, and in 1942 the Army converted her to a troop transport among the Hawaiian Islands. She was scrapped in San Francisco in 1952. The Octorara's brass bell hangs at the Dossin Great Lakes Museum at Belle Isle, Detroit, where it is rung each year during the annual blessing of the fleet in memory of ships and sailors lost to the Great Lakes.

STEAMER JUNIATA (right). Built in 1904, the Juniata was retired in 1936 but rebuilt over the winter of 1940–1941 and renamed the Milwaukee Clipper. From 1941–1970, the Milwaukee Clipper ran between Milwaukee and Muskegon, Michigan. It was renamed simply Clipper when a businessman bought it in 1977 to convert it into a museum ship. But the deal fell through, and a year later it moved to Chicago for use as a boutique-flotel at Navy Pier. In 1990, the ship moved to Hammond, Indiana, to be renovated into a tourist attraction with retail and office space.

STEAMER TIONESTA (bottom right). The Tionesta was built in 1903, the first of the Anchor Line triplets. Like her sisters, she was taken out of service in 1936, but was scrapped by Steel Company of Canada, at Hamilton, Ontario, in 1940.

STEAMER TIONESTA, DULUTH, MINN.

PASSENGER STEAMER NORTH WEST (right). Built in Cleveland, Ohio, in 1894 by the Globe Shipbuilding Company, the North West was operated by the Northern Steamship Company out of Buffalo, New York. Her days as a passenger ship ended in 1911, when she was gutted by fire while in Buffalo. In 1918 she was cut in half, lengthened, and rerigged as a saltie. In 1920 she was renamed the Maplecourt. She met her fate in the North Atlantic in 1941, torpedoed by a German U-Boat. All thirty-seven hands were lost.

STEAMER MINNESOTA (below). The Minnesota began life as the Harlem, one of two twin package freighters built in 1888 at Detroit Dry Dock in Wyandotte, Michigan. In 1898 she stranded on a reef near the entrance of Isle Royale's Siskiwit Bay. She was abandoned, salvaged, rebuilt, and sold (many times) until the Chicago & Duluth Transportation Company got ahold of her in 1911 and renamed her Minnesota. The ship traded hands several more times before becoming a hospital ship in 1917 for service in World War I. In order to get through the canals to the East Coast, she had to be cut in half in Cleveland, transported to Quebec, and reassembled. After the war she found herself in Jacksonville, Florida, where for a time she was operated as a floating hotel. Renamed Feliciana in 1928, she was abandoned just two years later and most likely scrapped in 1930.

NAVAL RESERVE SHIP GOPHER (bottom). The Gopher went from the warmth of the Florida Keys to the cold of Lake Superior. At her launch in 1871 she was christened the Fern and sailed along the East Coast carrying coal and other cargo and using her guns to destroy shipwrecks that blocked safe navigation. In 1898 she was transferred to Key West to carry supplies and mail to the growing U.S. armada gathering at Santiago and Guantanamo Bay for the Spanish-American War. Decommissioned in 1898, she eventually became part of the Minnesota Naval Militia and was renamed the Gopher in 1905. She later served as a training vessel in Chicago and, later still, with the Naval Reserve in Toledo, Ohio. On her way to Boston in 1922 she rammed and damaged a lock in the Soulanges Canal. The Canadian government apprehended her and held her in Quebec. In 1923, after her release, a northwest gale sank her in the Gulf of Lawrence.

11285. Steamer Minnesota in Duluth-Superior Harbor.

THE PASSENGER STEAMER, NORTHWEST, IN SUPERIOR BAY, SUPERIOR, WIS.

4877. U. S. Naval Reserve Training Ship "Gopher" Duluth, Minn.

STEAMER SINALOA UNLOADING COAL AT PITTSBURGH COAL DOCK, NO. 7, DULUTH, MINN.

STEAMER WILLIAM COREY LEAVING DULUTH-SUPERIOR HARBOR, LOADED WITH ORE.

FREIGHTER SINOLOA (left). The Sinoloa was originally named the William F. Rapprich when she first steamed out of West Bay, Michigan, in 1903, on her way to Duluth to serve for the Superior Steamship Company. In 1928 her new owners, the Clifton Steamship Company, renamed her the Sinoloa, the name she held until 1960, when she was rechristened the Stoneflax. In 1966 she collided with the Arthur Steven, a Norwegian freighter, in Welland Canal, and sank. She was raised later that year and was eventually scrapped in Santadar, Spain, in 1971.

FREIGHTER WILLIAM COREY (bottom left). The Pittsburgh Steamship company commissioned the Chicago Shipbuilding Company to build the William E. Corey, which launched in 1905. In her first year on the lakes she beached on Gull Island in the Apostle Islands and in 1917 she stranded on Lake Superior's Gros Cap Reef. She later became part of the U.S. Steel fleet and, in 1963, Toronto's Upper Lakes Shipping bought her and renamed her Ridgetown. In 1970 she was purposely sunk for use as a temporary breakwater during construction of harbor facilities in Nanticoke, Ontario. Raised, she was sunk purposefully again four years later for another breakwater in Port Credit, Ontario. The ship's namesake was president of U.S. Steel from 1903–1911.

Steamer Thos. F. Cole (Length 605½ ft.) Entering Duluth Harbor on her Maiden Trip, Duluth, Minn.

FREIGHTER THOMAS F. COLE (bottom right). The Pittsburgh Steamship Company of Cleveland, Ohio, ordered the Cole from the Great Lakes Engineering Company, and she was delivered in 1907. For forty-five years she hauled ore for PSC before being sold to U.S. Steel. In the fog on November 12, 1964, she collided with the Inverewe, a British motor vessel, off Pipe Island where the St. Mary's River empties into Lake Huron, severely damaging her port bow. She sold for scrap in 1980 and was hauled to the Western Metals Corporation in Thunder Bay, Ontario. She was named for Duluthian Thomas F. Cole, president of Oliver Mining from 1902–1909.

8686. The Wm. Livingstone coming into the Duluth Superior Harbor.

162-D—S. S. "Wilfred Sykes." One of the Largest Ore Boats on the Great Lakes

WILFRED SYKES

OC-H1325

STEAMER FITZGERALD LOCKING DOWN

IN DECEMBER AFTER A SEVENTY TWO HOUR BATTLE WITH A ZERO STORM ON LAKE SUPERIOR.
112948

According to the card, the sailors on the W. E. Fitzgerald successfully weathered a long and nasty storm on Lake Superior not long before the photo was taken that became the postcard above. Years later the Edmund Fitzgerald, named for the son of this ship's namesake, wouldn't be so lucky.

FREIGHTER WILLIAM LIVINGSTONE (above left). Great Lakes Engineering Works of Ecorse, Michigan, put the Livingstone together in 1908 for the Mutual Steamship Fleet. In 1936 the ship was renamed the S.B. Way, and twelve years later her name changed again, to the Crispin Oglebay, when she was converted to a self-unloader. She sold for scrap in 1973.

FREIGHTER W.E. FITZGERALD (left). It's no misprint—this is not the Edmund Fitzgerald of Lake Superior lore. The first "Fitz" was named for William Edmund Fitzgerald, president of the Milwaukee Drydock Company and father of Edmund. Built by the Detroit Shipbuilding Company of Wyandotte, Michigan, the ship first hit the water in 1906. It was scrapped in Humberstone, Ontario, in 1972.

ORE BOAT WILFRED SYKES (above). Built in 1949 by the American Shipbuilding Company of Lorain, Ohio, the Wilfred Sykes was declared "one of the largest ore boats on the Great Lakes." Named for an Inland Steel Company president, it is also the most modern boat featured in this book. Superior's Fraser Shipyard converted her to a self-unloader over the winter of 1974–75. She still plies the waters of the Great Lakes. This card is unique for two reasons: it is a linen card printed after 1945, and it has a white border, rarely found on linen cards.

Nor'easters in the Midwest?

The American Meteorological Society defines a Nor'easter as "A cyclonic storm of the East Coast of North America, so called because the winds over the coastal area preceding the storm's passage are from the northeast." Essentially, Nor'easters are very much like hurricanes, but they occur in much cooler climates and have cooler cores. They don't reach the same wind speeds, but they often last longer and cover a larger area. Lake Superior is far from the East Coast—so why do we have Nor'easters here? In part because Nor'easters are also defined as "extratropical cyclones, mid-latitude storms, or Great Lakes storms" (they can produce high winds and lake-effect snow in areas such as Buffalo, New York, and Cleveland, Ohio). But more than likely it is because folks are calling storms "Nor'easters" when they should be calling them "Alberta Clippers." Formed east of the Canadian Rockies, these low pressure systems gather force and "sail" (like a clipper ship of old) down through the Dakotas, across the Great Lakes, and on to New England. Unlike Nor'easters and hurricanes, Clippers usually produce very little precipitation—until they reach the Great Lakes. Once over water, they can create bands of lake-effect snow that hit snow belts (such as Lake Superior's Wisconsin South Shore) particularly hard.

A Late Arrival, Duluth, Minn.

32:—Mammoth Freighter, Covered

Ice Covered, unloading cargo of coal, Duluth-Superior Harbor.

A "Nor'easter," Duluth, Minn.

Lake Superior Tugboats

Tugboats of all shapes and sizes have long served the Great Lakes. The tugs include those designed to gently tow giant lakers and salties safely in and out of port, ice-breaking tugs like the *Record* and *Sinclair*, fire tugs like the *McGonagle*, and dredgers that helped dig out the St. Lawrence Seaway. Today the tow tug *Edna G.* is on display in Two Harbors and the dredger *Col. D. D. Gaillard* is part of a tourist attraction at Barker's Island in Superior, Wisconsin, along with the *Meteor*, the last of the Great Lakes whalebacks, which was designed and built in the Twin Ports (see page 47).

Ice Breaking in Harbor, Duluth, Minn. Always Cool.

Tugs "Record" and "Sinclair" breaking Ice in Duluth Harbor, Duluth, Minn.

ICE-BREAKING TUG RECORD. *The Globe Shipbuilding Company of Cleveland, Ohio, put the Record together in 1884, giving her an iron hull to smash through ice. She came to Duluth in 1887 as part of the Inman Tug Line, and later Union Towing & Wrecking Company. The Record had a record of sinking. She collided with tug Joe D. Dudley in 1895, and she crossed the Robert Fulton's bow during a heavy storm and sank in 1898, taking three lives with her. She was raised only to be rolled and sunk again in 1899 after the whaleback James B. Neilson increased speed while the Record was towing her (and another life was lost). Even at rest she was at risk: in 1902 while docked in Superior, she was struck by the Bradford and sank, at the cost of another life. She was moved to Michigan in 1927, later rerigged as a barge, and finally scrapped in 1975.*

ICE-BREAKING TUG SINCLAIR. *In 1907 the Dunham Towing Company of Chicago assembled the James R. Sinclair for Duluth's Union Towing & Wrecking Company. She served the Twin Ports until 1938, when the Roen Steamship Company of Sturgeon Bay, Wisconsin, bought her and changed her name to the John Roen, Jr. She then served ports in the U.S. and Canada. At Frankfurt, Michigan, in 1969, her crew tied her up in a dispute over back wages. She sank at City Dock and was later raised and renamed the Apollo in 1971.*

DIVING THROUGH THE ICE?
The postcard at left offered no explanation as to why a diver would brave the icy waters of Lake Superior or the St. Louis Bay during the winter. Perhaps something very valuable had to be salvaged, or a cable needed to be unwound from a ship's propeller. Whatever the case, it must have been mighty cold work in the days before insulated wetsuits.

DIVERS AT WORK THROUGH THE ICE, DULUTH, MINN.
No. 670. V. O. Hammon, Pub. Co., Minneapolis and Chicago.

18268

Dredging in Duluth Harbor, Duluth, Minn.

DREDGING TUGS (*above*). Steam dipper dredgers like the unidentified vessel pictured at right helped create the Duluth Ship Canal and the Duluth-Superior Harbor. The last and most famous of these dredgers was the 116-foot-long Col. D.D. Gaillard, built in 1916 by the U.S. Army Corps of Engineers and responsible for most of the work widening the St. Lawrence Seaway. The Gaillard was named for Lieutenant Colonel D. D. Gaillard, who served in the U.S. Army Corps of Engineers and was an engineer on the building of the Panama Canal. In 1915 President Wilson ordered a portion of the Panama Canal known as "Culebra Cut" renamed "Gaillard Cut" in honor of the late Lieutenant Colonel. Wilson said Gaillard had "ability of the highest class, untiring zeal, and unswerving devotion to duty."

FIRE TUG MCGONAGLE (*left*). Built in 1908 in Lorain, Ohio, by the American Shipbuilding Company for the Duluth, Missabe & Iron Range Railroad Company, the McGonagle was a 110-foot fire tug. She served the Twin Ports until 1935, when she was sold and her name changed to the Marguerite W. In 1953 she became the Ruth Hindman (and later the Lynda Hindman). In October 1966 her hull was stripped for conversion to a fish tug at Goderich, Ontario. Her superstructure was eventually scrapped at Ashtabula, Ohio, in November 1966. William McGonagle was president of the DM&IR railroad from 1909-1930.

FIRE TUG MC GONAGLE IN ACTION, SUPERIOR, WIS.

U.S. Government Building (Old Post Office)

431 W. 1st Street • 1894–1934

Oliver Traphagen & Francis W. Fitzpatrick, architects

A fine example of the many stone Romanesque Revival buildings that once graced Duluth, the U.S. Government Building's square stone tower reached five stories into the sky and its arched windows were trimmed in Bedford stone. The building stood at Fifth Avenue West and First Street, across the street from what is now the home of the *Duluth News-Tribune*. The heavy stone structure was often called the Post Office building, because it also held Duluth's central post office.

When it was dismantled in 1934, its arched doorway was supposed to go to Leif Erikson Park to act as a gateway to the park (if it did indeed move to the park, it is no longer there). A single nine-ton piece of stone featuring a carved eagle was also removed and was to be given to the Naval Reserve Station on Minnesota Point, but it was too heavy. Workers dismantling the building found a bottle within its walls; the bottle contained a cloth written with the message "goodby, Friends." It was dated November 11, 1892, and signed by "James Peterson, 14th Ave. E. and Charles Bowman, 465 23rd W."

The postcard above shows the U.S. Government Building after the new county courthouse was built in 1909. Note the courthouse behind the old post office.

9860 POST OFFICE AND CUSTOM HOUSE, DULUTH, MINN.

DETROIT PUBLISHING CO.

Whitewashed? Hardly. The card at left is another example of how colorists in Germany sometimes worked without the benefit of an accurate description of the building. In this case, the building's Lake Superior red sandstone is shown as white.

The undivided back card at the lower left shows a splendid bird's-eye view of the old post office before the courthouse was built, while the white border card below shows the building a few years later from a slightly different perspective. In the bottom card the house and large garden of the earlier card have been replaced with a manicured lawn where City Hall would eventually stand. The Incline Railway can be seen in the background.

BIRD'S-EYE VIEW DULUTH, LOOKING UPWARDS.
POSTOFFICE BUILDING TO LEFT

No. 698. V. O. Hammon Pub. Co., Minneapolis and Chicago

POST OFFICE AND COURT HOUSE, DULUTH, MINN.

71911

Civic Center Historic District

St. Louis County Courthouse • 1909
Daniel H. Burnham & Company, architects

St. Louis County Jail • 1923
Abraham Holstead & William J. Sullivan, architects

Duluth City Hall • 1928
Thomas Shefchik & Peter Olsen, architects

Federal Building/U.S. Courthouse and Customs House
1929 • Federal architects

Duluth's one-stop shop for some very impressive Classical/Renaissance architecture, the Civic Center includes the St. Louis County Courthouse, Duluth City Hall, and the U.S. Federal

ST. LOUIS COUNTY COURTHOUSE DULUTH. MINN.

747-30

CITY HALL, DULUTH, MINN.

362-30

Building—as well as a county jail, the Cass Gilbert-designed Soldiers & Sailors Monument (*Fortitude Defending the Flag*), and a fountain. The courthouse was designed by Daniel H. Burnham and went up in 1909; other architects designed the county jail, Duluth City Hall, and the Federal Building, but did so in a manner in keeping with Burnham's original idea. The gray granite building includes features such as Doric columns and lions heads. The jail is adorned with symbols of justice, including Roman fasces (a bundle of birch rods wrapped around an axe). The whole complex was part of the "City Beautiful" movement, a progressive reform movement of architecture and urban planning popular in the late 1890s and early twentieth century—it was thought that a beautiful city would create moral and civic virtue, people would behave, and the lives of inner-city poor would improve.

The card below shows the Soldiers & Sailors Monument—Fortitude Defending the Flag—in front of the St. Louis County Courthouse (top, center). Cass Gilbert designed the monument, which was added to the Civic Center in 1919.

The fountains shown in the card at lower left were never built, but a fountain was added to the mall near the Soldiers & Sailors Monument in the 1960s.

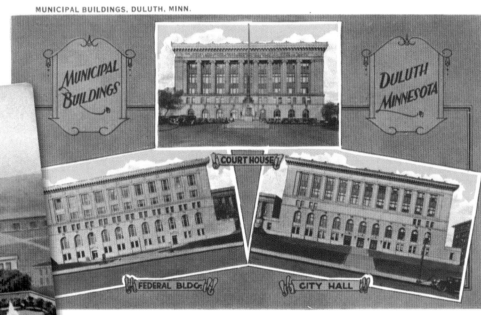

PUBLIC LIBRARY, DULUTH, MINN.

Duluth Public Library

102 W. 2ND STREET • 1902
ADOLPH F. RUDOLPH, ARCHITECT

When Duluth began to outgrow its first library, it used a $25,000 donation from Andrew Carnegie to help build a Neo-Classical brick sandstone structure that ultimately cost $65,000. The building includes a central dome and once held two Tiffany windows depicting the area's history (the windows are now on display at the Union Depot). An addition was built on the rear of the building in 1927. When a new library was built in 1980, the Carnegie building was converted to office space and is still in use today. Duluth's first library was housed on the second floor of the Temple Opera Building at 201 E. Superior Street and shared space with an opera house and a Masonic temple.

National Guard Armory

1305 LONDON ROAD • 1915
CLYDE KELLY & OWEN WILLIAMS, ARCHITECTS

Besides acting as headquarters for Duluth's Minnesota National Guard, the Duluth Armory also hosted hundreds of cultural events and national acts, including Louis Armstrong, Johnny Cash, Charlie Chaplin, Will Rogers, and many others. The armory also housed refugees from the 1918 Cloquet fire, and played host to the largest funeral ever held in Duluth: that of Albert Woolsen, the last surviving Union soldier from the Civil War, who died in 1956 at age 109. Woolsen, a drummer boy who never saw action but witnessed Sherman's march to the sea, lied about his age to enlist. Bob Dylan claims to have sat in the Armory's front row during a Buddy Holly concert at the Armory just days before Holly, Richie Valens, and the Big Bopper died in a plane crash. The Guard moved to new headquarters in 1977. Plans are underway to convert the building to the Armory Arts & Music Center.

NEW ARMORY, DULUTH, MINN.

U.S. Government Fish Hatchery

6008 London Road • 1880s
ARCHITECT UNKNOWN

U. S. Gov't Fish Hatchery, Duluth, Minn.

Because of its location at the mouth of the Lester River, the U.S. Government Fish Hatchery is more commonly known as the "Lester River Fish Hatchery." The simple stick-style building with Queen Anne features was built in the 1880s to raise native Lake Superior fish. The card at right shows the bins used to rear the fish. The University of Minnesota Duluth took over ownership when operations closed in 1948, and in 1955 converted it to a freshwater research station. Three other buildings, a carriage barn, a well house, and a cottage also make up the complex. Today it is called the Large Lakes Observatory. (A view of the Observatory from upstream in Lester Park can be found on page 93).

FOUNTAIN AT LAKEWOOD PUMPING STATION IN WINTER.
DULUTH, MINN.

There is no postcard of the Lakewood Pumping Station, but the card at left is of a fountain that once stood on the pumping station's grounds—frozen over and adorned with an American flag.

Lakewood Pump House

8120 Congdon Boulevard • 1897
ARCHITECT UNKNOWN (LIKELY DESIGNED BY CITY ENGINEERS)

People often wonder about the origins of the castle-like structure that sits along the road about three miles north of the Lester River. The short answer is this: keeping Duluth typhoid free. Before the Lakewood Pump House (with its Romanesque Revival-styled tower and battlements) was built, Duluth had a very primitive water system. In early years it was little more than a hog's head filled with lake water carted down Superior Street by a man hired by Camille Poirer, who started Duluth Tent and Awning. Typhoid epidemics in the city were the catalyst for both St. Luke's and St. Mary's Hospitals. Fearing that water close to the city could be contaminated by waste, city leaders had the pump built on the outskirts of town. It originally ran on steam power, but today's electric pumps supply the city with 20 million gallons of water a day. The tower's conical roof and a smokestack were removed during renovations in 1932.

Endion School

1801 E. 1ST STREET • 1890
ADOLPH F. RUDOLPH, ARCHITECT

Built in the Romanesque Revival style of red pressure brick, the Endion School hosted students from Duluth's Endion neighborhood for eighty-seven years until closing its doors in 1977. In 1970 vandals victimized its belfry, which subsequently had to be removed from the building. Today the building houses the Endion School Apartments.

The name "Endion" comes from a town site registered in 1856 and is Ojibwe for *my, your,* or *his home*. When the town was absorbed by a growing Duluth, it became a neighborhood. Endion Station, now found along the Lakewalk at the very corner of Lake Superior, once stood at Fifteenth Avenue East and South Street, but was relocated in the 1980s when Interstate 35 was extended through Duluth to Twenty-sixth Avenue East.

ENDION SCHOOL, DULUTH, MINN.

No. 676. V. O. Hammon Pub. Co., Minneapolis and Chicago

THE NEW DENFELD HIGH SCHOOL, DULUTH, MINN.   115476

Denfeld High School

4405 W. 4TH STREET • 1926
ABRAHAM HOLSTEAD & WILLIAM J. SULLIVAN, ARCHITECTS

Built in a style dubbed Collegiate English Gothic, Denfeld High School (home of the Hunters) reflects Renaissance ideals. The building is shaped like an **H** with a rising clock tower that stands for "aspiring idealism." The building's eight buttresses were intended to represent "the eight types of human beings who supported the human kingdom: masters, rulers, philanthropists, philosophers, magicians, scientists, devotees, and artists." Stone carvings of Renaissance symbolism adorn the school. The building is still in use as a high school today; it takes its name from Robert E. Denfeld, Duluth's superintendent of schools for over thirty years beginning in 1885.

Old Central High School

Lake Avenue & E. 2nd Street • 1892
Emmet S. Palmer & Lucien P. Hall, architects

Most everyone who has visited Duluth knows Old Central—its 230-foot clock tower rises above downtown and simply cannot be ignored. The Romanesque brownstone building is modeled after the Allegheny Courthouse in Pittsburgh, Pennsylvania. The building ceased operating as a school in 1971 and is now home to the Duluth School District's administrative offices. It was featured in the 1980s movie *Iron Will*, filmed in Duluth. In his description of Old Central's stone gargoyles, architectural historian James Allen Scott wrote that "about the cavernous entrance in the tower angelic cherubs lovingly smile while overhead grotesque animal figures leer their prurient intents." Those figures were carved by Duluth's master stone artisan, Norwegian immigrant O. George Thrana. The building's brownstone came from Fond du Lac's Krause Quarry and other quarries along the Wisconsin south shore. A tradition at Old Central held for seniors to climb the clock tower and sign their names on its walls.

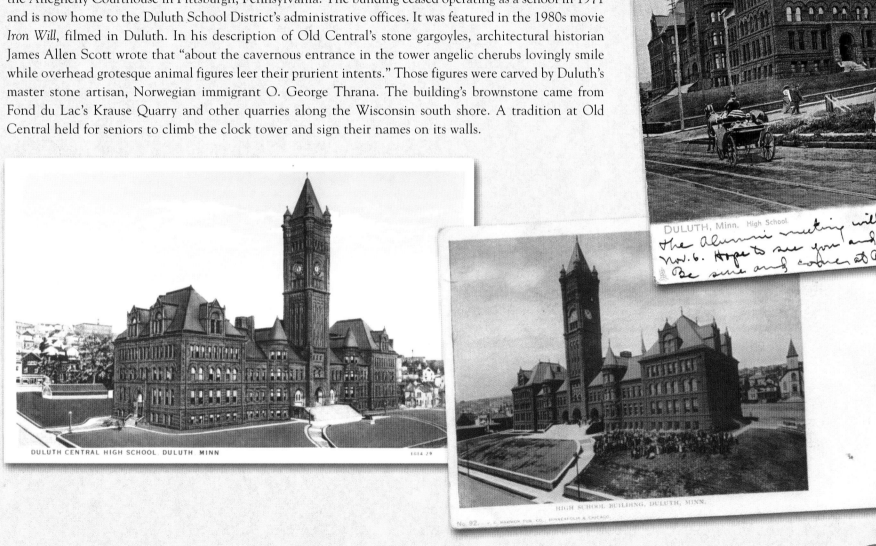

DULUTH, Minn. High School.

DULUTH CENTRAL HIGH SCHOOL, DULUTH, MINN

HIGH SCHOOL BUILDING, DULUTH, MINN.

College of St. Scholastica

KENWOOD AVENUE & COLLEGE STREET • 1909, 1938
ARCHITECT UNKNOWN

Duluth's College of St. Scholastica is the only independent private college in northeastern Minnesota, with a 186-acre campus set on a hill overlooking Lake Superior. St. Scholastica began as Sacred Heart Institute, a high school, in 1898. Tower Hall (the building shown in the card below and at the far right in the card to the right) went up in 1909. The school became a junior college in 1913 when a group of pioneering Benedictine sisters offered college courses to six young women. By 1924 it had developed into a four-year college for women. The chapel and library, seen at the center of the card at right, were built in 1938. The building to the left of the chapel was originally Stanbrook Hall, a residence for students.

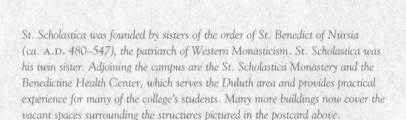

D-149—College of St. Scholastica, Duluth, Minn.

ADMINISTRATION BLDG., COLLEGE OF ST. SCHOLASTICA, DULUTH, MINN.—10

St. Scholastica was founded by sisters of the order of St. Benedict of Nursia (ca. A.D. 480–547), the patriarch of Western Monasticism. St. Scholastica was his twin sister. Adjoining the campus are the St. Scholastica Monastery and the Benedictine Health Center, which serves the Duluth area and provides practical experience for many of the college's students. Many more buildings now cover the vacant spaces surrounding the structures pictured in the postcard above.

Duluth Normal School

2205 E. 5th Street • 1898
Palmer, hall, & Hunt, Architects

In 1895 the State of Minnesota created the Normal School at Duluth. It was damaged by fire while under construction and opened in 1902. In 1905 it became the Duluth State Normal School. A west wing was added in 1909, an east wing in 1915. Its name was changed to the Duluth State Teachers' College in 1921, and finally, in 1947, to the University of Minnesota, Duluth Branch ("Branch" was dropped in 1959). In 1948 ground was broken for the first building of the new campus. The old campus continued to serve UMD students for years. Its central building, "Old Main," was used as a theater (performances are now held at the University's Marshall Performing Arts Center, built in 1974, and the Weber Music Hall, built in 2003).

Old Main was consumed by fire in February, 1993. The building was an architectural hybrid of Romanesque and renaissance features, but today only its arches stand preserved as a monument—the site has become a Duluth city park. Most of the buildings that surrounded Old Main are still in use by the university as research facilities. Torrance Hall, a former dormitory, has been converted into apartments.

State Normal School, Duluth, Minn.

12402. Normal School, Duluth, Minn.

State Normal School, Duluth, Minn.

Main Building

Torrance Hall

Washburn Hall

St. Mary's Hospital

404 E. 3RD STREET • 1898
ARCHITECT UNKNOWN

The first home of St. Mary's was in Lincoln Park, at Twentieth Avenue West and Third Street, where Benedictine sisters opened their hospital in 1888 due to the eruption of a typhoid epidemic. It moved to its building on East Third Street in 1898—and it's been expanding ever since.

The first addition was made in 1911, and a facility for X-rays was added the following year—the same year the St. Mary's School of Nursing graduated its first class. (That school is now an apartment building, and today in Duluth students can learn nursing at the College of St. Scholastica, another Benedictine organization.) St. Mary's doubled its patient capacity in 1922 when a six-story addition went up. The 1950s saw further growth, first with a psychiatric unit in 1955 and again in 1957 when a nine-story wing was added. Many more buildings have since been added, including a towering parking ramp that was completed in 2006. The hospital's campus now covers several city blocks, and that doesn't include various clinics in Duluth, Superior, Hermantown, and the Iron Range.

ST. MARY'S HOSPITAL, DULUTH, MINN.

A thrifty printer salvaged the above postcard of St. Mary's Hospital, originally mislabeled as St. Luke's Hospital. But, by the looks of it, the color couldn't be corrected.

Lumberjack Insurance

St. Mary's was certainly innovative in its early years. In the days when the timber industry reigned in northern Minnesota, long before medical insurance, St. Mary's own Sister Amata sold those who worked the lumber camps "lumberjack hospital tickets" for seventy cents a month. The cards guaranteed the jacks—who performed dangerous work and weren't always flush with money—medical care and a bed. It was one of the first plans of its kind in the nation.

St. Luke's Hospital

9TH AVENUE E. & 1ST STREET
1902 • ARCHITECT UNKNOWN

115-D—St. Luke's Hospital, Duluth, Minn.

Like St. Mary's, St. Luke's was started when an outbreak of typhoid threatened Duluth, but that epidemic was in 1881. Reverend J. A. Cummings of St. Paul's Episcopal Church responded to the threat by furnishing an old blacksmith shop with a few chairs, three beds, and a stove donated by British officials at the Duluth emigrant station. His first patient was a destitute old man who was treated for free. Cummings placed an ad in local papers and within a week housed twelve patients. Three years later the hospital relocated to a larger space at Second Avenue East and Fourth Street that could accommodate thirty-eight beds.

The building depicted in the postcards, at the hospital's present Ninth Avenue East and First Street location, first opened in 1902 with ninety-five beds. Like St. Mary's, its expansion has been ongoing. In 1926, five years after the hospital's management changed hands from St. Paul's to a nonsectarian board, a second wing was added and a nurse's dormitory went up on the upper side of the block. The hospital campus grew again in 1950, and in the late 1960s the original 1902 section, sometimes called the "old west building" was replaced with a new wing. Since then there has been so much development the old building is hardly recognizable behind layers of new construction.

Why was typhoid such a problem in Duluth that it prompted the start of the town's two major hospitals? Because *typhus bacillus* develops in tainted water supplies, and until nearly 1900 Duluth used a very primitive system to deliver fresh water to its residents: a hog's head filled with Lake Superior water and transported in a horse-drawn cart.

The card below shows one of Duluth's first skywalks, connecting hospital facilities across Tenth Avenue East. The brownstone structure behind the hospital is Jefferson School.

115-D. ST. LUKE'S HOSPITAL
DULUTH, MINN.

St. James Orphanage, Duluth, Minn.

Bethany Children's Home, Duluth, Minn.

Charitable Facilities

Besides opening hospitals to care for the sick, Duluth churches found other ways to provide for those in need, including setting up homes for homeless children. Missionary societies and social organizations helped as well. Many of these groups' members were of Duluth's upper class and often instilled with a sense of noblesse oblige—the belief that the wealthy and privileged are obliged to help those less fortunate. And at the turn of the last century, Duluth had more than its fair share of wealthy and privileged.

St. James Orphanage • 1910
4321 Allendale Avenue • Architect Unknown

(Top left) The Catholic Diocese operated St. James Orphanage (top left), which opened as a four-story building made of brick with Bedford stone trim in 1910. Besides housing children, the facility offered farm and industrial training. Kindergarten for neighboring St. John's School was taught at St. James, and in turn orphans from St. James were educated by Benedictine sisters at St. John's. In 1971 St. James became Woodland Hills, a residential treatment center for young people.

Bethany Children's Home • 1892
39th Avenue W. & 9th Street • Architect Unknown

(Left) The Bethany Children's Home (left) was originally the home of Alfred and Jane Merritt of the iron-mining Merritts. In 1916 the Swedish Lutheran Church established Bethany as an orphanage. The grand structure burned in 1920. A new facility was built in 1922 and another in 1975, but the children's home closed just five years later.

1765. Bethel Building, Duluth, Minn.

The Bethel Association Building • 1911
23 Mesaba Avenue • Vernon Price, Architect

(Right) Founded in 1873 as a missionary society to serve sailors visiting Duluth, the Bethel Association first put up a building in 1889 at 245 South Lake Avenue. It included a restaurant and also provided shelter for the area's homeless. That building came down in 1948, but the society had relocated to the building in the postcard at right in 1911. The society later expanded to serve workers (and their families) laboring in the lumber, mining, and rail industries. The building is now a drug and alcohol treatment facility and residence for those on work-release programs.

Y.W.C.A. Building

202 W. 2ND STREET • 1909
FREDERICK GERMAN & A.W. LIGNELL, ARCHITECTS

The Young Women's Christian Association came to Duluth in 1896 to offer assistance to "every unprotected young woman in Duluth" and opened its first building six years later. That facility's "narrow and inconvenient quarters" led to a fundraising drive to bankroll and furnish a new building, seen in the postcard at right. They raised much more than the $138,000 they had sought, and a good thing they did: the Neoclassical Revival structure cost $150,000.

The Y.W.C.A.'s objective is to "improve the spiritual, intellectual, social, and physical condition of young women." To this end the Y offered classes in everything from cooking to swimming, provided traveler's aid, arranged for interviews in its employment office, and of course provided living quarters for any "unprotected" girls who needed them. The Duluth Y even operated a summer camp, Camp Wanakiwin, which opened for ten weeks a year. In 1927 alone 527 local girls spent a week or more at the Barnum, Minnesota, facility.

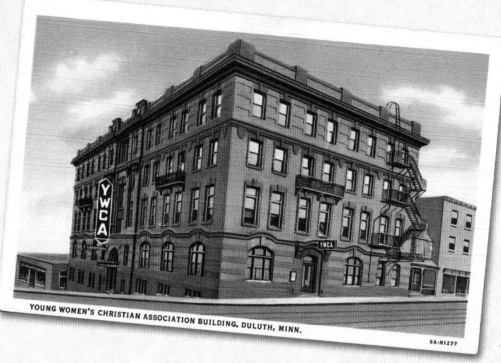

YOUNG WOMEN'S CHRISTIAN ASSOCIATION BUILDING, DULUTH, MINN.

6A-H1277

7565. Y. M. C. A. Building. Duluth, Minn.

Y.M.C.A. Building

302–312 W. 2ND STREET • 1907
FREDERICK GERMAN & A.W. LIGNELL, ARCHITECTS

One of the oldest organizations in Duluth, the Young Men's Christian Association has been serving the community since 1882, when it set up a free reading room and library association at 18 East Superior Street. Since then the Y has grown and spread throughout the city. Indeed, the building shown at left isn't the only Y.M.C.A. building in Duluth, but it has served as its central building since 1908. Local businessmen Julius Barnes and Ward Ames, Jr. also donated much of the cost of building branches on Lake Avenue and in West Duluth.

The Y got its start in the U.S. when a Boston sea captain named Thomas Sullivan tried to duplicate the efforts of the Y.M.C.A. in England, hoping to "put Christian principles into practice through programs that build a healthy spirit, mind, and body for all."

Protestant Churches

Long before any Protestant churches went up in Duluth—indeed, before there even was a Duluth—missionary Edmund F. Ely, a Massachusetts minister and teacher, had established himself as a Protestant force. At Fond du Lac he apparently berated the French Canadians who ran the American Fur Company post for practicing Catholicism. He later became one of Oneota's first residents, where he promoted business and shared his faith.

UNITED PROTESTANT CHURCH • 1922
88TH & ARBOR STREETS • FREDERICK GERMAN & LEIF JENSSEN, ARCHITECTS

(Below, lower-left corner) Built in Morgan Park for U.S. Steel's employees (the company also built a Catholic Church), United Protestant, like all the buildings in the company town, was made of cement stucco on concrete blocks.

PILGRIM CONGREGATIONAL CHURCH • 1916
2310 E. 4TH STREET • FREDERICK GERMAN & LEIF JENSSEN, ARCHITECTS

(Below, lower-right corner) This English Gothic church includes five Tiffany windows.

ST. PAUL'S EPISCOPAL CHURCH • 1913
1710 E. SUPERIOR STREET • BERTRAM GOODHUE, ARCHITECT

(Below left, top center) In 1913 the congregation at the first church built in Duluth—an 1869 Episcopalian structure located on the northwest corner of Lake Avenue and 2nd Street—chipped in to build a new one. Bertram Goodhue designed the church in the English Gothic style, very like an English country parish church. The original church was often called "Jay Cooke's Church" because the financier made a major contribution to its construction expenses.

FIRST PRESBYTERIAN CHURCH • 1891
300 E. 2ND STREET • TRAPHAGEN & FITZPATRICK, ARCHITECTS

(Below left, upper-left corner, below) This Romanesque building, constructed of varied shades of brown Lake Superior sandstone blocks and adorned with carvings and stained-glass windows, seems to erupt from the steep hillside. Its corner bell tower reaches 125 feet above Second Street, and inside it has enough pews to seat one thousand parishioners.

PRINCIPAL PROTESTANT CHURCHES OF DULUTH, MINN.

1st Presbyterian Church, Duluth, Minn.

The card at left has mislabeled two of the churches. The church at the lower left is the United Protestant Church in Morgan Park; the church in the lower right is the Pilgrim Congregational Church.

First Methodist Episcopal Church • 1892–1966
215 N. 3rd Avenue W.
Charles McMillen & Edwin S. Radcliffe, Architects

(Left) Built for $120,000 in 1892, the Gothic red sandstone First Methodist Episcopal Church seated 2,200 parishioners when all its galleries were open. All of its windows were stained glass, and paintings adorned the interior walls. Its chimes were the first to be installed in Duluth. The ten bells, the largest of which weighed 1,200 pounds, played in two keys and were the gift of Thomas and George Martin, who paid $10,000 for them in 1921. The chimes rang each day at noon, before Sunday services, and on national holidays and other special occasions.

Because most of its parishioners had moved away from the downtown area, the church closed its doors after its last service on November 6, 1966. It was replaced by the Pietro Belluschi-designed First United Methodist Church, known as the "Coppertop Church," at Skyline Parkway and Central Entrance.

The church also held a historic pipe organ made by the Austin firm of Hartford, Connecticut. The organ, a gift from a parishioner, had 1,500 pipes and was originally water driven. The instrument was dismantled before the church was torn down. Its cathedral chimes and stops were transplanted into the new church's organ.

FIRST M. E. CHURCH, DULUTH, MINN.

No. 761. V. O. Hammon Pub. Co., Minneapolis and Chicago

A view of the front of First Methodist Episcopal (left) and another looking at the rear (top).

NORWEGIAN LUTHERAN CHURCH, DULUTH, MINN.

No. 662. V. O. Hammon Pub. Co., Minneapolis and Chicago

Norwegian Lutheran Church • 1895
31 E. 3rd Street • Architect Unknown

(Right) The Norwegian Lutheran Church, a simple wooden structure, was built behind Central High School just three years after that brownstone monument first graced the hillside. The church changed its name to First Lutheran Church around 1930 and moved when a new church was built on East Superior Street in 1950. The original building was razed in 1972.

Catholic Churches

Jesuit missionaries traveling with French explorers made maps and spread Catholicism to Lake Superior's shores as early as the seventeenth century. They called Lake Superior *Lac Tracy*, after the provincial governor of New France, which included the Lake Superior region.

CHURCH OF THE BLESSED MARY MARGARET • 1918
1467 88TH AVENUE W. • DEAN & DEAN, ARCHITECTS

(Below, top left corner) U.S. Steel built this church for its Catholic workers; like United Protestant and all the buildings in the company town, it is made principally of concrete block.

ST. ANTHONY OF PADUA • 1922
1028 E. 8TH STREET • FREDERICK GERMAN, ARCHITECT

(Below, top-right corner) This Spanish Colonial-style church closed for services in 1984 and is now used for Benedictine Childhood Programs.

ST. CLEMENT'S CHURCH • 1911
2024 W. 3RD STREET • ARCHITECT UNKNOWN

(Below, bottom right corner) Although it closed its doors in 1974, this grand church graced Lincoln Park for over eighty years before it was demolished in 1992.

CATHEDRAL OF SACRED HEART • 1896
201 W. 4TH STREET
GEARHARD TENBUSCH, ARCHITECT

(Below, bottom left corner; right; bottom) Once the home of the archdiocese of Duluth, the Cathedral of Sacred Heart served Catholics in Duluth for eighty-seven years. Although it was replaced as the seat of the archdiocese in 1957 when the Cathedral of Our Lady of the Rosary opened its doors, masses were held here until Sacred Heart merged with St. Mary Star of the Sea in 1985. The postcard below shows Sacred Heart's parish house as well, also built in 1896, which acted as a rectory and the home of the diocese bishop. It was razed in 1956.

The church is now the home of the Sacred Heart Music Center, which presents a wide variety of concerts and houses a recording studio. The former cathedral has also retained its historic 1898 Felgemaker pipe organ, considered one of the finest instruments of its kind in the entire state. The center often provides visitors opportunities to hear (and even play) the organ. The building has retained some of its original beauty, including an Italian marble altar; unfortunately, the church's wooden pews have been replaced by chairs that distract considerably from the building's beauty.

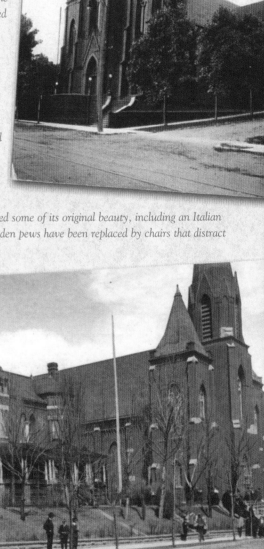

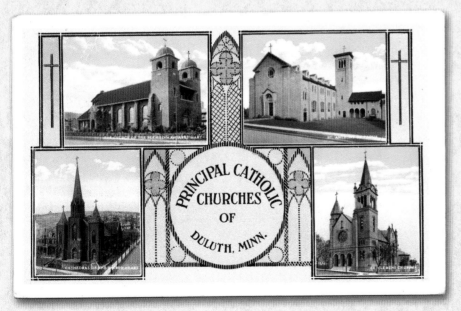

PRINCIPAL CATHOLIC CHURCHES OF DULUTH, MINN.

CATHEDRAL AND PARISH HOUSE. DULUTH, MINN.

Duluth's Grand Hotels

Duluth has been home to hotels both simple and opulent since before the town even had a name. In 1855 Robert Jefferson, who surveyed and platted the Town of Duluth in 1856, built a two-story frame structure at 430 Lake Avenue South and operated it as a hotel catering to settlers and visitors. One of the hotel's early residents was Thomas Preston Foster, who founded the *Minnesotian*, Duluth's first daily newspaper, on April 24, 1869. Foster also coined the phrase from which this book takes its title, calling Duluth "The Zenith City of the unsalted seas." The Jefferson House was taken down some time in the 1920s. Duluth's earliest "luxury" hotel, the Clark House (financed by Jay Cooke), opened on the 100 block of West Superior Street in 1870. It became the social center of Duluth, hosting dinners, dances, and meetings until it burned in 1881.

COCKTAIL LOUNGE

HOTEL HOLLAND

DULUTH, MINNESOTA

LOBBY OF THE HOTEL HOLLAND, DULUTH, MINNESOTA   114534

Hotel Holland. 250 Rooms. 150 with Baths. The Only Fire Proof Hotel in The City. Duluth, Minn.

HOTEL HOLLAND • 1910
5TH AVENUE W. & SUPERIOR STREET
WILLIAM T. BRAY & CARL E. NYSTROM, ARCHITECTS

The Holland was originally built as a four-story structure (right), but more floors were added just a year after it went up (left). When the addition was complete, the hotel boasted 250 rooms ("150 with Baths") and included such amenities as an opulent lobby (above) and a cocktail lounge (top). The Holland was also the first "fire proof" hotel in town.

DULUTH'S NEW $2,400,000 HOTEL

HOTEL DULUTH, DULUTH, MINN.—A SCHROEDER HOTEL   104581

Bear and Drunk Square Off

Although the story has been repeated time and again, no book can mention the Hotel Duluth without telling the tale of how the hotel's Black Bear Lounge got its name.

Early on a Sunday morning in August 1929, Arvid Peterson was driving down London Road with a truckload of fish fresh from the North Shore. At Twenty-sixth Avenue East he noticed a large black bear following his truck. The bear trailed him all the way to the corner of Superior Street and Third Avenue East—to the Hotel Duluth.

The bear apparently lost its taste for fish when it smelled the food being prepared in the hotel's coffee shop. It stood on its hind legs, swung a paw, smashed through a fifteen-foot-tall plate-glass window, then entered the hotel through the broken window and ran straight to the coffee shop.

A man described by newspapers as a "local drunk"—either up very early or still out quite late from the night before, if his reputation was deserved—grabbed a hammer and followed the bear through the broken window. The would-be hero yelled and waved the hammer, facing down the bear. All the commotion woke night watchman Albert Nelson, who ran to the lobby to see what was the matter. When Nelson saw the bear, he quickly alerted the assistant manager, who called police.

Nelson and the drunk occupied the bear, the inebriated man waving his hammer as the night watchman threw tables and chairs at the hungry bruin. As the battle went on, guests rushed to the lobby, and the faces of curious passersby filled the windows. Soon a crowd had gathered.

Duluth police officers Sergeant Eli Le Beau and Patrolman John Hagen answered the assistant manager's call. Along with members of the crowd, the officers used a rope to try to lasso the bear. After avoiding capture, the bear appeared to be bearing down on Nelson. Fearing that the watchman's life was in danger, Sergeant Le Beau raised his rifle and fired once, striking the bear in the head. The bear stood on its hind legs, wobbled for a moment, then fell down dead.

The bear's carcass was stuffed, mounted, and displayed in the front window of the hotel. When prohibition ended in 1932, the bear was moved to the coffee shop which then became, appropriately enough, the Black Bear Lounge. The lounge has since closed.

Grandma's Marketplace in Canal Park displays a stuffed bear, standing on its hind legs, long thought to be the fish-hungry bruin dispatched by Sergeant Le Beau, but some claim photos of the taxidermied bear show it was mounted posed on all fours.

THE HOTEL DULUTH • 1925
227 E. SUPERIOR STREET • MARTIN TULLGREN & SONS, ARCHITECTS

The Hotel Duluth, built in 1924 for a cost of $2.4 million, is made of reinforced steel and concrete and boasts many wonderful architectural features, such as a Classic Revival façade, a lobby and mezzanine designed in the Italian Renaissance style, and what its builders called a "typical Spanish dining room." One of the Schroeder chain's finest hotels, it is also the largest in

Duluth. Over the years the Hotel Duluth hosted such celebrities as Pearl Bailey, Charles Boyer, Henry Fonda, and Liberace. President John F. Kennedy stayed in the hotel in the summer of 1963, two months before he was assassinated in Dallas. Today it is known as Greysolon Plaza and its rooms are dedicated to senior housing while its ballroom hosts wedding receptions, proms, and other large gatherings; the building also houses the Chinese Garden restaurant. In 2005 new owners announced plans to bring the hotel back to its former glory—and purpose.

THE SPALDING HOTEL • 1889–1963
5TH AVENUE W. & SUPERIOR STREET • JAMES EGAN, ARCHITECT

When William Witter Spalding and his brother I. C. Spalding arrived in Duluth in 1869, they opened a general store at the southeast corner of Fifth Avenue West and Superior Street. Twenty years later a two-hundred-room hotel seven stories high and made of brownstone, brick, and terra cotta stood on the same corner and bore the brothers' name. Arguably Duluth's finest hotel, the Spalding featured the lavish Palm Dining Room and a rooftop pavilion that provided a spectacular harbor view for its guests. A grand opening was held on June 10, 1889, and the next day the Duluth Evening Herald lavished the building with praise, calling it "A noble piece of architecture" and "A magnificent pile of brick, iron, and stone towering eight stories above the street level." (The newspaper apparently counted one floor too many.) The Spalding closed its doors on July 1, 1963, and was razed just four months later.

HOTEL SPALDING,
DULUTH. MINN.

SPALDING HOTEL LOUNGE, DULUTH, MINN.

7569. Spalding Hotel, Duluth, Minn.

HOTEL LINCOLN, LOBBY, DULUTH, MINN.

ARROWHEAD HOTEL • 1925
225 N. 1ST AVENUE W.
ARCHITECT UNKNOWN

(Above) When this small hotel went up in 1925 it included
fifty-five rooms, a dining room, and a "women's reading room."
It is now a boarding house called Arrowhead House.

HOTEL REX • 1913
2001 W. SUPERIOR STREET
ARCHITECT UNKNOWN

(Above) The Rex has gone through
significant renovations and at least two
name changes since it first opened its
doors. From 1930 to 1942 it was called
the Curtis Hotel; it was the Milner
Hotel from 1942 to 1958; and since
1959 it has been known as the Seaway
Hotel. When it was built it stood just
two stories high, but two additional
floors were added at an unknown date.
Today the building is once again two
stories high, but it is not known when
the addition was removed. Today the
Seaway is a residential hotel.

HOTEL LINCOLN • 1926
309-317 W. 2ND STREET
STARIN & MELANDER, ARCHITECTS

(Left; above) The Lincoln, a patterned-brick building with limestone trim boasting
105 rooms, a restaurant, and a beauty parlor, opened in 1925. In 1973 it became
low-income housing, and in 1981 senior housing. It closed in 1988 and sat vacant
until it was demolished in 2004. The land it stood on is now a parking lot.

Hotel Lenox, Duluth, Minn.

Cascade Hotel • 1923
101 W. 3rd Street • Architect Unknown

(Below) The three-story brick Cascade Hotel was originally built for use as residential apartments. In 1942 the Coast Guard leased the entire building for its sailors. In 1996 the hotel became an apartment building called Olde Worlde Inne.

Hotel Lenox • 1904
601 W. Superior Street
John J. Wangenstein, Architects

(Above) The six-story Lenox held two hundred rooms, a cocktail lounge that sat 190 people, and had a separate "Ladies Entrance" until its doors closed in 1961; it was demolished soon after.

McKay Hotel • 1902
430 W. Superior Street • Architect Unknown

(Below; lower right) The McKay, with a grand fireplace and animal trophies adorning its lobby, became apartments in 1957 and was razed in the 1960s.

CASCADE HOTEL, DULUTH, MINN.

111060

Lobby, Hotel McKay, Duluth, Minn.

McKay Hotel, Duluth, Minn.

St. Louis Hotel • 1893
318-324 W. Superior Street
Traphagen & Fitzpatrick, Architects

(Above) The original St. Louis Hotel, built in 1882, burned in 1893. The 114-room structure pictured above replaced it. The St. Louis served as a gathering place for financiers and politicians and was the unofficial home of the Duluth Snowshoe and Toboggan Association and the Duluth Ski Club. In 1932 it met with the wrecking ball.

West Superior Street's Lower 300 Block

The lower or lake side of the 300 block of West Superior Street features some of Duluth's most prominent office buildings, as the title of the postcard below indicates. Except for the Moore Memorial building (the smaller structure to the left of the Torrey Building) and the building at the right edge of the card, all the structures pictured in the postcard below—a linen card printed some time after 1933—still stand today.

LONSDALE BUILDING • 1895
300 W. SUPERIOR STREET • PALMER, HALL, & HUNT, ARCHITECTS

(Below, far left) Before the Lonsdale occupied the southwest corner of Third Avenue East and Superior Street, it was the site of the first Board of Trade building. Fire claimed the original Board of Trade in 1894, and the Lonsdale went up just a year later.

TORREY BUILDING • 1892
314-316 W. SUPERIOR STREET • TRAPHAGEN & FITZPATRICK, ARCHITECTS

The Torrey was named for its owner, Captain Robert A. Torrey, a Civil War veteran. Eleven stories high, newspapers of the day called the building Duluth's "first skyscraper."

ALWORTH BUILDING • 1910
306 W. SUPERIOR STREET
DANIEL H. BURNHAM, ARCHITECT

Alworth Building, Duluth, Minn.

Sixteen stories of concrete and steel covered in buff-colored brick and terra cotta made the Alworth Building the tallest in Duluth—and almost one hundred years later, it remains the city's highest. You have to have a good eye to see its ornamental features, most of which appear at the top floor. The building is crowned with an ornate cornice and oval window openings on the top floor and features lion heads carved from stone. Constructing what the Duluth News-Tribune once called "a cosmopolitan office building, one that dwarfs the Tower of Babel" and "an epoch in the architectural history of Duluth" cost a mere $500,000. It took workers just nine months to build the Alworth, as much a feat today as it was in 1910—and most of the work was done during winter months. The building was named for prominent Duluth attorney Marshal W. Alworth.

MEDICAL ARTS BUILDING • 1933
324 W. SUPERIOR STREET • ERNEST R. ERICKSON, ARCHITECT

The newest kid—in this postcard, at least—on West Superior's 300 block, the Medical Arts Building is one of the few Art Deco structures in Duluth. Area physicians petitioned to have the $1 million building constructed. Today it still serves its original purpose.

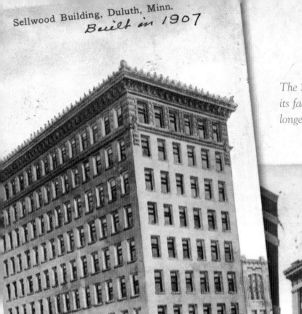

Sellwood Building, Duluth, Minn.
Built in 1907

Published by Hoyt E. Boylan

The Sellwood Building still stands, but its façade has been altered so that it no longer resembles the postcard at left.

Sellwood Building

202 W. SUPERIOR STREET • 1907
WILLIAM A. HUNT, ARCHITECT

The Sellwood Building (far left), designed in the Classical Revival style, offered space for 113 offices. Unfortunately, its façade was altered in 1967. The building takes its name from Captain John Sellwood, a miner who in 1865 set out from his home in Cornwall, England, for the copper mines in northern Michigan. After finding great success in various mining partnerships, he moved to Duluth and built three homes at the corner of Eighteenth Avenue East and Superior Street, one for himself and two as wedding presents for his daughters.

BOARD OF TRADE, DULUTH, MINN.

Board of Trade Building

301 W. 1ST STREET • 1895
TRAPHAGEN & FITZPATRICK, ARCHITECTS

Fire has shaped the history of this great old building (center and right). It was built after the original Board of Trade building burned in 1894, and its cornice was removed after another fire damaged the building in 1948. Built of steel, stone, brick, and marble, the ornate Romanesque structure with a two-story entrance and elaborate O. George Thrana stone carvings cost $350,000. Today the building is used as office space for attorneys and architects. In the 1990s the trading floor was renovated and it now serves as rehearsal space for the Minnesota Ballet.

BOARD OF TRADE, DULUTH, MINN.

Gowan–Lenning–Brown Building

525 S. LAKE AVENUE • 1915
FREDERICK E. GERMAN, ARCHITECT

Built in the shadow of the Aerial Transfer Bridge, the Gowan-Lenning-Brown Building has been a fixture of Canal Park since 1915. The firm was started by Henry Patrick Gowan and his partners in 1878 and operated until 1935. Stone medallions featuring the likeness of George Washington adorn the building's facade. Today the structure is called the Paulucci Building for its owner, Jeno Paulucci, who returned from World War II with an idea to can ready-to-eat meals and grew it into an enterprise that once included Chun-King Foods. Members of his family operate the Grandma's restaurant chain and other Canal Park restaurants.

GOWAN-LENNING-BROWN BUILDING, DULUTH, MINN.

Today the Gowan-Lenning-Brown Building is known as the Paulucci Building, and includes Grandma's Marketplace.

Wolvin Building

227 W. 1ST STREET • 1902
JOHN J. WANGENSTEIN, ARCHITECT

When the Wolvin first went up in 1902, it was six stories high—another three were added in 1909, as shown in the postcard above. Built by Captain August B. Wolvin, the building's primary tenants included subsidiary companies of U.S. Steel and the Duluth, Missabe & Northern Railroad. Ironically, Wolvin and others had also acquired and modernized the West Duluth Blast Furnace Company, turning it into a profitable operation that competed with its tenant, U.S. Steel in Morgan Park. By the 1970s the building's name had changed to the Missabe Building.

Marshall-Wells Hardware

325 S. LAKE AVENUE • 1900
ARCHITECT UNKNOWN

In 1893 Albert Marshall bought a wholesale hardware business and renamed it Marshall-Wells, and then he built himself a warehouse on South Fifth Avenue West. His business prospered, and soon he was shipping throughout the Midwest and Canada. Marshall-Wells got in on the manufacturing end as well, making everything from tools to appliances to paint under the "Zenith" house brand name. Business was going so well that in 1900 Marshall built the huge plant and warehouse seen at right. The building was designed in two sections and straddled railway tracks. Ten years later the company became the world's third largest hardware wholesaler and the largest in the United States. The company also operated over one thousand retail stores in the U.S. and Canada. But by the late 1950s the company had liquidated, and the buildings were sold. Today the complex has been divided into a hotel, restaurants, and various offices.

Aeroplane View, Marshall Wells Main Building, Duluth, Minn.

4922. Wholesale District, Duluth, Minn.

Stone-Ordean-Wells (et al)

203-211 S. 5TH AVENUE W. • 1893
TRAPHAGEN & FITZPATRICK, ARCHITECTS

Stone-Ordean-Wells began in 1872 as a wholesale grocer operated by William R. Stone; the name changed when he became partners with Albert Ordean and Benjamin Wells. Their house brand was called "Nokomis." The warehouse shown in the postcard was built in 1893 and was part of Duluth's Wholesale District.

The seven-story building to the left of Stone-Ordean-Wells—built in 1903 and also designed by Traphagen's firm—housed the F. A. Patrick Company, which operated as a dry goods wholesaler beginning in 1900. Further down Commerce Street (look for the "Hickory" sign) Kelley-How-Thomson specialized in wholesale hardware—the firm called its house brand "Hickory"—and competed with Marshall-Wells. The building went up in 1888 as the Wells-Stone Mercantile; Kelley-How-Thomson moved there in 1896. All the buildings along Fifth Avenue West near Commerce Street were razed in 1966.

McDougall Terminal

9TH AVENUE W. & RAILROAD STREET • 1923
S. SCOTT JOY, ARCHITECT

Built in 1923 as a cold-storage warehouse, the McDougall Terminal was served by its own fleet of boats outfitted with refrigeration units that brought food to and from Duluth and New York—the largest such operation in the world at the time. The building's operations were under the direction of A. M. McDougall, son of famed local shipbuilder Alexander McDougall (see page 147). By the 1940s the name had been changed to Duluth Terminal Building, and in the 1960s the building also became home to an electronics firm. The building was demolished some time around 1980.

7571. "Soo" Line Depot, Duluth, Minn.

McDOUGAL TERMINAL BUILDING, DULUTH, MINN.

Engineers blasted a tunnel through Point of Rocks and under Superior and Michigan Streets so that trains could reach the Soo Depot, shown above and at left.

The card below left includes a typo: there should be two Ls in "McDougall."

"Soo Line" Passenger Depot

602 W. SUPERIOR STREET • 1910
BELL, TYRIE & CHAPMAN, ARCHITECTS

A lot of engineering went into the creation of the passenger depot for the Soo Line—more formally known as the Minneapolis, St. Paul & Sault Ste. Marie Railroad. It was not so much building the Classical Revival structure as it was figuring out how to get trains to the station at Sixth Avenue West and Superior Street, adjacent to but above the Union Depot. To avoid disrupting street traffic, a tunnel was blasted through Point of Rocks from Eighth and Twelfth Avenues West and under Superior and Michigan Streets. Passenger service ended in 1964; the building was razed in 1972.

Union Depot, Duluth, Minn.

Duluth, Minn. Union Depot.

The many colors of the Union Depot, at least as far as postcards go. The real Depot looks most like the card in the center: yellow bricks and a green roof.

Union Depot

505 W. MICHIGAN STREET • 1892
PEABODY & STEARNS, ARCHITECTS

7563. Union Depot, Duluth, Minn.

Designed by Boston architects Robert Swain Peabody and John Goddard Stearns to resemble a French Norman chateau on a grand scale, Duluth's Union Depot—including track, a roundhouse, and a shed system—was built in 1892 for a cost of $615,000. At one point, it serviced over sixty trains a day from the St. Paul & Duluth, Northern Pacific, and other railways. In 1910, trains from seven railroads carried five thousand people to and from the Depot each day. It closed as a railroad depot in 1969 and is now home to the St. Louis County Heritage and Arts Center, which houses museums, offices, the St. Louis County Historical Society, a theater, and studio space for five performing arts organizations including the Duluth Children's Museum, the Duluth Art Institute, the Minnesota Ballet, and the Duluth Playhouse. It also houses the Lake Superior Railroad Museum, which operates the North Shore Scenic Railway. The train shed behind the Depot (as seen in the postcards above) was razed in 1924.

Commercial Club Building, Duluth, Minn.

Kitchi Gammi Club

402 W. 1st Street • 1912
Bertram Goodhue, Architect

In 1883 sixteen Duluth men—including Chester Congdon and Guilford Hartley—formed the Kitchi Gammi Club, the first men's club in the state (female guests used a side entrance as late as the 1980s). After renting several locations, including rooms in the Grand Opera House, the club built itself a $304,000 home in 1912 (below). The building features elements of Gothicism mixed with Georgian pilasters and Tudor details along with the stone carvings of O. George Thrana. Many wealthy men from out of town became members so that they could stay at the Kitch rather than a hotel when in town on business. One, Andrew Carnegie, was expelled for not paying his dues. The building was designed by Hartley's friend Bertram Goodhue, who also drew the plans for the Hartley Building across the street from the Kitch (734 East Superior Street), and St. Paul's Episcopal Church (1710 East Superior Street), about a half mile down the road.

Commercial Club

402 W. 1st Street • 1908
Bray & Nystrom, Architects

Duluth's Commercial Club (above) was an organization much like today's Chamber of Commerce or the Duluth Convention and Visitors Bureau: a booster organization made up of locals, mostly business owners, to promote Duluth as a great place to open a business or take a vacation. In the 1940s and 1950s the building was home to the Duluth Athletic Club. (Unfortunately, while renovating the building, the Athletic Club had its brick façade covered over.) Club members enjoyed workout facilities, courts for handball and other sports, and a small restaurant. Between 1976 and 1994 the building played host to one of Duluth's most popular restaurants, the Chinese Lantern, along with its companion business, the Brass Phoenix nightclub. Fire put an end to the Chinese Lantern. In recent years a new restaurant with an old name has taken the Chinese Lantern's place: The Duluth Athletic Club.

KITCHI GAMMI CLUB, DULUTH, MINN.

48537

Elks Hall

309-311 W. 1st Street • 1909
Radcliffe & Price, Architects

The Benevolent and Protective Order of Elks was started by a group of New York actors and entertainers in 1867 so they could get together for a drink on Sundays, an act prohibited by New York's "blue laws." When one of the group died, leaving his family destitute, they became a benevolent society. Why "Elk"? Because "the elk is a peaceful animal, but will rise in defense of its own in the face of a threat." The Elks left their hall in 1975. The building has since lost its ornate façade.

THE MASONIC TEMPLE, DULUTH, MINN.

Elks' Hall, Duluth, Minn.

Before they got serious as a benevolent society, the Elks called themselves the "Jolly Corks" after a drinking game their founder enjoyed.

Masonic Temple

4 W. 2nd Street • 1912
Architect Unknown

Mystery surrounds the Masons. George Washington belonged to the order, and some say they remain a force behind global politics. Whatever the truth, they've left more than a few interesting buildings in their wake. Home to the Palestine Lodge #79, first established in 1869, the Masonic Temple is one of many buildings the Masons have constructed in Duluth (their first permanent home was the ornate Temple Opera Building; see page 131). The Second Street building once boasted Moorish onion-shaped domes at each corner of its roof, but they have since been destroyed (and an elevator has been added). Its cornerstone was laid August 10, 1904, by Masonic Grand Master of Minnesota William A. McGonagle. Many say the Masons were quite influential in Duluth's development. J. B. Culver, Duluth's first mayor, was also the first Master of Palestine Lodge…coincidence?

Northland Country Club, Duluth, Minn.

The original 1903 Northland Country Club (left) and the 1919 replacement (below). In 2005 the Club announced plans to build a new structure in the same style as the first.

NORTHLAND COUNTRY CLUB, DULUTH, MINN.

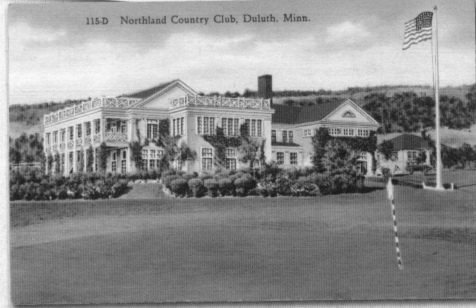

115-D   Northland Country Club, Duluth, Minn.

Northland Country Club

3901 E. Superior Street • 1903 & 1913
Architects Unknown

The first Northland Country Club burned in the 1918 Cloquet Fire that destroyed thousands of acres and turned Duluth's National Guard Armory into a refugee shelter. During the early years of the club, a herd of sheep was used to keep the grass down to playing level. For the first twenty-eight years of the course (first played in 1899), six of its holes were positioned across Superior Street (the three-hundred yard number five actually played across the street; six, seven, and eight were entirely on the lower side; and nine crossed back over Superior). In 1927 a redesign positioned all the holes safely above Superior Street. Club member Albert Ordean bought the newly vacated land below Superior Street and donated it to the city for use as an athletic field. That land is now home to Ordean Middle School, soccer and football practice fields, and Ordean Stadium.

The second Duluth Boat Club on the bay side of Park Point near 10th Street (below). The clubhouse at right was the former home of the Duluth Yacht Club— which the Boat Club purchased and moved to Park Point at Oatka Beach. The Club had another boathouse on Spirit Lake (see page 102) and a facility at Pike Lake.

Duluth Boat Club

10TH STREET, PARK POINT (BAY SIDE) • 1903
OATKA BEACH, PARK POINT (BAY SIDE) • 1906

In 1886 eleven local men got together to form the Duluth Boat Club and soon after built a grand clubhouse along the lake at Seventh Avenue West on the Northern Pacific Slip in St. Louis Bay. A second clubhouse was built at Tenth Street on the bay side of Minnesota Point in 1903. Three years later, the club acquired the former Duluth Yacht Club and moved it to Oatka Beach, three miles down the Point.

The club was a mecca for sports wet and dry: tennis, swimming, rowing, canoeing, sailing, and others. At its peak in 1912 the exclusive club had 1,400 members (the largest club of its kind in the nation) and became the hub of social activities for Duluth's elite, hosting lavish parties, banquets, dances, and other events. When the second clubhouse opened in 1903, five hundred people attended the gala event. The society columns of Duluth's newspapers called the dance floor "the most exclusive ballroom in the city."

The Boat Club produced twenty national-champion rowing crews led by coach James Ten Eyck, Jr. (who had been hired by Duluth businessman and Boat Club benefactor Julius Barnes) and in 1916 played host to the national championships. But by 1926 Ten Eyck had left and automobiles were all the rage. Starving for funds, the club closed its doors.

CURLING CLUB, DULUTH, MINN.

Duluth Curling Club

1330 LONDON ROAD • 1912
FREDERICK G. GERMAN, ARCHITECT

Curling is a shuffleboard-like sport played on a sheet of ice with brooms and rocks with handles—Scottish bocce ball, if you will. Local residents have participated in organized curling since Christmas Day 1891, when players first slid their stones across the ice of St. Louis Bay, where snow had been cleared. The Duluth Curling Club was born a year later on a $400 rink at Third Avenue East and Superior Street. Built in 1912, the London Road Curling Club eclipsed all other curling facilities in sheer number of rinks, with twelve. Ice skaters and hockey players used rinks on the second floor and in the summer the space was used for roller skating. In 1984 the curling club caught fire and was demolished just before work on the I-35 extension began. The space on which it stood is now a parking lot next to the Rose Garden. Today, the Curling Club practices and competes at its facility inside the Duluth Entertainment and Convention Center. (By the way, Superior's Raymond "Bud" Somerville led the U.S. Olympic curling team to a bronze medal in 1992; he was fifty-five years old.)

Duluth's Sporting Life

Curling wasn't the only sport to find a natural home in Duluth. In fact, the town has produced national champions in a variety of athletic events, some common to us, some that seem, well, a little bizarre (at one time, horse races were held on the Lake Superior ice).

Duluth's earliest success in competition came through the success of the Boat Club's rowing team, lead by coach James Ten Eyck, Jr. During Eyck's tenure between 1911 and 1923, Duluth rowers defeated their foes forty-seven times in fifty-eight tries (they were 22-0 before World War I interrupted the sport), bringing home the hardware in twenty national championships, plus nine second-place and one third-place trophies. (More about the Duluth Boat Club can be found on page 69.)

Duluth's ski jumpers also rose to national glory. In November 1905, jumpers gathered at the St. Louis Hotel to start the Duluth Ski Club; a year later the club's Ole Feiring won the national championship—and did it again the next year with a record jump of 112 feet, shattering the previous record by 30 feet. (Seventy years later, Duluth's Jim Denney launched himself 325 feet at Squaw Valley, California, taking home another national title.) Duluth's jumpers used facilities in Fond du Lac at Mission Creek near the old Krause brownstone quarry and at Chester Park (for more on Chester Park, and some postcards of jumpers, see page 90). Between 1926 and 1979, Duluth produced twelve world champion jumpers. National and Olympic jumpers from Duluth include Jon Denney (1984), his brother Jim Denney (1972, 1980), John Broman (1980), Terry Kern (1976), Greg Swor (1968), Adrian Watt (1968), Gene Kotlarek (1960, 1964), Dave Hicks (1964), and George Hovland, Jr. (1952).

Both the men's and women's Bulldog hockey teams from the University of Minnesota Duluth regularly make the national playoffs (the women have three national titles) and its high school teams regularly appear in the Minnesota State High School Tournament; ice hockey fans have a lot to love about Duluth—and they have since 1895. That was the year the YMCA first put a team together, followed a few years later by the Zenith Polo Club (hockey was sometimes called "polo on ice"). Local parks and the Curling Club played host to most games in Duluth. By 1906 Duluth's

Northern Hardware team took home the U.S. Amateur title. In 1917 a team from Duluth's West End was champion of the American Hockey Association. In 1920 the Duluth Hornets formed, playing in the U.S. American Hockey Association. By 1924 the Hornets were fully professional and the town built an amphitheater for them to play in; they won the league title in 1927-28. In 1936 the Duluth Zephyrs were the first to join the International Amateur Hockey League and won the league in its inaugural season. When the amphitheater's roof collapsed in 1939, so did the Zephyrs. Since that time, the game has been played in youth and high school leagues. Today Duluth hosts many adult leagues, but no national or regional teams.

And of course no American city could go without a baseball team. Duluth hosted minor league teams affiliated with the St. Louis Cardinals in 1903 and the Chicago White Sox in 1904, 1905, 1908, and from 1913 to 1916; competing in the Northern League, the Duluth Dukes played here from 1934 to 1942 (and in 1941 moved into the new Wade Stadium), and from 1946 to 1955. Tragedy struck the team in 1948, when four of its players died and fourteen others were injured in a bus crash. Duluth and Superior shared a White Sox franchise from 1956 to 1958, and the Dukes again from 1959 to 1970. A new Northern League formed in 1993, and the Duluth-Superior Dukes took the field once more, playing until 2002. Recently, the Duluth Huskies played at the Wade.

The postcard above doesn't identify where in Duluth this scene was captured, but it shows that throughout the years Duluthians haven't let a little cold prevent them from getting outside and having fun. Today the city's residents fill the cold months with skating, skiing (Alpine and Nordic), snowshoeing, hockey, broomball, and, although it's played exclusively indoors theses days, curling.

Duluth: Home of the Washington Redskins

Most folks expect Duluth, with its frigid winters, to be the home to great winter sports teams, but not many are aware that Duluth was once the home of the Washington Redskins—back when they were known as the Duluth Eskimos.

The Eskimos actually started in 1923 as the Duluth Kelleys (named for their sponsor, Kelley-Duluth Hardware), later playing as the Eskimos from 1926 to 1928. They were a traveling team featuring future NFL hall-of-famers Ernie Nevers, Walter Kiesling, and Johnny "Blood" McNally (McNally also played for the Green Bay Packers). The Eskimos played against teams such as the Potsville Maroons, the Milwaukee Badgers, and the Canton Bulldogs (as well as the Chicago Bears and the Packers).

The 1926 Eskimos, featuring all-American fullback and Superior-native Nevers (a ticket attraction rivaling Red Grange), were called "The Iron Men of the North." The team played twenty-nine exhibition and league games—twenty-eight of them on the road—and Nevers played almost every minute of every game. The team earned a 6-5-3 record that season and played from September until February. Nevers had a good year in 1927. He played professional football, baseball, and basketball that year—the only man ever to do so—scrimmaging with Red Grange and pitching against Babe Ruth.

The Eskimos folded in 1928, and in 1929 the franchise was sold to New Jersey's Orange Athletic Club. They were renamed the Tornadoes, played one season in East Orange, and moved to Newark in 1930. The National Football League then reclaimed the franchise and sold it to a Boston group who renamed it the Braves and, later, the Redskins. The Redskins moved to Washington in 1932. (Eskimos, Braves, Redskins—not the most ethnically sensitive names.)

The Duluth team has not been forgotten by all. You can buy Eskimo hats and sweatshirts from Internet retailers, and *Sports Illustrated* writer Rick Reilly co-authored a screenplay centered on the 1927 Eskimos, a romantic comedy entitled *Leatherheads* (the Eskimos played to a 1-8-0 record that season).

Lyceum Building,
Duluth, Minn.

The Lyceum Building,
Duluth, Minn.

The Lyceum Theatre

5TH AVENUE W. & SUPERIOR STREET • 1891
TRAPHAGEN & FITZPATRICK, ARCHITECTS

When the Lyceum Theatre opened for business in July 1891, it was proudly hailed as the "handsomest and costliest building in the Northwest." The building stood six stories high in a style the *Duluth Daily Tribune* called "reposeful and majestic Romanesque" and contained an auditorium surrounded by business offices. Its façade was a treat for the eyes.

The Lyceum featured a triple-arched, two-story entryway on Superior Street complete with stone lions to guard the entry and the ornate carvings of O. George Thrana. The Lyceum seated 1,500 and its stage was the second largest in the "Northwest." Opera divas, actors, and vaudevillians graced its stage for thirty years before it was converted to a movie theater; it also served as the home of Duluth's first radio station, WJAP. The movie house operated until November 1960, and in January 1966 was destroyed to make room for KDLH-TV's studios.

You can still see some remains of the Lyceum: its stairway's stone lions, appropriately enough, have found a home at the Lake Superior Zoo, and the drama and comedy masks that flanked its entrance now grace the Depot's Duluth Playhouse Theater.

The Orpheum Theatre

8-12 N. 2ND AVENUE E. • 1910
J. E. O. PRIDEMORE, ARCHITECT

Orpheum Theatre, Duluth, Minn

The Orpheum was Duluth's premier vaudeville house; such greats as Ethyl Barrymore, Groucho Marx, W. C. Fields, Al Jolson, and Charlie Chaplin once trod its boards. Designed in the Classical Revival style, the Orpheum was built by Guilford Hartley in 1910, attached to the back of the Temple Opera Building, which he also owned.

The Temple Opera Building was built in 1889 on the corner of Second Avenue West and Superior Street. It housed the first Duluth Public Library, a Masonic lodge, an opera house, and business offices. The six-story building was designed in the Moorish Romanesque style complete with an onion-shaped dome at its top. It had an ornate entrance on Second Avenue.

With the building of the Orpheum, that entrance was replaced with a façade sporting an awning and Classic Revival pillars. Hartley later had the top three floors and the dome of the Temple Opera Building removed. Later, the Orpheum itself would be compromised.

The Orpheum closed in the 1930s. In 1941 the building was dramatically converted into the NorShor Theatre, an art deco movie house featuring the world's first milk bar. Three-dimensional art deco reliefs decorate the stairway walls and those adjacent to the main stage. A balcony level lounge features a classic wooden bar. Portions of the Orpheum are actually still inside the structure of the NorShor, whose entrance is on Superior Street. When first built, the NorShor featured a tower of lights that reached sixty-five feet in the air. (Some say Hartley had the Temple Opera Building altered to make the tower more visible, but he had died in 1922.)

The NorShor has operated sporadically over recent years. In the late 1980s its balcony was turned into a stage and movie house (it had shown films in its 1,500-seat theatre for years). In the late 1990s and early 2000s, the theatre played host to a burgeoning music scene. Desperately in need of expensive repairs, the NorShor was closed by the Duluth Fire Marshall in 2005. There is a great deal of public support to keep the NorShor alive as both a historic site and a cultural center.

Duluth's Grand Opera House

There is no known postcard of Duluth's most opulent showcase, the Grand Opera House. Built on the Northeast corner of Fourth Avenue West and Superior Street in 1883, its brick walls and terra cotta trim rose four stories into the air. Designer George Wirth included retail stores, offices, and rooms for rent (the Kitchi Gammi Club rented space in the building), and its theatre seated one thousand patrons. On a cold January night in 1889 the Opera House was consumed by fire; a bookstore owner died when the east wall collapsed on him. The aptly named Phoenix Building was built in its place.

The Flame Restaurant

1400 LONDON ROAD • 1930
ARCHITECT UNKNOWN

Jimmy Oreck and Alex Zurovsky opened The Flame in the heart of the Great Depression as a simple barbecue stand on London Road. A year later Zurovsky dropped his end of the bargain, and Oreck and his wife Ruth ran the stand, eventually turning it into Duluth's premier restaurant. The Flame building on London Road boasted large picture windows that looked out over a garden of "trees and shrubs, a waterfall, trout pool, and stuffed wild animals." It also had the town's first custom-made semi-circular booths, strolling musicians, and a dwarf decked out in a red bellhop uniform hired to pass out cigarettes. On tap they served Fitger's Beer, brewed less than a mile away.

Fire claimed the Flame in 1942, and the business moved to the waterfront at the base of Fifth Avenue West. It closed in 1971, later becoming the Anchor Inn. The Lake Superior Aquarium now stands on the site.

ROOSTER TERRACE

THE FLAME, 14TH AT LONDON ROAD, DULUTH, MINNESOTA

LAKE VIEW TEA AND DINING ROOM, 728-730 EAST SUPERIOR STREET, PHONE HEMLOCK 1394-W, DULUTH, MINN.

LOCATED ON THE SHORE OF LAKE SUPERIOR WHERE YOU CAN VIEW THE LARGE STEAMERS COMING AND GOING.

Lake View Tea & Dining Room

730 E. SUPERIOR STREET • 1915
ARCHITECT UNKNOWN

The building shown in the postcard at left first operated as a confectionary. It became the home of the Lake View Tea and Dining Room in the 1940s and remained so into the next decade. The postcard takes some geographic liberties: From that perspective, the actual canal and Lift Bridge wouldn't be in the frame, and the speedboat would be in danger of running out of lake. But this card was designed to draw business, and even then the Lift Bridge was the biggest tourist draw in the region. Today the building sits among a row of historic buildings bookended by the Hartley Building and the Fitger's Brewery Complex.

JOE'S PICKWICK TAVERN — 508 EAST SUPERIOR STREET, DULUTH, MINN.

6A-H752

The Pickwick

508 E. SUPERIOR STREET • 1914
ANTHONY PUCK, ARCHITECT

When he opened the Brewery Saloon in 1915, Fitger's brewmaster August Fitger commissioned John Frey to paint murals of his boyhood home in Delmenhorst, Germany, on the walls; his partner Percy Anneke added a lion plaque imported from Pompeii, Italy. Brewery Saloon bartender Joseph S. Wisocki took over the operation before Prohibition struck in 1918. When the country went dry the brewery turned to making candy, distributing cigars, and producing non-alcoholic beverages. In 1919 they introduced an alcohol-free drink called "Pickwick." It became so popular (alone and as a mixer) that patrons began referring to the saloon itself as "The Pickwick." Owned and operated by Wisocki's grandsons, it remains one of Duluth's favorite restaurants, but its façade looks very different from the one shown in the postcard's detail, and the interior has changed a little as well.

Fitger's Brewery

In 1857 four jobless young men in Duluth, one with some brewing skills, started brewing beer along a creek near what is now Seventh Avenue East, on land owned by Sidney Luce. That creek has since been called Brewery Creek, but the brewery itself barely survived Duluth's tough economy of the 1860s. In 1865, Luce sold the brewery to Nicholas Decker. Decker died in 1875, and two years later his family leased the brewery to Michael Fink. In 1882 Fink hired August Fitger to run his brewery; less than half a year later Fitger and his partner Percy Anneke bought the Brewery from Fink and changed the name of the Decker Brewery to A. Fitger & Co. Lake Superior Brewery.

Fitger and Anneke had much greater success than their predecessors. The company grew throughout the late nineteenth and early twentieth centuries, adding buildings and employees as the years progressed. In 1890 the brewery installed the first ice machine in Minnesota. Sales continued to grow.

That growth stopped abruptly in 1918, when Prohibition shut down beer manufacturing and sales. Fitger and Anneke scrabbled to keep the brewery operational and Duluthians employed. They made candy and non-alcoholic beverages and even distributed cigars. They survived prohibition to become a major regional brewery, but they couldn't survive the post-war consolidation and expansion of breweries such as Miller and Budweiser. On September 19, 1972, the final shift reported to the bottling house.

The Fitger's Brewery corporate stationery, circa 1905. Some of the buildings, like the stables at left, were never built. Plans for the rooftop of the main office building included lavish gardens and a large statue of Gambrenius, the mythical Flemish King of Beers. The brewery closed in 1972 and is now a hotel and retail complex with many fine shops and restaurants.

Skyline Parkway: "An absolutely perfect road, graded & macadamized

The twenty-eight-mile roadway known as Skyline Parkway sits almost five hundred feet above Lake Superior and stretches along a ridge which was—thousands of years ago—the beach of Glacial Lake Duluth. The road once reached from Occidental Boulevard (Seven Bridges Road) along Amity Creek near the Lester River all the way into Jay Cooke State Park. It can still be accessed at Occidental and East Superior Street, but now terminates in the west where it intersects with Becks Road near Gary-New Duluth.

The parkway was first imagined by William K. Rogers, president of Duluth's first park board, and was presented to the Duluth City Council in 1888. By 1900 it was only five miles long. During the 1920s, Mayor Sam Snively—dedicated to making Duluth "the most beautiful city in the Northwest"—saw to it that the roadway was extended. The mayor had already built Seven Bridges Road with private funds. By 1927 the parkway ran to Jay Cooke State Park and in 1929 it was named Skyline Parkway. (Before that, the road had been named Carriage Drive, Rogers Boulevard,

Around the turn of the twentieth century, when the parkway was still in its infancy, people commonly took part in what they called "Tally-ho" parties, day-long excursions along the parkway with stops for picnicking. The postcards on this page show just how large these coaching parties could be; the image at lower left was captured at Gem Lakes, known today as Twin Ponds.

Duluth, Minn. Tally-Ho Party, Boulevard Drive.

TALLYHO PARTY ON BOULEVARD DRIVE, DULUTH, MINN.

Boulevard Drive, Duluth, Minn.

by nature...it holds such a gift of nature in trust."

and Terrace Parkway.) In 1935 Snively began work to connect Skyline to Seven Bridges Road, a task that would not be completed until 1939, two years after he left office.

Today, much of the parkway is interrupted by larger thoroughfares that took priority over a leisure route. Starting at Spirit Mountain and heading west, the road remains unpaved. One of its original stone bridges can be seen along this stretch, which features a stunning view from Bardon's Peak.

Perhaps the highest praise for the parkway came from Chicago Landscape Engineer Olaf Benson, who said, "I have seen nothing approaching it in this country, or in foreign lands in all my experience, for the purpose for which it is wanted—an absolutely perfect road, graded and macadamized by nature up nearly five hundred feet above the level of the lake overlooking the city and commanding a view in every direction of its superb surrounds, that Duluth may well be proud of, and should not fail to show every visitor. The city, I think, should recognize that it holds such a gift of nature in trust—to develop it in every appropriate way."

When automobiles replaced horses, Skyline was still a popular excursion route. Enterprising individuals used large touring cars and buses (like the one at right, operating out of Chester Park) to take groups of locals and tourists along the roadway.

SKYLINE PARKWAY SIGHTSEEING BUS IN CHESTER PARK B

ard Drive, Duluth,- Minn.

RIVE, CHESTER PARK, DULUTH, MINN.

SIGHT SEEING CAR ON BOULEVARD DRIVE, DULUTH, MINN.

Lester Park, Duluth, Minn.

One of Duluth's Beautiful Driveways, Duluth, Minn.

116-D

LESTER PARK ABOUNDS WITH BEAUTY SPOTS

7A-H1057

Seven Bridges Road

Back in 1899, Sam Snively had an idea while strolling through his four hundred-acre spread near Hawk Ridge and Lester Park: a roadway to rival any other found in the city. He donated sixty acres of his own, then convinced his neighbors to donate land or provide rights-of-way for his vision. He even raised some cash. Although Snively had originally wanted his road, which would take thirty years to complete, to be called Spring Garden Boulevard, it became known as Snively Road. It has long been called Seven Bridges Road, but that name is somewhat misleading. In 1910 the road became the property of the Park Board, which hired a landscape architect to draw up plans which included blueprints for ten stone-arch bridges to replace the ten wooden spans Snively and his crew had built, but in the end only nine were necessary. Plans also included connecting the road to Rogers Boulevard (later Skyline Parkway), which pleased Snively to no end. When it reopened in 1912, it was named Amity Parkway for the creek its bridges crossed nine times.

Today, the road technically has seven bridges, although from Superior Street to Skyline travellers cross eight. Two of the original nine were abandoned when Skyline Parkway was completed, and a newer bridge near Superior Street is not considered part of Mr. Snively's road. The bridges, damaged by misuse and neglect, were restored in the 1990s.

104-D VIEW OF DULUTH AND LIFT BRIDGE FROM SKYLINE PARKWAY

24-H304

122-D House and Rock Garden on Skyline Drive, Duluth, Minn.

UNIQUE RESIDENCE ABOVE
BOULEVARD DRIVE, DULUTH, MINN.

House of Rock

ARTHUR P. COOK HOUSE • 1900
501 W. SKYLINE PARKWAY
I. VERNON HILL, ARCHITECT

Most Duluthians know the Arthur P. Cook house (named for its first owner, a Duluth druggist who dabbled in real estate) as the "House of Rock" both for the rocky lot it sits on and the incorporation of the same stone by architect I. Vernon Hill, who was just thirty-one years old when he designed it. With arguably one of the best views of the Duluth-Superior harbor, the house was built of stone and timber for just $5,000. It became the most photographed house in Duluth and in 1931 was featured in an advertisement for the Duluth Builders' Exchange, touting the future of Duluth as a "metropolis serving the great Northwest Empire and its Atlantic Gateway." Those cruising Skyline Parkway today (Boulevard Drive at the time the house was built) would be remiss if they don't pull over for a long look at this much-coveted home.

Fairmount Park & Municipal Zoo

The Municipal Zoo at Fairmount Park—also known as the Duluth Zoo—began its life as simply Fairmount Park, another of Duluth's parks built along a Lake Superior tributary, in this case Kingsbury Creek (named for Wallace Kingsbury, an Endion pioneer and delegate to the Territorial Congress). In 1923 West Duluth printer Bert Onsgrad outlined a plan for a game farm menagerie, and city leaders liked the idea. The zoo's first resident was Onsgard's pet deer, Billy. His pen was built with fencing donated by the Pittsburgh Steel Company. Three years later a cassowary and a pair of lions were purchased with funds raised by school children. Bears were acquired by trapping them when they wandered into town. One of the early zoo's stranger policies called for not feeding carnivorous animals on Sundays, as they "should fast on Sundays." By 1928 the zoo held about two hundred animals and birds.

The zoo grew considerably over the following twenty years. Regional animals like bear, wolf, moose, and elk were joined by exotics including hyenas, monkeys, and elephants. Buildings went up, many constructed by the Works Project Administration during the Great Depression. An American bomber unit serving in the Pacific in World War II adopted a Himalayan black bear as a mascot and even took the bruin on several bombing runs. A year after the war ended, that bear was donated to the zoo.

Boys enjoying the cool waters of Fairmount Park's Kingsbury Creek on a hot summer day, before the park became home to the town's municipal zoo. Certain days of the week were once designated for either boys' or girls' bathing. Note the typo on the card, identifying Fairmount Park as "Fremont Park." Throughout the years spelling of the park's name has varied, sometimes with the u, sometimes without.

For years the zoo had been administered by the city, with policies changing each time the town elected a new mayor. That ended in 1959 with the organization of the Arrowhead Zoological Society, which operated the zoo for the next twenty-eight years. During that time the zoo's population grew, adding a giant tortoise, chimpanzees, kangaroos, and large cats, including a jaguar and a cougar. That period also saw the zoo playing host to its most popular tenant, an Indian mongoose named Mr. Magoo. A merchant seaman had smuggled the exotic weasel into the U.S. in 1963, but a federal ban on mongooses threatened Magoo's very existence. Duluthians were outraged, and their anger spread across the country and up the government. During his last months in office, President John F. Kennedy signed a presidential pardon, sparing Mr. Magoo's life. The mongoose spent the rest of his life at the zoo; he died in 1968.

In 1987, life at the zoo changed in a big way. With $4 million from the state and $3 million from the city, zoo officials began initiating a three-part plan that included more naturalistic facilities for its residents. The municipal zoo's name changed to the Lake Superior Zoo. The plan's second stage went forth in the 1990s and included renovating the zoo's old main building from animal cages to offices, a restaurant, and a gift shop. The third stage is in limbo, having had its budget cut by a gubernatorial veto in 1996.

Besides enjoying the animals, children visiting Duluth's Municipal Zoo at Fairmount Park could at one time ride a miniature train, as seen in the above linen postcard, printed some time between 1930 and 1945.

The gentle cascade seen in the postcard at the upper right-hand side of this page forms Lincoln Park's natural "slip-and-slide" in late summer and fall, when the water level is low.

The women seen in the above postcard have chosen a much safer way to cross Lincoln Park's Miller Creek than their male counterpart, who appears to be ready to step out onto a warped plank to traverse the stream.

Lincoln Park

Just about every town in America has a Lincoln Park, and Duluth is no exception. The park was one of Duluth's first four parks, along with Chester (Garfield), Cascade, and Portland Square. The park surrounds Miller Creek below Skyline Parkway down to West Third Street. Through development and land acquisition, the park has grown over the years, most significantly in 1926 when Lincoln Parkway—roughly six thousand feet of roadway alongside the creek—was constructed. Prior to that two stone-arch bridges and a wooden pavilion (seen in the left postcard on the opposite page) were constructed.

In 1934 the Public Works Administration added a stone pavilion on the park's central grounds, an expansive groomed lawn surrounded by the pavilion to the south and, to the north, Elephant Rock, an outcropping so large it looks out of place. The pavilion was built for public gatherings and was recently renovated. Behind the pavilion, the creek cascades gently down

Duluth, Minn. View in Lincoln Park.

Lincoln Park, Duluth, Minn.

DULUTH MINNESOTA LINCOLN PARK, THE STONE ARCH BRIDGE.

large, flat rocks (shown in the postcard at the top right of the opposite page); when the creek is low in late summer or fall, many local kids can be found hydroplaning down the creek. North of Elephant Rock, one and a half miles of trails line either side of Miller Creek and connect via several small footbridges, making it a popular spot for dog walkers. The creek itself is lined with rocks as it runs through the park and features several waterfalls and cauldrons large enough to serve as swimming holes.

Today Lincoln Park is the centerpiece of Duluth's West End, a neighborhood that in recent years has adopted the name "Lincoln Park" to promote business. Many Duluthians, West End residents among them, have never warmed to the name change—just as many proud West Duluthians refuse to call their neighborhood "Spirit Valley."

(Some historians have mistakenly written that Lincoln Park was originally called Garfield Park, but that's not true; it was actually Chester Park that was first called Garfield Park. It does seem like an odd coincidence that two of Duluth's first four parks were named for U.S. presidents who died from gunshot wounds inflicted while they were in office.)

The wooden pavilion shown above left is now gone, replaced by a stone structure built by the Public Works Administration in 1934.

Originally called the Gem Lakes, Twin Ponds (right) were created when Buckingham Creek was dammed.

Enger Memorial Tower (below) sits five hundred feet above Lake Superior, providing a stunning view of the Duluth-Superior Harbor. The structure was built in 1939, eight years after Bert Enger's death.

138-D—Enger Memorial Tower, Duluth, Minnesota

Enger Park & Twin Ponds

Some think Enger Tower was once an active lighthouse; others, a tribute from a grieving husband to his dead wife. Neither story is true. The sixty-foot-high, five-story octagonal structure was built in 1939 to honor Bert Enger, a prominent area businessman and Norwegian immigrant who came to this country penniless and made a fortune in furniture and real estate. When the tower was finished, Crown Prince Olav of Norway visited Duluth to dedicate it. Since then, it has provided visitors with a great look at Duluth's harbor.

The park itself was created after Enger gave the city six hundred acres of land on which the Tower and surrounding gardens, and the Enger Park Golf Course were built. Today Enger Park contains a gazebo, a pavilion, gardens, and the Peace Bell, a replica of a cherished temple bell in Ohara, Japan, one of Duluth's sister cities. At the end of World War II American sailors on the *USS Duluth* took the original bell as a spoil of war (it was almost melted down by the Japanese as part of the war effort), then returned it to Ohara years later.

Just east of the park sit Duluth's Twin Ponds. Known as the "Gem Lakes" in the 1890s, the pools were created by damming Buckingham Creek. Many of the old Tally-ho parties along Skyline Parkway stopped at the tiny lakes for picnics. The ponds are used today as swimming holes.

114-D—A Replica of Leif Erikson's Boat, Duluth, Minnesota

LEIF ERIKSON VIKING SHIP, LEIF ERIKSON PARK ON LONDON ROAD, DULUTH, MINN.—71

When I-35 was expanded through Duluth in the 1980s, Leif Erikson Park was changed dramatically. One of those changes resulted in the creation of another park: Duluth's Rose Garden, a lovely spot featuring stone benches, a gazebo, and an incredible variety of roses and shrubs. It also includes the horse fountain that sat where London Road once split off from Superior Street (see page 111). The Rose Garden actually sits on top of I-35; highway traffic passes through tunnels beneath it.

Leif Erikson Park

A statue of Leif Erikson crediting the Viking explorer with discovering America one thousand years ago marks the entrance to Leif Erikson Park, perhaps Duluth's best-known greenspace. Across a footbridge and down next to the Lakewalk a vast groomed lawn forms a natural amphitheater and, at its base, a wonderfully whimsical stone stage framed by castle-like "towers". This pavilion/stage, designed by Abraham Holmstead and William Sullivan (who also designed Denfeld High School and the St. Louis County Jail), has made the park a natural site for such events as the Duluth International Folk Festival and the Lake Superior Shakespeare Festival. Behind the stage the park meets the lakeshore. The beach is lined with stones, some boulders large enough to explore and others small and ideal for skipping.

Leif Erikson Park was originally Lakeshore Park, part of William Rogers' dream of a park that paralleled Terrace Parkway (now Skyline Parkway); the parkway and Lakeshore Park would be connected by "a string of pearls"—parks, like Chester and Lincoln, built along the creeks that fed Lake Superior. But Lakeshore Park was forever changed by Bert Enger (see page 84). In 1926

Captain Gerhard Folgero and his crew sailed the replica Viking ship *Leif Erikson* to Boston from Bergen, Norway, and then on to Duluth. The ship was featured in the opening celebration of the Arrowhead Bridge in 1927 (see page 26). Enger bought the boat and donated it to Duluth, but there was a catch: he insisted that Lakeshore Park be renamed Leif Erikson Park. The boat is currently wrapped in blue shrink wrap to protect it. The *Leif Erikson* Restoration Project (LERP) is raising funds to create a roof to cover the ship to protect it from the elements—and vandals.

CASCADE PARK AND BOULEVARD DRIVE, DULUTH, MINN.

Cascade Park

William Rogers' plan for Duluth's park system called for three of the first four parks (and other future parks) to run along creeks starting at the proposed roadway that would become Skyline Parkway. When he announced his idea in 1889, two of his first four designated parks were already in place, and one of them fit his plan precisely. Cascade Park, with the Clark House Creek running right through it, was plotted between Cascade Drive and Mesaba Avenue in 1886 (Portland Square was also established in 1886). And of all of Duluth's early parks, Cascade was by far the grandest. Originally planned to be a forty-nine acre spread, the three-acre park sat on a bluff above downtown Duluth's business section; many beautiful, meticulously tended gardens and carefully groomed pathways graced the park.

In 1895 the city added a sandstone pavilion and bell tower at the heart of the park, giving it a whimsical, castle-like atmosphere. The structure had

CASCADE PARK, DULUTH, MINN.

7552. Cascade Park, Duluth, Minn. McKenzie, Photo.

several levels and picnic facilities and played host to many garden parties and social events. Clark House Creek flowed directly through the pavilion, cascading out through an opening on the building's lakeside façade. (The creek was diverted below ground at First Avenue West.) The park quickly became a popular spot for picnickers and others seeking escape from the smoke and noise of Duluth's busy waterfront. Unfortunately, the bell tower was destroyed during a storm in 1897. Portions of the creek were altered to flow underground as the area surrounding the park developed.

Today only two and a half acres of Cascade Park survive. When Mesaba Avenue was widened in 1975 to accommodate traffic heading toward the Duluth Heights neighborhood and the Miller Hill Mall and surrounding retail developments, a large part of the park was sacrificed. Its sandstone structures were destroyed and the remainder of the creek was forced underground. The city then rebuilt the bell tower, though in a different design than the original.

Cascade Park, Duluth, Minn.

"Cascade Park", Duluth, Min.

Duluth, Minn. Cascade Square, Cascade Park.

7722. Chester Creek Falls, Duluth, Minn.

"Chester Creek", Duluth, Minn.

Falls on Chester River, Chester P...
Duluth, Minn.

Chester Park

The postcards on this page feature Chester Creek Falls, found just below Skyline Parkway. The old wooden bridge shown in the center card is actually part of Skyline Parkway (more likely "Rogers Boulevard" at the time the image was captured). While the cards show a forceful cascade that churns into a cauldron, during most summer months the top of the falls can be traversed on stepping stones.

Many Duluthians believe that Chester Park was named for Chester Congdon, the iron mining lawyer who, along with his wife, Clara, built Glensheen, Duluth's most famous mansion. Not true. The park takes its name from Charles Chester, who homesteaded a property along the creek near what is now Fifth Street, just east of Thirteenth Avenue East, on May 31, 1856. (The park was originally called Garfield Park for President James Garfield; the name was changed in 1903.)

One of Duluth's first four parks, Chester Park lies roughly between Thirteenth and Fourteenth Avenues East and stretches from Kenwood Avenue to Fourth Street, where the creek runs under the street and, a few blocks later, disappears beneath the city before it emerges near Leif Erikson Park and empties into Lake Superior. When the first leg of Skyline Parkway was completed, it stretched from Lincoln Park's Miller Creek to Chester Creek. The park became both a launching point and destination for Tally-ho excursions along the parkway. Later, bus tours operated out of the park.

CHESTER PARK, DULUTH, MINN.

FALLS, CHESTER PARK, DULUTH, MINN.

NO. 31. CHESTER CREEK, DULUTH, MINN.

The park's 108 acres include 2.5 miles of hiking trail, much of it on either side of the creek in Lower Chester (the area from just below Skyline Parkway to Fourth Street); parts of the trail run high above a gorge created by erosion while at other points the path follows the creek just a few feet from the water's edge. Lower Chester is home to a pair of footbridges, several waterfalls, and a cauldron known as Devil's Hole. Stone retaining walls constructed by the Work Projects Administration in the 1930s still hold back the sloping hillside. Upper Chester, also known as Chester Bowl, sits above Skyline Parkway. It holds four miles of cross-country ski and hiking trails as well as soccer fields (flooded in the winter for ice skating), a small ski hill, and three old and famous ski jumps (see page 90). Behind the ski jumps the terrain flattens out for several acres, providing visitors with one of Duluth's best views of the lake from a natural setting.

The card at top center of this page shows two men standing on rocks at the edge of Devil's Hole, formed by a small waterfall that drops directly under the footbridge. During the dog days of summer kids can be found cooling themselves in the cauldron's waters, some of them jumping from the ledge just below the bridge on the east side of the gorge. The wooden bridge in the postcard has long since been replaced.

Chester Park's Ski Jumps

Chester Park's ski jumps were the training grounds for several national champions and members of the U.S. Olympic Ski Jumping Team (see page 70). The first slide at Chester was built by the Duluth Ski Club in 1907, but it blew down three times before World War I, and the club disbanded. It reorganized in 1922 and built a larger slide at upper Chester. In 1924 that slide was replaced by what was then the largest ski jump in the world. By 1940, Chester Park's parking was insufficient to keep up with the number of spectators who came to watch the sport, and its position didn't protect enthusiasts from the north wind. The club began searching for a new site.

The club next built a slide in Fond du Lac, near Mission Creek and the old Krause brownstone quarry. With labor help from the Work Projects Administration, the slide went up in 1941, and Fond du Lac replaced Chester Park as the scene for national tournaments (but many a Duluth ski-jump hopeful still trained at Chester; see page 70). The jump at Fond du Lac has since washed away due to erosion (helped by vandalism), but three unused slides still stand atop Chester Park.

SKI JUMPING, DULUTH, MINN.

Ski Tournament, Duluth, Minn.

Lester River's Rustic Bridge

After heavy rains washed out all the bridges crossing the Lester River in 1896, Duluth's Park Board commissioned Civil War veteran John Busha to build a bridge across the river. In the winter of 1897 Busha and his sons Abraham and George set to work felling and hauling Lester Park's cedar trees to a site along the river. Then they started putting the unpeeled logs together until they spanned the river. The "Rustic Bridge," as it was called, became a popular tourist stop, with picnic tables on the bottom deck and lounging on the upper promenade. The lower deck even featured large square viewing holes (surrounded by rails) that allowed picnickers to look down on the Lester's roiling brown waters as they made their way to Lake Superior. Unfortunately, nature took its toll on the bridge, and the upper deck had to be removed in 1916 due to safety concerns. In 1931 the lower deck met the same fate. Because its footings cannot be located, no one is sure exactly where the rustic bridge stood. A transcript from a 1948 radio show claims that "more picture postcards of that rustic bridge were sold than any other attraction in the city." Postcard collectors today will tell you the same thing.

7560. Rustic Bridge in Lester Park, Duluth, Minn.

Rustic Bridge, Lester Park, Duluth, Minn.

RUSTIC BRIDGE. LESTER PARK. DULUTH, MINN.

8546 A SWIMMING HOLE, LESTER PARK, DULUTH, MINN.

Put some clothes on! Apparently the publisher of the postcard at left (printed some time between 1915 and 1930) saw no problem in releasing a card showing boys skinny-dipping in the Lester River. The shorts most of the boys are shown wearing were actually added in the coloring process.

The bottom center card shows the Lester Park Pavilion, at which park-goers gathered for activities and refreshments.

The Lester River Bridge (lower right) near where London Road becomes Congdon Boulevard.

PARK, DULUTH, MINN.

LESTER RIVER BRIDGE, HIGHWAY No. 1, DULUTH, MINN.

Lester Park

Lester Park follows the Lester River upstream roughly a half mile starting a few blocks north of the river's mouth. Its eastern boundary runs along Lester River Road, and it is bordered on the west by Amity Creek and Seven Bridges Road (see page 78). Lester measures forty-seven square acres; because it is adjacent to Amity Park, the two parks together create a greenspace that stretches from Superior Street all the way to Skyline Parkway. It has long been thought that the park was, like Chester Park, named for a homesteader, although some believe it was named for a five-year-old boy who drowned in the river. But long before Europeans reached the Lester's banks the Ojibwe called it *Busabikazibi*, "river where water flows through a worn place in the rocks."

The park's natural beauty includes several waterfalls and at least two swimming holes: the eastern branch's "Shallows" and "The Deeps" of the western branch. Foot paths were groomed and bridges built so visitors, many of whom travelled by streetcar from central Duluth, could stroll through the park and across the river. Oriental Boulevard, a carriage path, ran through the park's center between the Lester's two branches; carriages could access the park over a bridge that connected with Occidental Boulevard.

At one time a development of summer homes, Pinehurst on the Lester, sat along the river's east branch. They burned in the 1918 Cloquet Fire that roared through the region. Many of the park's trees were also destroyed in the blaze, but most of the larger trees survived.

From 1897 until 1931 a handmade rustic bridge graced the park (see page 91), decorated with Ojibwe designs described as resembling "Indian embroidery." They were made by the bridge's builder, John Busha, who was of Ojibwe descent. The park was also home to the Lester Park Pavilion, operated by one Mr. L. A. Fungerson, which offered visitors a variety of ways to enjoy themselves, including a merry-go-round, refreshment parlors, a dance hall, a shooting gallery, and even a small zoo. Nearby stood Harmony Hall, decorated with the same Ojibwe designs that graced the pavilion and the bridge, and which also played host to dances and other social gatherings. Both the pavilion and Harmony Hall burned in the early years of the last century.

Today Lester includes miles of hiking and cross-country ski trails and a central park area outfitted with playground equipment, picnic tables and grills, and portable toilets in the summer. Hiking and ski trails lead along both Lester River and Amity Creek. Portions of the river run through a fairly deep gorge in parts of the park, and hikers can either stroll on the smooth trails above the river or along rough trails next to the water.

Trout fishing is still popular near the mouth of the Lester. Starting in the early 1940s, smelt (planted in Lake Superior earlier in the century) began appearing at the mouth of the river to spawn each spring. Hundreds of people would gather at the mouth of the Lester (and other Duluth creeks) during the smelt run, each netting pounds and pounds of the tiny silver fish. Other exotic species have dramatically reduced the smelt population since the 1980s.

Amity Falls, Lester

Mouth of Lester River and Fish Hatchery.

TROUT FISHING, LESTER RIVER, DULUTH, MINN.

LESTER RAPIDS IN WINTER'S GRASP, DULUTH, MINN

CONGDON PARK, DULUTH, MINN.

71906

7734. Congdon Park,
Duluth, Minn.

7572 RUSTIC BRIDGE IN CONGDON PARK
DULUTH, MINN.
© McKENZIE

Congdon Park

The thirty-eight acres along Tischer Creek that make up Congdon Park were donated to the city in 1908 by mining attorney Chester Congdon and his wife Clara, who built Glensheen—Duluth's most noted estate—further downstream where the Tischer empties into Lake Superior. Plans for the park were drawn up by the same men who spent years designing Glensheen's gardens and landscaping: Anthony Morell and Arthur Nichols. (Morell and Nichols also laid out Lester Park, parts of Skyline Parkway, Morgan Park, Duluth's Civic Center, and Duluth's Central Park, which was never completed.) Congdon's own staff executed the plan, creating gravel-covered trails, stone stairways, wooden bridges, and even a bridle path. Congdon accessed the park from Glensheen using a path beneath London Road.

The park rests between Superior Street and Vermilion Road and winds along the creek near Thirty-second Avenue East. A stairway leads down to trails within the deep walls that form the park's boundaries. High cliffs of red rock, produced by lava roughly one billion years ago, show how much the

creek has eroded the stone over the eons. White
cedars appear to grow straight out of the cliffs (a trick of erosion), Norway pines
and a variety of hardwood trees line the creek, and several waterfalls grace
Tischer Creek, one forming a large swimming hole. The park fell into disrepair
over time; trails became overgrown with brush, erosion created large gullies,
and trail markings were lost. In 1971 and the following year the Duluth Junior
League, along with the Department of Parks and Recreation, restored the park
as a nature trail with the help of local Boy Scouts and UMD students.

Tischer Creek was central to Chester and Clara Congdon's vision of
Glensheen. According to family legend, the mansion was named for both
Congdon's ancestral home (Sheen, in Surrey, England) and for the way the
sun shone on the waters of Tischer Creek. For years the Congdons had trouble keeping trespassers off the estate in the springtime during the smelt run,
as many sought to harvest the tiny fish where they gathered to spawn at the
mouths of Lake Superior north shore tributaries.

Minnesota Point

Park Point is actually not a park at all, but a community built on Minnesota Point, the northern half of the world's largest freshwater sand bar. Most of Minnesota Point is a residential area, but the entire stretch of shore on the lake side—all of it sandy beach—remains open to the public. At the end of Minnesota Avenue the Minnesota Point Hiking Trail cuts through an old-growth forest of naturally regenerating red and white pines (some two hundred years old) to the end of the point. The forest is home to the ruins of the oldest lighthouse on Lake Superior (see page 99) at the point where surveyor George Stuntz began plotting what would become Duluth.

Park Point was once a township separate from Duluth; when other surrounding townships folded into Duluth in the late 1880s and early 1890s, Park Point refused until the city promised to build a bridge over the ship canal (they got their bridge, but not until sixteen years after joining Duluth). At one time Park Point was advertised as "Hay Fever Haven"—those who could afford it summered on Park Point for relief from allergies. Opportunists even considered building a "Hay Fever colony" on the point.

The card above touts Duluth's Minnesota Point as Duluth's "Far Famed Hay Fever and Summer Resort." A stand of white pines on the Point was once planned to be used as the site of a "Hay Fever colony," complete with cabins for allergy sufferers.

Minnesota Point in winter—the mail managed to get delivered even if the trolley couldn't always make it through the snow.

THE TROLLEY ROAD ON MINNESOTA POINT IN WINTER, DULUTH, MINN.
No. 668. V. O. Hammon Pub. Co., Minneapolis and Chicago

No. 667. V. O. Hammon Pub. Co., Minneapolis and Chicago

DELIVERING MAIL ON MINNESOTA POINT IN WINTER, DULUTH, MINN.

ICE FORMATION ON MINNESOTA POINT

A WINTER RESIDENCE ON MINNESOTA POINT, DULUTH, MINN.

No. 701. V. O. Hammon Pub. Co., Minneapolis and Chicago

The publisher of the heavily retouched postcard above had a little fun with Duluth's one-time reputation as a town full of hearty pioneers living on the edge of the wilderness.

AMES-HUNTLEY CO., 215 W. FIR...

THE WHITE CITY,
DULUTH AND SUPERIOR'S AMUSEMENT PARK.

Duluth, Minnesota. Minnesota Point, White City

BEACH ON
MINNESOTA POINT
AT "WHITE CITY"
NEAR DULUTH,
AND EXCURSION
STEAMER

White City

On the last day of June, 1906, Oatka Park opened on Park Point between Thirty-ninth and Fortieth Streets. Reports claim ten- to fifteen thousand people enjoyed the park on its first day even though the park had little more to offer than a public dance pavilion. Soon after, the park became White City, an amusement park operated by the Duluth Amusement Company. Rides were added, including the "Mystic River" boat ride, a miniature railroad (operators claimed it had the smallest steam locomotive in the United States), and the "Fun Factory," where ticket payers lost themselves wandering on twisted paths and "[ran] up against all kinds of funny and startling adventures." Other attractions included an automated baseball game, a Ferris Wheel, a water slide, free acrobats and burlesque performances, sitting rooms (for the ladies), cafés and restaurants, bath houses, swimming lessons, and vaudeville performances. The park also featured a corral of deer, and at one time its owners commissioned the construction of a $7,500 gasoline-propelled airship to be named *Duluth No. 1*. It was never built, and, after a brief name change to "Joyland" in 1908, the park shut down in 1909. If the postcard at the top of page 81 is any indication, the miniature railroad may have later been donated to the Municipal Zoo.

Minnesota Point Lighthouse

Lake Superior's first lighthouse once stood fifty feet tall and served mariners for twenty years, from 1858 to 1878. R. H. Barrett, its first and only keeper, and his family lived in a simple cottage next to the tower of red Ohio brick wrapped in limestone. Barrett kept the light burning and, when the fog became thick, actually used his own lungs to blow a warning through a logging camp dinner horn. Local residents called the horn "Barrett's Cow."

The lighthouse was abandoned in 1878. The keeper's cottage was destroyed, and the tower now stands barely thirty feet high and has to be protected by a fence, but its French lenses are still used in the west pier-head light of the Superior Entry.

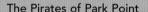

Duluth, Minn. Old Light House, Minnesota Point.

Ruins of the oldest lighthouse on Lake Superior can still be found, although in not as good shape as shown here, by walking the Minnesota Point Hiking Trail (found behind Sky Harbor Airport) which leads to the end of Minnesota Point.

The Pirates of Park Point

Back in 1889, Minnesota Point—at the time, the village of Park Point—was not nearly as heavily populated as it is today. Few houses stood along the world's largest sand bar, and no roads had been built. It was mostly sand dunes and scrub pine, the perfect place to hide pirate booty.

Park Point's pirates weren't your typical, cutlass-wielding "aaargh"-exclaiming, peg-legged, hook-handed, eye-patch-wearin', parrot-totin' buccaneers of the Caribbean, and they hardly plundered ships for gold doubloons and pieces of eight. Duluth's pirates were a band of about six young men who apparently had an aversion to labor and turned to crime on the not-so-high seas to earn their keep.

They dug themselves a cave on Park Point at a site close to Thirty-ninth Street, near what in 1906 would become the Duluth Boat Club's Oatka Branch. With open water on both sides, this was a strategic spot for their operation. While they hardly fit the stereotype, their style was not much different than traditional pirates. They plundered various vessels, sawmills, and warehouses.

Apparently, the cave was a temporary lair, and the pirates' goal was to set up permanent housing on the point, as the lumber they stole was used to build a house. Much of that lumber was taken from the mill of Duluthian R. A. Gray, and Gray had had enough.

When Duluth's buccaneers tried to make off with more of his lumber one night, Gray decided to do something about it. He watched, then pursued the thieves. But the band of ne'er-do-wells had a large sailboat and managed to escape in the Lake Superior darkness. The patient Mr. Gray eventually found their cave—and his lumber, in use in the unfinished house—and captured the gang after a struggle that history books called a "fierce battle." The half-dozen or so thieves all ended up in the penitentiary.

Smaller Parks

Starting with just four parks proposed in 1889, Duluth's greenspaces now count over one hundred, some smaller than an acre. Even with all this, what was to be one of Duluth's grandest parks was never even completed. The rocky plateau rising above First Street up to Skyline Parkway between roughly Thirteenth and Eighteenth Avenues West is not welcoming to home-builders, and Duluth planned to turn most of it into its own Central Park. Plans for the park, which was originally to be be called Zenith Park, included an arboretum (complete with labeled plantings, gardens, and viewing areas). The idea died when population growth slowed in the 1920s.

The card below depicts "Lookout Point," most likely a group of rocks behind Leif Erikson Park. The shoreline in the card at upper right is just east of Leif Erikson. When he proposed Boulevard Drive (Skyline Parkway), William K. Rogers also proposed a park along the lakeshore running parallel to the roadway above; Lakeshore Park would eventually become Leif Erikson Park.

The card below, "Lakeside Scene at Lester Park," appears to capture the shoreline near Kitchi Gammi Park. Many people think the park's original name was Brighton Beach, but it has always been Kitchi Gammi Park; the park was also home to the Brighton Beach Tourist Camp, hence the confusion.

LAKESIDE SCENE AT LESTER PARK, DULUTH, MINN.

Lookout Point, Duluth, Minn.

North Shore, 9th Ave. East, Duluth, Minn.

PORTLAND
SQUARE,
DULUTH, MINN.

Along with Lincoln Park, Cascade Park, and Chester Park (Garfield Park), Portland Square was one of Duluth's first four parks. One square city block, Portland Square takes its name from the former township of Portland (roughly today's East Hillside), which became part of Duluth when it and other townships joined the city's ranks at the end of the 1880s and in the early 1890s. Portland Square has been reported as being the first square park in the United States. The park no longer features the hand-carved fountain shown in the postcard at left.

Miller Creek winds its way nine miles from bog land above Duluth and Hermantown, through the Heights and Lincoln Park, then goes underground until it empties into St. Louis Bay. Once considered one of the best brook trout streams in Minnesota, it has been threatened by increased development since the early 1980s. There never was a mill built along the creek; it was named for Robert P. Miller, a Duluthian and Civil War veteran who served with the 50th U.S. Colored Infantry in 1863.

The whimsical card at lower left appears to depict some eager young men prepared to canoe on an unnamed body of water in Duluth—if they can only find some female companionship. But there is doubt the image is local; the postcard publisher also produced a card with the very same image with a different caption: "Girls Wanted, Minneapolis, Minn."

GIRLS WANTED, DULUTH, MINN.

514—Miller's Creek, Duluth, Minn.

Spirit Lake

SPIRIT LAKE, DULUTH, MINN.

Spirit Lake, Minnesota. Duluth Boat Club,
Boat House and Steamboat Landing.

The Duluth Boat Club's Spirit Lake boathouse, built in 1907, included a dining room and dance floor; club members could rent a launch for $2 for the twelve-mile boat ride from the Club's main facility on Park Point. It closed in 1915 when U.S. Steel put up a plant on Spirit Lake.

Spirit Lake, the island that sits in it, and the hillside that rises behind it have long been revered by native peoples. Today that hillside is known as Spirit Mountain, or *Manitoushgebik* in Ojibwe. The hillside holds particular significance for the Ojibwe, as it was the sixth and final stop of their migration from the "great salt water in the east." For generations Ojibwe have used Spirit Mountain for vision quests and other spiritual events; they may have even used it as a burial site.

Spirit Lake is often overlooked, even by locals, because it can appear simply as an extension of the St. Louis River. It was once home to the Duluth Boat Club's Spirit Lake boathouse. Built in 1907, the boathouse included a dining room and dance floor. The entire facility consisted of cottages, a dormitory, picnic tables, and even two clay tennis courts. The Spirit Lake Boat Club was open year round, in the fall for duck hunting and in winter for snow shoeing, skiing, skating, and even hockey. It shut down in 1915 when U.S. Steel put up a plant on Spirit Lake near the boathouse.

A Legend of Spirit Island

A legend tells of Chaska, the son of a Dakota Chief, who accidentally entered Ojibwe territory while hunting and encountered Wetona, the daughter of Ojibwe Chief Buckado. He was handsome, she beautiful; soon they were in love. They would secretly meet at *Manitoushgebik* overlooking the St. Louis River—a spot known today as Bardon's Peak (named for James Bardon, a pioneer of Superior).

The Dakota planned a surprise attack on the Ojibwe, prompting the lovers to flee to a small island on the river. After the battle, Buckado rewarded one of his warriors, Gray Fox, by offering him Wetona's hand in marriage. When it was discovered that Chaska and Wetona had run off, Buckado became angry, vowing that his daughter would not marry a Dakota. A party of Ojibwe warriors saw a light on the island, paddled over to it, and found Wetona's canoe beached there.

But there was no trace of the lovers, just two pair of moccasins: Wetona's puckered Ojibwe footwear and Chaska's made in the Dakota fashion. They were never found.

Loon Feathers, Wetona's grandmother, said, "I am brave and strong, but now a great fear comes over me. I hear strange sounds like music. This is the voice of the Love Spirit, who has carried the lovers to the Moon of Perpetual Honey in his sky canoe."

The Love Spirit's magic was said to be stronger than death, so in order to not anger the spirit, Buckado had his warriors return to their village. Since then the island has been known as Spirit Island—and the lake Spirit Lake, and the hillside nearby Spirit Mountain.

Jay Cooke State Park

Jay Cooke State Park, located just south of Duluth on the St. Louis River, covers a region from Fond du Lac to Carlton, Minnesota (it is actually within Carlton County), and plays host to 223,000 visitors each year. Spanning both sides of the St. Louis River, the park's beauty has been enhanced by eons of seismic activity and erosion, which has exposed the slate bedrock, creating stunning rock formations.

The park is named for Philadelphia financier Jay Cooke, whose investments in the area pulled Duluth and surrounding communities out of a depression in the 1860s. The park contains some land that was once owned by Cooke and at one time included a cemetery used for residents of Thomson, a nearby lumber town. (The cemetery was abandoned when Cooke gave his land to the state of Minnesota.)

In 1915 the St. Louis Power Company donated 2,350 acres for the park (additional land was added later), but it wasn't until 1933 that the park really took shape, thanks in no small part to the Civilian Conservation Corps, which set up camp and constructed picnic sites, worked on soil erosion prevention, and built the park's famous Swinging Bridge. The camp closed in 1935.

The Swinging Bridge spans a particularly rocky and narrow portion of the river where rapids run rough. The bridge's pilons are made of native stone, and steel cables support the wood-and-steel structure. It is one of just two suspension bridges in all of Minnesota's state park system. First built in 1933, it was reconstructed in 1939, when the CCC returned and set up camp once more.

That same year the CCC built the park's River Inn, one of the largest buildings in the state park system. Like the bridge, the Inn and its accompanying water tower, latrine, and other structures are all made of logs and stone in the Rustic Style tradition.

In 1945 the state purchased another large piece of land for the park and has since added even more property to the site over the years; its original 2,350 acres have grown to 8,818.

SWING BRIDGE, JAY COOKE STATE PARK, DULUTH, MINN.—3

Swinging Bridge over St. Louis River, Jay Cooke State Park, near Duluth, Minn.

Fond du Lac

French for "Bottom of the Lake," Fond du Lac is the oldest settled neighborhood in Duluth. Once a township, Fond du Lac is where Sieur du Lhut first brought the Dakota and Ojibwe together; it later became a major trading center and the location of John Astor's American Fur Company, a trading post that was the site of a treaty signing in 1826. (Much more of Fond du Lac's early history can be found in this book's introduction.)

By the 1870s the population of Fond du Lac was a mix of Ojibwe, settlers of European stock, and the children of mixed marriages (French fur traders had been marrying Ojibwe women for decades). At this time a logging industry had developed in the area and three brownstone quarries began operation: Michael Chambers' quarry on the the St. Louis River's north side, J. H. Crowley's Duluth Brownstone Company on its south, and C. A. Krause's quarry on Mission Creek. They thrived until brownstone went out of fashion after the turn of the century. In 1895 the township was incorporated into the city of Duluth, instantly becoming the town's oldest neighborhood, which was fitting: it included the home built in 1867 by fur trader Peter J. Peterson, the first frame house built in "Duluth."

Old Fond du Lac Indian Trading Post on St. Louis River, Duluth, Minn.

9492. THE RETURN OF THE HUNTERS.

The card at top is of the 1935 reconstruction of the American Fur Company Post, made of logs, some of which were reportedly salvaged from the original trading post (the claim has been disputed); it was razed in 1968 after it had been compromised by neglect.

The card directly above claims to be ruins of the original 1809 post, but it is obviously made of stone. It is actually the ruins of the home of Michael and Emily Chambers, which once boasted twenty rooms, including a dance hall. The house burned in the early 1890s and the land on which it stood has since become Chambers Grove Park. Michael Chambers owned one of Fond du Lac's sandstone quarries.

The scene captured in the card at left, on a white-border card produced sometime between 1915 and 1930, was obviously staged for tourism. Those times weren't nearly as educated about native cultures as are today's.

Fond du Lac's Excursion Boats

From before the advent of the automobile until about the 1940s, Fond du Lac was a popular spot for Duluthians and others to take day trips and longer breaks from their daily routine. Served by the railroad and steamers such as those shown on these pages, Fond du Lac offered picnic sites, fine hotel dining, and even some entertainment, including shows featuring native ceremonies billed as the "Chippewa Indian Medicine Dance" (the postcard at the bottom left of page 104 also indicates that native Ojibwe customs were often exploited as entertainment).

Three of the many excursion boats that once brought Duluthians to and from Fond du Lac. The Newsboy (left and top) was built in 1889 in West Bay, Michigan; records don't indicate when she first arrived in Duluth, but she was listed as "abandoned" in 1916. Also built in 1889, the Rotarion (bottom left), was first named the A. Wehrle, Jr. She became the Rotarian in 1919 and by 1930 she was tied up in Chicago and used as a restaurant and dance hall; she sank at her moorings that year. Perhaps the most famous Fond du Lac excursion boat, the Montauk, was built in Wilmington, Delaware, in 1891 but didn't get to Duluth until 1925. She ran the Duluth-to-Fond du Lac route for nearly fifteen years before being sold, stripped of her cabins, and converted to a barge. There are no records for the Montauk past 1947.

Duluth, Minn.   Excursion Steamer, Fond Du Lac Line.

Compliments of.... Clow-Nicholson Transportation Co... Both Phones.

Excursion Steamer "Newsboy" Returning from her Daily Fond du Lac Trip.

STEAMER ROTARIAN LANDING AT FOND-DU-LAC ON ST. LOUIS RIVER, NEAR DULUTH, MINN.

S. S. "MONTAUK", DULUTH, MINN.—28

MORGAN PARK, DULUTH, MINN.—69

INTERSECTION OF FOURTH STREET AND "A" AVENUE, MORGAN PARK, DULUTH, MINN.

NENOVAN CLUB, MORGAN PARK, DULUTH, MINN.

NORTH BOULEVARD AND SECOND STREET, MORGAN PARK, DULUTH, MINN.

Morgan Park

At the turn of the twentieth century, U.S. Steel decided to build a mill in the vicinity of Duluth to save on transportation costs (its ore came from Minnesota's Iron Range). After the State of Minnesota threatened to tax iron ore that crossed the state line—unless the plant was located in the state—a site near Gary-New Duluth was chosen. U.S. Steel built Morgan Park (named for the firm's founder, J. P. Morgan; it was originally to be named "Model City") to provide nearby housing for its employees. Construction began in 1913. At the time, Morgan Park had the most modern school, hospital, and community facilities in the nation, and one church each for Catholics and Protestants. All of the company town's buildings were made chiefly of concrete block produced at the U.S. Steel's own cement plant because the material needed little maintenance. The somewhat harsh look of concrete was softened by gables, eaves, and rooflines that concealed the appearance of monotonous regularity. The heart of the community was the Goodfellowship Club, a workers' association dedicated to serving sick or needy fellow employees. The club was housed in a large, multi-use building that included a gymnasium with a running track, an auditorium, an indoor swimming pool, and a bowling alley. It was torn down in 1981 when a more fuel-efficient building was built to replace it.

INTERIOR, ELECTRIC POWER HOUSE, U. S. STEEL PLANT, DULUTH, MINN

61:—View from Bardon's Peak, Skyline Parkway, Duluth, Minn.

Universal Atlas Cement Plant. $125,000,000 Minnesota Steel Plant—

Morgan Park Industry

When plans for a U.S. Steel plant in Duluth were first announced in 1907, wild predictions were made about the town's population tripling and that the plant would be the first of many "lining the shores of Lake Superior from Fond du Lac to Two Harbors…each striving to outdo its neighbor with smoke and noise." Morgan Park's U.S. Steel plant first went operational in 1915 and would grow to include a wire mill, a coke plant, and a fence-post fabrication operation.

It also included the Universal Atlas Cement plant (shown in the postcard above right) which made all of the concrete used to construct Morgan Park's homes, office buildings, retail stores, hospital, boathouse, and churches. In 1942 U.S. Steel sold all of its Morgan Park holdings to John W. Galbreath & Company, a Columbus, Ohio, real estate firm. Residents were given the choice to buy their homes or move. The plant shut down in the 1970s. Its buildings saw some use in the 1980s and early 1990s, but none are left. The community of Morgan Park is still a vital part of Duluth, and now includes some newer buildings and houses, many on the western part of town that was never developed by U.S. Steel. The hospital and boathouse met the same fate as the Goodfellowship Club (see page 106).

Blast Furnaces and Stoves, U. S. Steel Plant, Duluth, Minn.

ONE OF THE MANY BEAUTY SPOTS OF ST. LOUIS RIVER.

BETWEEN DULUTH-SUPERIOR HARBOR AND FOND-DU-LAC, MINN.

Fond du Lac, Minnesota.
Up the beautiful St. Louis, above Fond du Lac.

On the St. Louis River,
Duluth, Minn.

St. Louis River

The St. Louis River arcs its way roughly 180 miles from its headwaters at Seven Beaver Lake (which straddles the border between St. Louis and Lake Counties almost directly north of Duluth) down through the Iron Range and the old lumber town of Cloquet before emptying itself into Lake Superior at the very head of the lakes. The largest tributary feeding Lake Superior, the St. Louis itself is fed by several smaller rivers, including the Cloquet, the Whiteface, the East Swan, the Floodwood, the Embarrass, the Red, and the Pokegama. The silt it carries to the big lake formed Minnesota and Wisconsin Point, the largest naturally formed sandbar on the planet. It has also created three bays: St. Louis Bay (between Spirit Lake and Rice's Point), Superior Bay (between Rice's Point and Minnesota Point) and Allouez Bay, between Wisconsin Point and Superior's Allouez neighborhood. Before they were developed, the bays were mostly marshland and floating islands. The French explorer Verendrye named the river to honor being named to the order of St. Louis by Louis XV, the king of France, in 1749.

Great Northern Power Co. Dam, which furnishes the power for Duluth and Superior, developing 80,000 horse power.

Waterfall of the Great Northern Power Co., at Thompson, Minn., 18 Miles from Duluth, which will supply power for factories and other Plants at Duluth and Superior.

Thomson Dam

Electric light first lit up Duluth in 1906 after the Great Northern Power Company harnessed the St. Louis River by building a dam at the old logging town of Thomson in the heart of what would become Jay Cooke State Park (the land for the dam had been acquired from Cooke's estate). The dam was actually constructed by Boston's National Railway Construction Company (and a variety of subcontractors) according to a design by A. H. Albertson of New York and Duluth's own V. M. Holder. At the time it powered up, the Thomson Dam was the third largest waterpower plant in the world, and the *Duluth News-Tribune* called it "a water power second in potential to that of Niagara Falls." Designed to reach a capacity of 200,000 horsepower, it drew only 30,000 horsepower in its first year, which was part of a multi-stage plan. The company quickly added three power units, and soon it was up to 75,000 horsepower. Work on the dam was completed in 1907.

Beginning during World War I, Great Northern Power merged with Duluth Edison and several power companies on the Mesabi and Cuyuna iron ranges; in 1923, this conglomerate became the Minnesota Power and Light Company. When drought depleted the Minnesota watershed in the 1920s, Minnesota Power constructed a coal-fired plant in West Duluth.

The Thomson Dam wasn't the first time someone came up with a plan to use the St. Louis as a power source. In 1883 the Minnesota Canal Company proposed a grand idea: starting twenty-six miles upstream from Cloquet, dig a canal 120 feet wide and 20 feet deep to the top of the hill above Duluth's West End. From there, direct the water through giant conduits, turning waterwheels that would in turn fuel generators that would bring power and light to the Zenith City. The only problem was the cost: $7 million was a lot to raise back in 1883, today's equivalent to about $133,750,000.

Duluth in 1871

Despite prediction in the 1850s that Duluth's population would grow to eclipse Chicago's, in 1860 just 353 people called the town home. Nearby townships such as Fond du Lac and Oneota—both of which would eventually become part of Duluth—also found their populations depleted.

In 1866 the mood was nothing if not optimistic. Those who held on through the lean years called themselves the "Ancient and Honorable Order of the Fish Eaters," for they rarely had more to eat than what they could pull out of Lake Superior. It was that July 4 on Minnesota Point that newspaperman Thomas Foster gave the famous speech in which he dubbed Duluth the "Zenith City of the Unsalted Seas." That year Philadelphia financier Jay Cooke showed up, along with his money, and started investing heavily in the region. Cooke's arrival coincided with a gold rush—a small amount of gold was discovered at Lake Vermilion, but prospectors found little more. In 1869 just fourteen families lived in Duluth.

Cooke's injection of cash led to a land rush by those again speculating that Duluth would grow into a major urban center. And as Cooke continued to spend, Duluth continued to grow—laborers arrived to construct his grain elevators, lumberjacks showed up to clear timber, mill workers appeared to turn the timber into lumber, carpenters came to take that lumber and use it to build houses, and so on. These new arrivals, called "Sixty-niners" by the Fish Eaters, would help Duluth win a city charter in 1870.

That spring Duluthians elected J. B. Culver their first mayor. Promise was in the air, but that would not last. In 1873 Cooke himself went bankrupt, and by 1877 state officials allowed Duluth's charter to lapse, reducing it to village status. It wouldn't become a city again until 1887.

Superior Street, Duluth, 1871.

DULUTH Minn. Twenty Months old. June 3, 1871.
Photo Copyrighted by G. A. Sloan May 7th 1908

These postcards are made from photographs taken in 1871, but they weren't published as postcards until long after. The above card (copyright 1908), claims that Duluth was twenty months old in June, 1871, but that all depends on which of Duluth's "birth" dates you go by—1856, 1870, or 1887.

Street Scenes North and East of Downtown

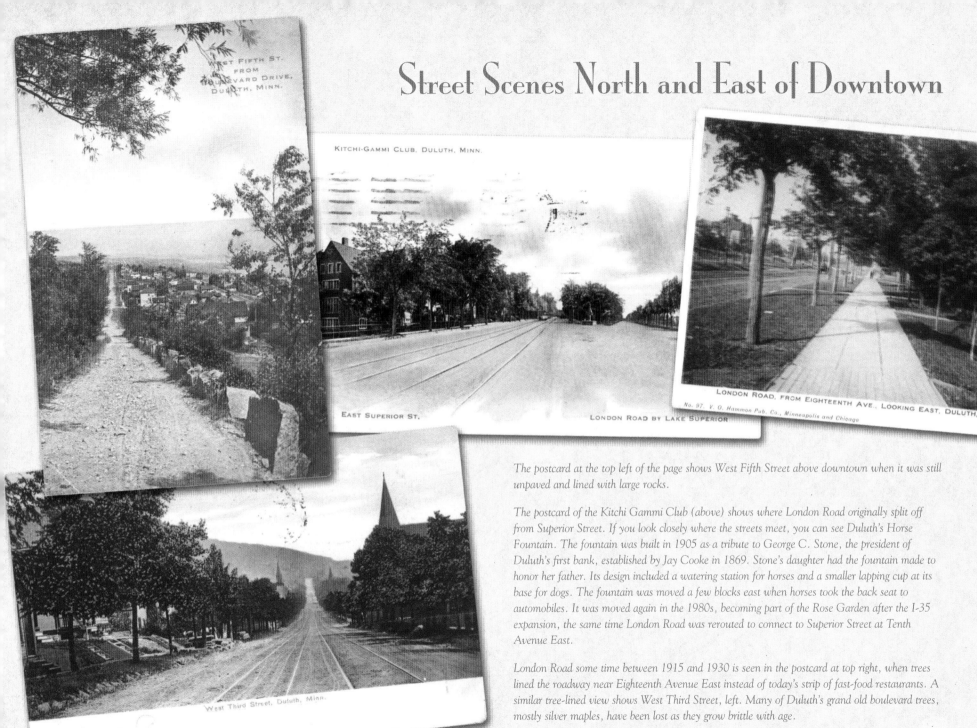

WEST FIFTH ST. FROM BOULEVARD DRIVE, DULUTH, MINN.

KITCHI-GAMMI CLUB, DULUTH, MINN.

EAST SUPERIOR ST.

LONDON ROAD BY LAKE SUPERIOR

LONDON ROAD, FROM EIGHTEENTH AVE., LOOKING EAST, DULUTH, MINN.

No. 97, V. O. Hammon Pub. Co., Minneapolis and Chicago

West Third Street, Duluth, Minn.

The postcard at the top left of the page shows West Fifth Street above downtown when it was still unpaved and lined with large rocks.

The postcard of the Kitchi Gammi Club (above) shows where London Road originally split off from Superior Street. If you look closely where the streets meet, you can see Duluth's Horse Fountain. The fountain was built in 1905 as a tribute to George C. Stone, the president of Duluth's first bank, established by Jay Cooke in 1869. Stone's daughter had the fountain made to honor her father. Its design included a watering station for horses and a smaller lapping cup at its base for dogs. The fountain was moved a few blocks east when horses took the back seat to automobiles. It was moved again in the 1980s, becoming part of the Rose Garden after the I-35 expansion, the same time London Road was rerouted to connect to Superior Street at Tenth Avenue East.

London Road some time between 1915 and 1930 is seen in the postcard at top right, when trees lined the roadway near Eighteenth Avenue East instead of today's strip of fast-food restaurants. A similar tree-lined view shows West Third Street, left. Many of Duluth's grand old boulevard trees, mostly silver maples, have been lost as they grow brittle with age.

Along Superior Street Near Fifth Avenue West

The white-border era card at left, made some time between 1915 and 1930, shows trolleys in front of the St. Louis Hotel, the Torrey Building, and the Alworth Building, Duluth's tallest building to this day. The card at the bottom left of the next page is of a similar view taken a few years earlier—before the Alworth was built.

SUPERIOR STREET, EAST FROM FOURTH AVENUE, DULUTH, MINN.

Duluth, Minnesota.
West Superior Street, showing Spalding Hotel and Lyceum Theatre

SUPERIOR ST., LOOKING EAST FROM 5TH. WEST, DULUTH, MINN.

The card at right and the one above take in the view from from Fifth Avenue West. Both show the Lyceum Theatre and Spalding Hotel, buildings that once shared the intersection of Fifth Avenue West and Superior Street. Both cards were printed some time after 1901 but prior to 1915.

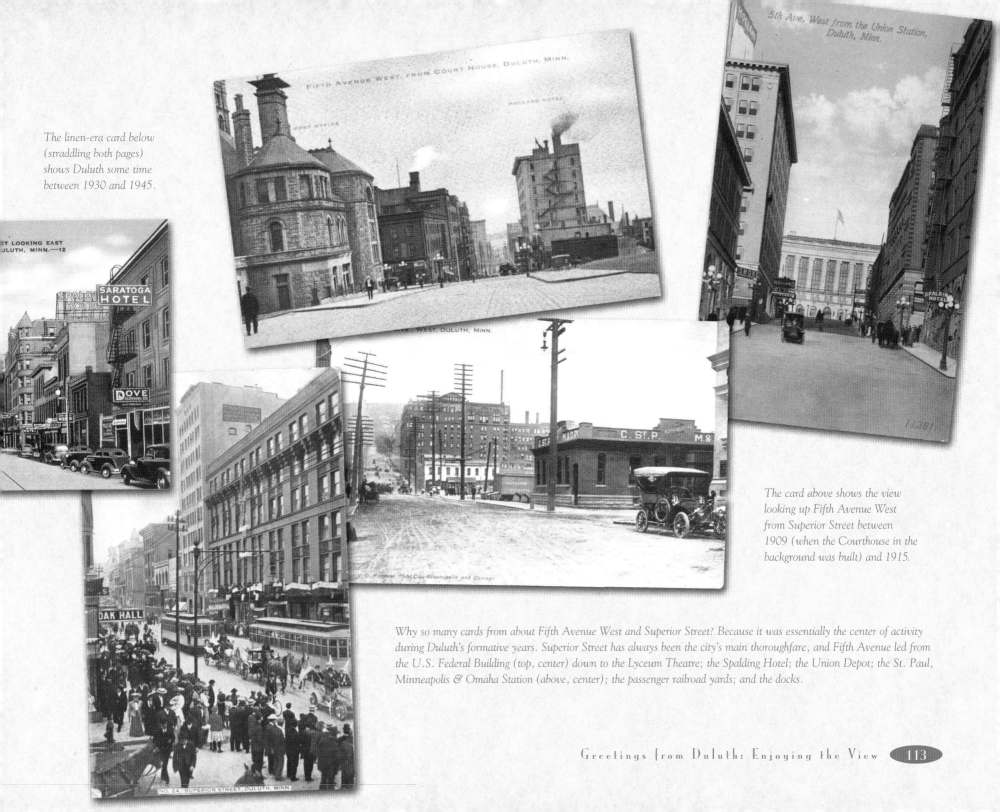

The linen-era card below (straddling both pages) shows Duluth some time between 1930 and 1945.

FIFTH AVENUE WEST, FROM COURT HOUSE, DULUTH, MINN.

POST OFFICE

HOLLAND HOTEL

5th Ave. West from the Union Station, Duluth, Minn.

...ET LOOKING EAST ...LUTH, MINN.—12

SPALDI... HOTEL

SARATOGA HOTEL

DOVE CLOTHING CO.

...E WEST, DULUTH, MINN.

C. ST. P. M. &...

V. O. Hammon Pub. Co., Minneapolis and Chicago

The card above shows the view looking up Fifth Avenue West from Superior Street between 1909 (when the Courthouse in the background was built) and 1915.

OAK HALL

NO. 24. SUPERIOR STREET, DULUTH, MINN.

Why so many cards from about Fifth Avenue West and Superior Street? Because it was essentially the center of activity during Duluth's formative years. Superior Street has always been the city's main thoroughfare, and Fifth Avenue led from the U.S. Federal Building (top, center) down to the Lyceum Theatre; the Spalding Hotel; the Union Depot; the St. Paul, Minneapolis & Omaha Station (above, center); the passenger railroad yards; and the docks.

Bird's-eye Views of Duluth's Downtown & Waterfront

The linen-era card below shows a bridge that once extended Sixth Avenue West over the railroad yards to the waterfront some time after 1930 and before 1945. (The Union Depot is visible in the lower left-hand corner.)

AERIAL BRIDGE AND PART OF

MERCHANDISE DOCKS AND PASSENGER TERMINALS, DULUTH, MINN.—67

FIREPROOF STORAGE

VIEW OF DULUTH-SUPERIOR HARBOR AND NEW AERIAL LIFT BRIDGE FROM EIGHTH AVE. WEST   1930-30

Duluth from Eighth Avenue West (right) in 1930. It was the last year of the white-border era, and the bridge shown includes the lift span, added in 1929, already in place (and the publisher's code, "1930-30" also makes a pretty good clue).

Lake Avenue crosses the railroad tracks in the undivided-back card above, made between 1901 and 1907. The image was captured after 1892, when Central High School (its clock tower shown rising above the horizon) was built.

Copyright 1905, T. A. Patrick & Co.

SKYLINE OF BUSINESS DISTRICT FROM HARBOR, DULUTH, MINN.—66

Water Front, Duluth, Minn.

BIRDSEYE VIEW, DULUTH, MINN.

The two waterfront images on this page show just how much Duluth changed from as early as 1907 (right) and as late as 1945 (above). The Alworth Building stands tall in both postcards, but in the linen card at top note how many more buildings line the waterfront and houses dot the hillside.

This oversized panoramic view and those on the following pages are linen cards, printed between 1930 and 1945.

usiness District from Harbor

BIRD'S-EYE VIEW OF DULUTH, MINN.

HOTEL LENOX

UNION STATION

SPAUL

Copyright by L. P. Gallagher

BIRD'S EYE VIEW OF DULUTH, MINN., AND WATER FRONT.

HOTEL LENOX

Incline Railway

Built in 1891, the Incline Railway was a system of steam engines and cables that pulled tram cars up and down two sets of elevated tracks on what is now Seventh Avenue West, carrying commuters back and forth from their homes at the top of the hill down to Superior Street and their jobs downtown. On weekends and evenings, downtown residents hopped on the Incline for a ride up to its expansive pavilion. There, Duluthians enjoyed dances, performances, or dined in one of its restaurants. Others picnicked outdoors or took a ride in a hot-air balloon.

Unfortunately, in 1901 a fire began in the pavilion and destroyed it. The blaze spread to the power station, and the heat melted the railway's cables, releasing a flaming trolley car that raced toward Superior Street, crashed through the railway's depot gates, crossed Superior Street, and came to a halt in the railyards near the Union Depot. No one was injured.

The Incline Railway served Duluth until Labor Day, 1939. After that, it was dismantled and sold as scrap.

The Incline Railway. A grand pavilion designed by Duluth architects Traphagen & Fitzpatrick once sat at the top, next to the engine house. It was destroyed by fire in 1901 and never rebuilt.

8671. Incline Railroad, Duluth, Minn.

COPR. DETROIT PUBLISHING CO.

-12452   UP THE INCLINE FROM SUPERIOR ST., DULUTH, MINN.

As indicated by the white-border card at left (printed some time between 1915 and 1930), a certain D. Donovan operated the Incline Saloon at the base of the Incline Railway where it met Superior Street.

Point of Rocks

Superior Street, looking East from 14th Avenue West Duluth, Minn.

Point of Rock, Duluth, Minn.

Since 1887 Duluthians have been chipping away at Point of Rocks, a giant rock outcropping near Thirteenth Avenue West and Superior Street. Early attempts to remove the stone were spurred both by safety concerns and in order to make Superior Street straight. Shortly after the first blast in 1887, a huge boulder narrowly missed a man on horseback. In 1924 a movement grew to remove the natural landmark after 100,000 tons of rock fell onto Superior Street (another 100,000 tons fell in 1931 after heavy rains).

Duluthians found a use for the Point: both painted and handbill advertisements found their way onto the stone, as the postcards at left attest. In 1919, city leaders decided to turn Point of Rocks into a work of art. They brought in Mount Rushmore sculptor Gutzon Borglum to blast the rock into the form of the city's namesake, Daniel Greysolon Sieur du Lhut. But Borglum found the stone too hard to carve and refused the job. (A bronze statue of du Lhut by famed sculptor Jacque Lipschitz stands in UMD's Ordean Court.) Despite blasting and plans for public art, Point of Rocks remains—albeit smaller—and Superior Street still bows around it.

The Elephants, Point of Rocks, DULUTH Minn.
Copyrighted by G. A. Sloan May 7th 1908

The circus must have been in town when someone took the image of a herd of elephants parading past Point of Rocks in the card at right, first published in 1908.

Rice's Point and the West End (a.k.a. Lincoln Park)

The Glenn Rock housing development was built in the shade of Point of Rocks between Twelfth and Thirteenth Avenues East off Superior Street in about 1890, before Duluth's more modest homes enjoyed the convenience of indoor plumbing (note the outhouses). There is no record of the houses past 1930; they were most likely razed due to safety sometime before the city dynamited parts of Point of Rocks in the late 1910s or 1920s.

An early township which its founder, Orrin Rice, thought would become a major city, Rice's Point (above and right) has played home to Duluth's grain elevators. coal docks, lumber mills, and railroad yards since the 1870s. The roundhouse shown in both cards belonged to the Northern Pacific Railroad and operated as a repair shop.

Bird's-eye views of the West End, the earliest captured some time between 1901 and 1915 (right) and the latest (below) from a photo taken between 1930 and 1945.

WEST END DULUTH FROM HILLTOP DRIVE, DULUTH, MINN.—35

WEST DULUTH, MINN.

Duluth, Minnesota. Bird's Eye View of

19th Ave. and Superior St. looking West, Duluth, Minn.

The white-border era card above shows the West End business district some time between 1915 and 1930. Today the same area is sometimes referred to as the "Furniture District" because of the many furniture stores along this stretch of Superior Street.

The View from Skyline Parkway, a.k.a. Boulevard Drive, Carriage Drive,

Skyline Parkway was designed to take in the view, and the cards say enough without captions. But if you want to read about the parkway, turn to page 76.

113-D View from Rest Point, U. S. Highway 61, Entering Duluth. Minn.

"Bird's Eye View looking South".

Duluth, Minn.

113-D—View from Rest Point, Entering Duluth, Minnesota

No. 90. Y. C. HAMMON PUB. CO., MINNEAPOLIS

Rogers Boulevard, Terrace Parkway...

26:—Panoramic View of Duluth-Superior Harbor from Skyline Parkway.

Main Duluth Business Section and Aerial Lift Bridge in Foreground.

Duluth, Minnesota. Bird's Eye View, Minnesota Point

...OTA POINT, AND HARBOR.

DULUTH, MINN., FROM THE HILL TOP.

64165

The Zenith City Lit Up After the Sun Went Down

It must have been difficult to take night photos with cameras that would be considered primitive by today's standards. In fact, many "night scene" postcards were actually made from photos taken in the daylight and then colored in the lithography process to appear as nighttime scenes.

Lyceum Theatre, Duluth, Minn.

102 Lift Bridge and Ship Canal at Night. Duluth-Superior Harbor

AERIAL BRIDGE BY NIGHT. DULUTH, MINN.

MISSABE ORE DOCKS AT NIGHT, DULUTH.

A Bit Too Much Artistic License?

It's easy to understand how colorists working in Germany without proper guidance could have colored a column-adorned brownstone building white, assuming it was made of marble, or a yellow brick building such as the Union Depot red, the most common color of bricks. One can even see how an artist might have some fun with a town's reputation, such as the card on page 97 titled "A Winter's Residence on Park Point." But the postcard at right causes one to wonder: did photographer Hugh McKenzie think he was fooling anyone when he scratched the image of Halley's Comet and some stars into his photo? The comet may well have been visible in the night skies over Duluth when it made its 1910 pass, but it would never have appeared so large, and photo equipment of the day would have had a hard time capturing any image of it.

Halley's Comet Seen At Duluth Minn
Photo by McKenzie

140-D—Bird's-Eye View from Skyline Drive at Night, Duluth, Minn.

Hunting near Duluth, Minn.

ENGER TOWER, DULUTH, MINN.—65

The Storm of 1905 and Wreck of the *Mataafa* (and others)

STEAMER "UMBRIA" SAFE IN DULUTH HARBOR AFTER A FORTY-EIGHT HOURS' BATTLE WITH THE STORM OF NOV. 28, 1905. HER PILOT HOUSE WHEEL AND BINNACLE WERE DESTROYED BUT HER CREW SUCCEEDED IN CONTROLLING HER FROM THE STEERING DECK "AFT."

Wrecked
Pilot House
of
Str. "Umbria"
Nov. 28, 1905

The gales of November that famously wrecked the *Edmund Fitzgerald* in 1975 have been claiming watercraft since boats first dared to navigate Lake Superior. The costliest storm on record, in terms of ships damaged or destroyed and lives lost, occurred seventy years before the *Fitz* failed to make Whitefish Bay, and thousands of Duluthians witnessed the worst of it.

Vessels navigating Lake Superior on Tuesday, November 28, 1905—two days before Thanksgiving—found themselves battling hurricane-force winds. That day and the next, twenty-six ships were wrecked or suffered damage, seventeen were stranded, and at least one foundered. The human toll was also heavy; the storm took thirty-three souls, nine of them just outside Duluth's ship canal. A crowd of thousands gathered near the ship canal to watch the ships attempt to ride out the storm. The *Mataafa*, hauling a load of iron, appeared out of the squall in midafternoon, steaming hard for the canal and the safety beyond it. As it entered the canal, currents and wind gusts forced the ship into the north pier; conditions then carried it back into the lake before slamming it broadside against the pierhead. About 150 yards from shore, the *Mataafa* settled to the lake bottom and split in two. Desperate

STEAMER "ELWOOD" MAKING THE HARBOR OF DULUTH SAFELY DURING THE GREAT STORM OF NOV. 28, 1905. SHE AFTERWARDS SANK FROM LEAKS SUSTAINED DURING THE STORM.

No. 359. V. O. HAMMON PUB. CO., MINNEAPOLIS AND CHICAGO

sailors in both the fore and aft cabins—which were still above water—signalled for help. Members of the U.S. Life Savers stood helplessly on shore, the storm too strong to launch their lifeboats. That night thousands of Duluthians lined the shore, standing vigil as the storm pounded the wounded ship. In the wee hours of the morning, the flickering light in the pilot house went dead. When the Life Savers finally reached the ship the next morning they found fifteen sailors—including the ship's captain—alive. They had survived their ordeal by burning furniture to keep warm. Unfortunately, nine of their crew either drowned or froze to death.

Other ships lost or damaged in the storm include the *Umbria*, the *Elwood*, the *George Spencer*, the *Amboy*, the *Ira H. Owen*, and the *John Smythe*, which the *Mataafa* had been towing when the storm hit. The *Crescent City* ran aground two miles east of Lester Park; its crew used a ladder as a gangway to escape the ship. The *Medeira* was under tow of the *William Edenborn*; the *Edenborn*'s captain cut the tow line thinking it would be safer for the *Medeira*. It wasn't. The ship struck Gold Rock, north of where Split Rock Lighthouse now stands. Crewman Fred Benson grabbed a coil of rope and climbed a sixty-foot cliff while the storm raged about him. He then dropped the rope to the *Medeira* and saved eight other crew members. Only the first mate perished, pulled down with the ship as he tried to climb the mizzenmast and jump to safety.

The steamer Crescent City ran aground during the November 1905 storm. Its crew was lucky: they were able to safely reach shore with the help of a ladder. Thirty-three men on other ships were less fortunate.

WRECK OF THE STEAMER "CRESCENT CITY"; DRIVEN ASHORE TWO MILES EAST OF LESTER PARK, DULUTH, MINNESOTA, DURING THE GREAT STORM OF NOV. 28, 1905. HER CREW ESCAPED TO SHORE BY USING A LADDER AS A BRIDGE.

No. 364. V. O. HAMMON PUB. CO., MINNEAPOLIS AND CHICAGO

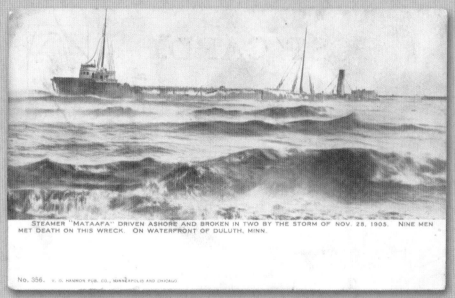

STEAMER "MATAAFA" DRIVEN ASHORE AND BROKEN IN TWO BY THE STORM OF NOV. 28, 1905. NINE MEN MET DEATH ON THIS WRECK. ON WATERFRONT OF DULUTH, MINN.

No. 356. V. O. HAMMON PUB. CO., MINNEAPOLIS AND CHICAGO

WRECK OF THE STEAMER "CRESCENT CITY"; DRIVEN ASHORE TWO MILES EAST OF LESTER PARK, DULUTH, MINNESOTA, DURING THE GREAT STORM OF NOV. 28, 1905. HER CREW ESCAPED TO SHORE BY USING A LADDER AS A BRIDGE.

No. 363. V. O. HAMMON PUB. CO., MINNEAPOLIS AND CHICAGO

The 1906 Wreck of the Interstate Bridge—a Very Costly Collision

INTER STATE BRIDGE BETWEEN SUPERIOR & DULUTH, WRECKED
AUG. 11, 1906. CAUSED BY COLLISION OF STEAMSHIP "TROY."
ONE OF THE WESTERN TRANSIT CO'S BOATS.

RUSSELL BROS. PUB.

About an hour past midnight on August 11, 1906, the 398-foot, 3,665-ton steamer *Troy* rammed the Interstate Bridge, knocking a 200-foot piece of steel into the bay and buckling the northern span, which collapsed, blocking all traffic on the bay and trapping thirty-three ships inside the upper harbor.

Captain Robert Murray had blown the signal on the ship's whistle (one long, one short, one long) to notify operators to swing the bridge open, but claimed he could not see the bridge well because of the structure's lighting, which he said "kind of blinds one at night." He explained to reporters that instead of slowing or stopping, as was required when the bridge failed to open, he didn't worry that the bridge wasn't immediately opening for the *Troy*, claiming "That seems to always be the custom of the bridge."

The collision did more injury to Murray's reputation than it did to the *Troy*, but the bridge was significantly damaged. Clearing the channel took almost a week, costing each trapped vessel's operators about $1,000 a day. Engineers spent nearly two years restoring the bridge.

More about the Interstate Bridge can be found on page 27.

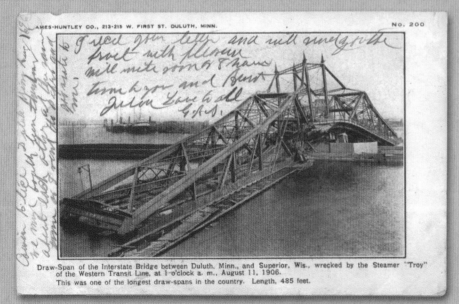

Draw-Span of the Interstate Bridge between Duluth, Minn., and Superior, Wis., wrecked by the Steamer "Troy" of the Western Transit Line, at 1-o'clock a. m., August 11, 1906.
This was one of the longest draw-spans in the country. Length, 485 feet.

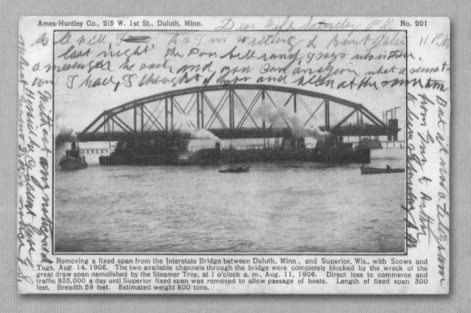

Removing a fixed span from the Interstate Bridge between Duluth, Minn., and Superior, Wis., with Scows and Tugs. Aug. 14, 1906. The two available channels through the bridge were completely blocked by the wreck of the great draw span demolished by the Steamer Troy, at 1 o'clock a. m., Aug. 11, 1906. Direct loss to commerce and traffic $35,000 a day until Superior fixed span was removed to allow passage of boats. Length of fixed span 300 feet. Breadth 59 feet. Estimated weight 800 tons.

Night Scene of $2,500,000 Fire in Superior Milling District

The High Cost of Fire

During Duluth's last big boom, when the city's grand old buildings were going up faster than you could count them, many were coming down just as quickly—and fire was the main culprit. Firefighting was still primitive in the days before hydrants, when the fire department used horses to bring water-pumping steam engines to the scene. In fact, Duluth's first fire hall burned to the ground in 1871 after a mishap with its steam engine as the fledgling department attempted to respond to its first call. Buildings destroyed by flame over the years include the Clark House Hotel (1881), an entire row of thirteen Superior Street buildings between Lake and First Avenues (1883), Grain Elevators A and Q (1886), the Grand Opera House (1889), the Incline Railway Pavilion (1901), the first Sacred Heart Cathedral (1892), the first St. Louis Hotel (1893), the first Board of Trade (1894), the first Northland Country Club (1918), and, ironically, the first Flame restaurant (1942). Fire even claimed the steamer *Winslow* as it sat at its moorings at the St. Paul & Duluth Railroad Dock in 1894. More recently, fire has taken the Curling Club and UMD's Old Main.

The High Cost of "Progress"

Perhaps the only good thing about the loss of historic buildings to fire is that often other architectural wonders take their place, just as the Phoenix Building rose from the ashes of the Grand Opera House. Duluth is indeed lucky to have many historic buildings still standing, giving parts of the city an old-world charm not found in other American cities of its size. And the Zenith City would still have many more of its treasures if not for the wrecking ball, as many of Duluth's brick and brownstone monuments have been torn down in the name of progress and pandering to architectural trends.

Gone are the Lyceum Theatre, the First Methodist Episcopal Church, the Old Post Office/Government Building, the McDougall Terminal, the Soo Line Depot, a string of hotels (the Spalding, the second St. Louis, the Holland, the Lincoln, the Lenox, and more), and the entire wholesale district—even the Incline Railway went down when it was deemed obsolete. Other buildings have been compromised: The top three floors of the Temple Opera Building (right) were removed, as were the bell towers from Endion School and Engine House Number 1; the Orpheum Theatre was gutted to create the NorShor Theatre; and the brick façade of the Commercial Club was sided over when it became the Duluth Athletic Club.

Temple Opera House and
Masonic Temple Building
as it appeared in 1889.

The Temple Opera Building as it looked in all its glory. Its Second Avenue East façade was altered by fire and again when the Orpheum Theatre was built; later its moorish dome and top three floors were removed.

The 1920 Lynchings

A lyric from "Desolation Row" by Duluth native Bob Dylan, "They're selling postcards of the hanging…the circus is in town," should hold particular poignancy to the people of his hometown. Like any city, Duluth has had some ugly moments in its past, but perhaps none more horrible than June 15, 1920. The John Robinson Show Circus was in town after two performances in West Duluth the previous day. Later that night, eighteen-year-old Duluthian James Sullivan claimed that a black man from the circus held a pistol to his head and forced him to watch five other black circus hands rape Irene Tusken, nineteen, also from Duluth. It was a lie. A doctor who examined Tusken found no signs of sexual assault, yet he did not report his findings to authorities. Police rounded up a group of black circus workers and held several of them, including Elmer Jackson, Elias Clayton, and material witness Isaac McGhie; all were between nineteen and twenty-one years old.

Though not reported in the newspapers, news of the alleged rape spread through West Duluth, where outraged businessman Louis Dondino began rounding up a mob, causing a chain reaction throughout the community. By 8:40 P.M. a riotous group of several thousand people stormed the downtown jail on Superior Street at Second Avenue East. By 9:30 they had broken through. The mob took Jackson and Clayton—and later McGhie—a block away to the corner of First Street and Second Avenue East. Some tried to stop the mob, including Reverend W. J. Powers, who climbed a light pole to address the crowd. The mob pulled him down and used the same light pole and some rope to hang Jackson, Clayton, and McGhie. The killers then posed for photographs next to their victims before a militia arrived and dispersed the crowd. Later, the photos were sold as postcards. Some members of the lynch mob were convicted of rioting; no murder charges were ever filed.

Clayton, Jackson, and McGhie were buried in pauper's graves in Duluth's Park Hill Cemetery. The following September the NAACP opened a Duluth branch, and Minnesota passed anti-lynching legislation in 1923. But by then much of Duluth's black population had left. In 1991 a granite headstone was placed at their graves with the message "Deterred but not defeated," and in 2003 the Clayton Jackson McGhie Memorial Committee installed a memorial to the lynching victims on the very street corner where they were killed.

A postcard commemorating the 1921 vigilante hanging of three innocent black men, their images blurred by the publisher out of respect for the victims and their families. At one time postcards of hangings were common. We present it here for what it is, another part of Duluth's history recorded in a postcard.

The Forgotten Lynching

Before lies and racial prejudice caused the death of three innocent black men, a group of Duluth vigilantes displayed their ignorance by hanging a man for his political beliefs. Actually, they tarred and feathered him first, then they hanged him.

Olli Kinkkonen was an immigrant from Finland and, like many Finns, a Socialist. He refused to join the American army to fight in World War I and renounced his U.S. citizenship. Some say Kinkkonen considered the war an imperialist conflict, a struggle for economic power, an unjust war. Others say he was simply a peaceful man, a dockworker and logger who wanted no part of war and was mistaken for a more outspoken antiwar Finn. Whatever the case, Kinkkonen had made plans to return to Finland, but he never made it. Historians say it may not matter whether Kinkkonen was against the war, as anti-Finnish sentiment flourished in the area in 1918. What happened to him may have been as much inspired by ethnic bias as by politics.

In September 1918, Kinkkonen was abducted from his boarding house bed by a group calling themselves the Knights of Liberty, vigilantes who labeled those who did not join the army "slackers." The group first phoned then sent a letter to a local newspaper, claiming that they tarred and feathered Kinkkonen as a warning to all slackers. Two weeks after the abduction, Kinkkonen was found hanging by his neck from a tree near Lester Park, covered in tar and feathers; $410 was found in his shoes. Duluth authorities ruled that Kinkkonen must have committed suicide because he was embarrassed about what had happened to him. His abductors—and probable murderers—were never charged. One local paper, *The Truth*, called the chief of police "unfit for office" and suggested that the *Duluth Tribune* knew the truth behind Kinkkonen's hanging.

Kinkkonen was buried in an unmarked grave in the poor section of Duluth's Park Hill Cemetery (two years later, Duluth's three other lynching victims would be buried just a few rows away). In 1993 a Finnish cultural group placed a marker on Kinkkonen's grave. It reads, "Olli Kinkkonen, 1881 to 1918, Victim of Warmongers."

Part II

G-14

MINNESOTA

INTERNATIONAL FALLS

COOK

ELY

GRAND MARAIS

TOWER

VIRGINIA

EVELETH

LITTLE MARAIS

CHISHOLM

HIBBING

BEAVER BAY

BEMIDJI

CASS LAKE

DEER RIVER

GRAND RAPIDS

TWO HARBORS

WALKER

DULUTH

CLOQUET

AITKIN

MC GREGOR

CARLTON

BARNUM

MOOSE LAKE

LAKE SUPERIOR

WISCONSIN

© CURT TEICH & CO., INC.

Greetings from "THE MINNESOTA ARROWHEAD COUNTRY"

Arrowhead Industry

In the 1890s drilling and blasting was used to loosen extremely hard iron ore (drilling was also used to locate the ore, as seen at left) in the open pit mining process. A compressed air drill with a diamond-tipped bit was used to bore holes three inches in diameter and about four feet deep; the holes were then filled with dynamite or nitro-glycerin and the explosives detonated. Blasts occurred every three hours and could be heard up to forty miles away. The explosions could also trigger the sides of mining pits to collapse and often covered nearby miners' homes with debris. Miners used a cut-and-slice back sloping system, which gave the mines a stepped appearance, as seen in the card at lower right.

Underground slope mining (shown below) was later used at mines with softer ore. If the ore was close to the surface, strip mining was employed; soil and other material was scraped away until the ore was exposed, then the ore was broken up by blasting.

Iron Mining

On July 3, 1884, the first shipment of iron ore from Charlemagne Tower's Minnesota Iron Company left the Soudan Mine near Lake Vermilion. It rode the Duluth & Iron Range Railway to the massive ore docks of Agate Bay (now Two Harbors), was loaded onto the steamer *Hecla*, and travelled to Philadelphia, ushering in an industry that the entire Arrowhead region's economy has relied on since (albeit to dwindling degrees). Six years later, at Mountain Iron, Lewis Merritt's sons drilled for ore. The next year they built the Duluth, Missabe & Northern Railway to transport the ore to Duluth, giving birth to the Mesabi Iron Range. Later, the Cuyuna Range would join the Mesabi and Tower's Vermilion Range to form the Minnesota Iron Range in the heart of Minnesota's Arrowhead country.

Iron mining would ebb and flow for the next one hundred years, booming during both world wars. The blast furnaces of Duluth Iron and Steel Company and U.S. Steel, fed by ore from the Iron Range, cranked out steel to feed the war machine. The Mesabi Range alone produced twenty million tons of ore during World War I. After World War II the Mesabi Range continued to produce impressive tonnage (and continues to do so), but the Vermilion shut down in 1963; the Cuyuna, which never obtained the production level of the others, closed in the mid-1970s.

SHAFT HOUSE AND STOCK PILE, UNDERGROUND MINE, NEAR DULUTH.

134-D—Open Pit Iron Ore Mine

Mesabi Iron Range, Northern Minnesota

PHOTO BY ROLEFF

One of the largest and most Powerful Engines in the World, used for handling Ore Trains on the Duluth, Missabe and Northern R. R.

PLANT OF ZENITH FURNACE CO., AT WEST DULUTH MINN.

NO. 34. STEAM SHOVEL AT WORK OPEN IN PIT IRON   E NORTHERN MINN.

Both the strip mining and open pit mining methods relied on steam shovels to load ore into railroad cars. A locomotive would pull a train of cars to the giant ore docks at Duluth and Two Harbors, where the ore was loaded onto ships or delivered directly to Duluth's blast furnaces. In the 1930s, when hauling by rail became impractical due to the terrain of newer mines, the mining companies turned to heavy trucking, and steam shovels were replaced by conveyor belts. Once the ore arrived at a blast furnace, it was turned into pig iron (an iron-carbon mix) in a process called smelting—essentially, extracting sulfur from the ore. The furnaces (huge chimney-like cauldrons lined with refectory brick) were loaded with ore, coke, and limestone, then pre-heated air was forced into the middle of the furnace—that's the blast. The mixture was heated in the middle for more even burning. Through this process, the unwanted materials formed a heavy liquid—slag— which was poured out of the bottom of the furnace through a valve. Another valve allowed the pig iron, lighter than slag, to be removed separately. But pig iron is very brittle and had to be processed further to lower its carbon content. To do this, the pig iron was placed in a special rotating container, which in turn was blasted with high-pressure oxygen. The impurities were removed from the pig iron, leaving behind both carbon monoxide and carbon dioxide. The purified pig iron was then used as wrought iron or converted to steel with the Bessemer process, wherein further impurities were removed by blowing air through the molten pig iron. Following World War II, high-grade iron ore was nearly mined out, so the industry turned to taconite, a flint-like rock with high silica and magnetite iron content. Taconite is processed by grinding it into a powder, then separating the iron from waste material with powerful magnets. Next, the powdered iron concentrate is mixed with limestone and bentonite clay and rolled into pellets, which are subjected to very high temperatures to oxidize the magnetite to hematite. The nuggets are then used to make steel.

HULL RUST MINE, HIBBING, MINN.

SELLERS MINE, HIBBING, MINN.

BUFFALO-SUSQUEHANNA MINE, HIBBING, MINN.

Mining Life on the Iron Range

Minnesota's Iron Range is actually made up of three distinct ranges: the Vermilion, the Mesabi, and the Cuyuna, and the work in all their mines was dirty and dangerous. Dynamite and nitroglycerin were used to break up ore; the blasting threw debris into the air, and the vibrations often created landslides at other points in the mine; and underground mines could collapse. The mines claimed the lives of many workers. Early mining operations left behind no clear records, but some claimed that in 1889, two men a week died in the Vermilion Range's Soudan Mine alone (others say no more than five that entire year). Between 1905 and 1910, more than seventy workers died in underground Iron Range mines each year. Perhaps the worst Iron Range tragedy occurred on February 5, 1924, at the Milford Mine near Crosby. A forty-eight man crew working a shaft near Foley Lake apparently struck an unknown underground stream, causing water and mud to flood the mine (some sources say it was the lake itself that broke through the mine). Seven men managed to climb a ladder up the side of a two-hundred foot shaft; the other forty-one perished.

The men who worked the mines were mostly immigrants from Norway, Finland, or Sweden, giving "Da Range" its decidedly Scandinavian flavor. Other miners came from Italy or Cornwall, England. The coal miners from England's West Country brought their own vocabulary to the mines. They called their shift boss "captain," downward mines weren't dug but "sunk," upward mining was "rising," and digging a horizontal mine was known as "drifting." In 1892 Vermilion underground miners worked 257 days a year and earned from $1.96 to $2.55 a day, actually a higher rate than miners were paid elsewhere. In today's money, the higher-paid employees would be taking down about $265 a week before taxes. Those shift bosses the Cornish called "captain," usually men who had a great deal of mining experience, held the authority of a ship's captain; anyone not responding promptly to a captain's orders could be immediately dismissed. To distinguish them, the captains wore a "somewhat formless hat, that resembled only slightly that of a ship's captain." Another Cornish tradition that became part of Iron Range life was the pasty (or pastie): beef, potatoes, rutabagas, and onions (often leftovers) wrapped in a pastry shell and baked; it was a hearty meal the miners could bring to work for their lunch break.

IRON MOUNTAIN MINE (LARGEST PRODUCER IN THE WORLD), NEAR DULUTH, MINN.

Copyrighted by Crandall & Maher, 1904

No. 505. V. O. Hammon Pub. Co., Minneapolis and Chicago

4917. Commodore Mine, Virginia, Minn.

Hundreds of mine pits dot Minnesota's Iron Range. Hibbing's Hull Rust Mine (opposite page, far left), the first strip mine on the Mesabi Range, was by far the largest. Actually made up of several mines—Mahoning, Webb, Agnew, Sellers (opposite page, middle) and Buffalo-Susquehanna (opposite page, lower right)—the Hull Rust became known as the "Grand Canyon of the North" and produced a quarter of all the iron ore produced in the United Sates during the 1940s. The Mountain Iron Mine (left) was the first Mesabi Range mine to produce ore, earning it the nickname "the birthplace of the Mesabi." The very first mine on the Range to produce ore was the Vermilion Range's Soudan Mine, which sent its first trainload of ore to Agate Bay the day before Independence Day, 1884. Twenty-five years later the Soudan had produced 8,202,900 tons of ore, about half of the 17,225,871 tons pulled from the ground at Mountain Iron.

Duluth's Ore Docks

In 1893 the Duluth, Missabe & Northern Railroad finished construction of Duluth's first ore dock at Thirty-third Avenue West. It was a long time coming: work on it had begun in 1884, but Charlemagne Tower had his first load of Vermilion ore shipped to Agate Bay (Two Harbors) instead of Duluth, so the dock wasn't needed until after the Merritt Brothers opened the Mesabi Range in 1892. In 1910 the DM&N had four docks in West Duluth at Thirty-fourth Avenue West. By the 1920s Duluth was home to ten ore docks with a storage capacity of 1,098,384 tons. By 1938 ore demand had lessened and the DM&N was down to two docks.

That same year U.S. Steel merged the DM&N with the Duluth & Iron Range Railway to form the Duluth, Missabe & Iron Range Railway. U.S. Steel had acquired the DM&N in 1901 from John D. Rockefeller, who had taken control of it when the Merritt Brothers' finances went sour; the firm purchased the D&IR from Illinois Steel that same year—Illinois had bought the railroad from Tower's Minnesota Iron Company in 1887.

DULUTH, MESABA & IRON RANGE RAILWAY CO. DOCK, DULUTH, MINN.—68

1288. Loading Ore in Duluth-Superior Harbor.

MESABA ORE DOCKS, DULUTH, MINN.—32

7736. Loading Ore at Missabe Ore Dock.

Various views of the Duluth, Missabe & Iron Range ore docks in West Duluth. The docks were originally built by the Duluth, Missabe & Northern Railway, which merged with the Duluth & Iron Range Railway to become the Duluth, Missabe & Iron Range Railway in 1938. Note the card's various spellings of "Mesabi."

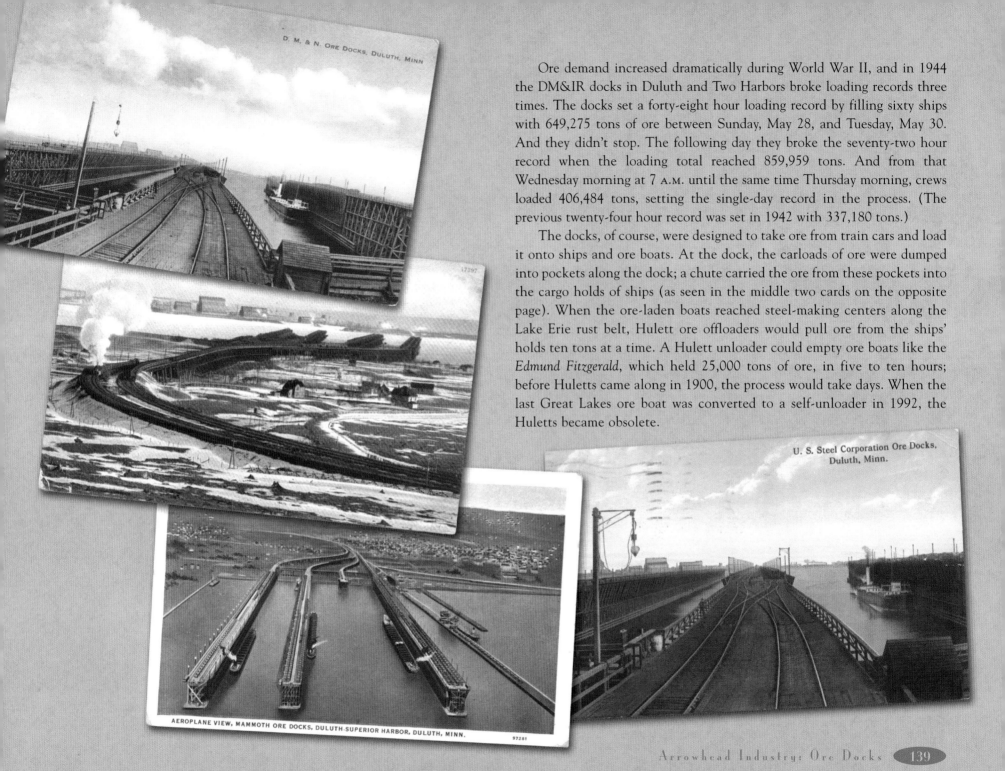

D. M. & N. ORE DOCKS, DULUTH, MINN.

Ore demand increased dramatically during World War II, and in 1944 the DM&IR docks in Duluth and Two Harbors broke loading records three times. The docks set a forty-eight hour loading record by filling sixty ships with 649,275 tons of ore between Sunday, May 28, and Tuesday, May 30. And they didn't stop. The following day they broke the seventy-two hour record when the loading total reached 859,959 tons. And from that Wednesday morning at 7 A.M. until the same time Thursday morning, crews loaded 406,484 tons, setting the single-day record in the process. (The previous twenty-four hour record was set in 1942 with 337,180 tons.)

The docks, of course, were designed to take ore from train cars and load it onto ships and ore boats. At the dock, the carloads of ore were dumped into pockets along the dock; a chute carried the ore from these pockets into the cargo holds of ships (as seen in the middle two cards on the opposite page). When the ore-laden boats reached steel-making centers along the Lake Erie rust belt, Hulett ore offloaders would pull ore from the ships' holds ten tons at a time. A Hulett unloader could empty ore boats like the *Edmund Fitzgerald*, which held 25,000 tons of ore, in five to ten hours; before Huletts came along in 1900, the process would take days. When the last Great Lakes ore boat was converted to a self-unloader in 1992, the Huletts became obsolete.

U. S. Steel Corporation Ore Docks, Duluth, Minn.

AEROPLANE VIEW, MAMMOTH ORE DOCKS, DULUTH-SUPERIOR HARBOR, DULUTH, MINN.

97281

Grain Elevators

In 1872 Jay Cooke built Duluth's first grain elevator at the very corner of Lake Superior, where Fourth Avenue East once met the shore next to Sidney Luce's warehouse. Well, Cooke didn't actually build it so much as finance its construction, just as he was financing everything else in town at the time. Cooke's Union Improvement and Elevator Company purchased wood from Roger Munger's Lake Avenue sawmill to build Elevator A, a grain terminal that could hold 350,000 bushels of grain and came equipped with a steam-powered conveyance system. Cooke's Lake Superior & Mississippi Railroad, along with Union Improvement, then brought rail to the elevator by building large docks. They also added docks along a timber-and-stone breakwater that protected vessels from Lake Superior's often turbulent waters. The steamer *St. Paul* took Elevator A's first load, 11,500 bushels

of wheat, on May 30, 1871, becoming the first boat to carry a cargo of grain out of the Duluth and down the lakes. Only one other grain elevator, Elevator Q, was built on the lake itself. When the ship canal opened, allowing ships passage to the safety of the bay, all of Duluth's grain elevators were built on Rice's Point. (All of Superior's were built on Connor's Point.)

By 1880 grain elevators had grown in capacity and could store 560,000 bushels each. In 1881, 3,332,176 bushels of grain passed through the Zenith City. So much grain poured through Duluth that year that it all but forced the organization of the Duluth Board of Trade (see page 61). Five years later, that number jumped to 22,425,730. One of the board's members, George G. Barnum, was a distant cousin of P. T. Barnum, of Barnum & Bailey Circus fame. Duluth's Barnum didn't prey on suckers; he was so admired for his leadership he was known as the "Grand old man of the Board of Trade." His Barnum Grain Company would merge with others to form General Mills.

One big problem with the early grain elevators was that they were made of wood, and grain dust is highly combustible. Many were lost to fire, including Elevators A and Q, which burned on November 27, 1886, taking with them about 500,000

Grain elevators fed the holds of ore boats by using chutes to empty their bins. Duluth's first grain elevator went up in 1872, and less than ten years later the city transported over three million bushels of grain.

bushels of wheat, corn, flax, and oats, and the lives of two men. The loss was so substantial it actually led to a rise in value of the Chicago grain market.

Elevators continued to pop up on Rice's Point, most built between 1885 and 1902, and by 1910 ten of the storage facilities lined the eastern side of the point. Ten years earlier Frank H. Peavey and Charles H. Haglin had graced Rice's Point with the first tubular concrete silo elevator (they had finished building an experimental version of such an elevator in St. Louis Park, Minnesota, earlier that year). Because of concrete's fireproof qualities, facilities like the Peavey elevator eventually replaced their wooden counterparts.

By 1920, Duluth's grain elevators could hold over 36 million bushels of grain and loaded 62,723,563 bushels onto ships. Despite this, over the years Duluth's importance in the grain trade declined, enough so that in 1946 the Duluth Board of Trade made its last futures transaction.

The Peavey Grain Elevator (upper right)—found, like all of Duluth's grain elevators, on Rice's Point—was the first tubular silo facility made of concrete.

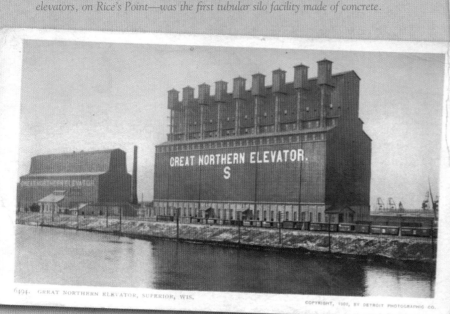

Rice's Point Elevators from Above

Except for Duluth's first two grain elevators, A and Q, all of the city's grain storage facilities have been built on Rice's Point. In 1856 Orrin Rice established the point, a peninsula of mostly marshland between Superior Bay and St. Louis Bay back to Point of Rocks, as a town site. Rice had big ambitions for the town he named after himself. He attempted to have Rice's Point made the St. Louis County Seat and even temporarily changed its name to "Port Byron" to give it a more glamorous appeal. His efforts failed, but the Territorial Legislature threw him a juicy bone: for fifteen years he alone held the rights to run a freight and ferry service between his township and Superior's Connor's Point across the bay. (The two points didn't connect until 1897 with the construction of the Interstate Bridge, which was later replaced by the Blatnik Bridge.) Grain elevators first popped up on Rice's Point in the 1870s. The postcards on this page testify to the number of elevators the peninsula once held. Today three companies—General Mills, Cargill, and AGP Grain—still operate elevators in Duluth on Rice's Point. The point was also home to coal docks, lumber mills, and Duluth's first blast furnace at the Duluth Iron and Steel Company. Rice's Point joined Duluth after the Zenith City regained its status as a city in 1887.

ELEVATORS OF DULUTH, MINN.

No. 559. V. O. HAMMON PUB. CO., MINNEAPOLIS AND CHICAGO.

BIRD'S-EYE VIEW OF ELEVATORS FROM SKY LINE DRIVE, DULUTH, MINN.—33

119-D   Airplane View of Grain Elevators, Lift Bridge, and Entrance to Duluth-Superior Harbor

7A H1051

Flour Mills

All the grain flowing from the Dakotas and Western Minnesota to Duluth's and Superior's mammoth grain elevators made the Twin Ports a natural spot for flour mills to flourish. In 1886, a year before Duluth regained its charter, Roger Munger organized the Duluth Roller Mill where Sixth Avenue West met the bay (about where Bayfront Park sits today; eighteen years earlier he had launched a lumber mill on Lake Avenue that produced the wood for Duluth's early grain elevators).

The Duluth Imperial Mill went up on the east side of Rice's Point in 1888. While Duluthians had been milling flour for years (551,800 barrels of the processed grain had shipped from Duluth in 1880), the Imperial Mill was considered "the most complete ever built" and at six stories high

was by far the largest. With crews working day and night, Imperial could pump out 250 barrels of flour each day in its new mill, which ran on the power supplied by a 600-horsepower Reynolds-Cross steam engine. By the end of 1889, the facility had increased production to 8,000 barrels a day. More flour mills popped up throughout Duluth; many, including one built by Peavey (who also operated grain elevators in Duluth), on Rice's Point in the shadow of the grain elevators. In 1920 flour leaving Duluth filled 5,294,576 barrels. But despite its strategic position, the Duluth flour industry never reached Minneapolis's milling capacity.

Roger Munger, a Connecticut native who first came to Duluth in 1869, was a powerful man in Duluth, called "a kingpin of commercial, civic, and social affairs." In 1883 he built Duluth's Grand Opera House (page 73), which hosted the best entertainment available in the country. Before arriving in Duluth, he and his brother Russel moved to St. Paul in 1859 and opened the Munger Brothers music publishing house. His little brother Gilbert was an extremely gifted artist quite well-known in Europe; the younger Munger's landscape painting of Duluth in 1871 graces page 10 of this book.

Unnamed flour mills along both Superior's and Duluth's waterfronts. The Twin Ports' position as a major grain storage and shipping center made Duluth and Superior ideal towns in which to set up milling operations.

Superior, Wis.

7735. New Pittsburg Coal Dock, Duluth, Minn.

THE CLARKSON COAL & DOCK CO., DULUTH, MINN.

98381

Coal Docks

When the Delaware and Hudson Canal Company first sent a cargo of coal from its deposits in Pennsylvania to Duluth in June of 1871, most locals just scratched their heads: why, when wood was so cheap and plentiful, would anyone use coal as fuel? After all, just a few dollars could buy enough wood to last a long Duluth winter, and if you had the time and the energy, you could cut all the firewood you wanted for free.

But Jay Cooke and others were building railroads to Duluth, and that provided an opportunity for another local industry. Not only did trains run on coal, but many other towns in the region needed it to heat buildings. Soon Duluth was supplying coal, most of it a high-sulfur grade mined in Pennsylvania and Ohio, to Minneapolis, St. Paul, and cities in at least seven other states.

The coal of course had to be taken off the boats and loaded onto the trains. The first contract for unloading coal was awarded to Jack Lewis, and he had no modern machinery. Men shoveled coal from the ships' holds into baskets, which were hoisted to a tramway by horse, where their load was transferred to wheelbarrows. Eventually steam replaced horsepower, and they used bigger baskets. Between 8,000 and 20,000 tons were shipped to Duluth that first year.

In 1875 Northwestern Fuel built Duluth's first dedicated coal dock; it remained Duluth's only coal company until 1881, bringing in 60,000 tons of coal for use in the Twin Ports in 1880. Eventually a system of giant coal docks and their support machinery lined the waterfront from Rice's Point to Seventh Avenue West. Beginning in 1881 docks were built for use by the Lake Superior Coal and Iron Company, New Pittsburgh, Clarkston Coal, Ohio Central Coal, St. Paul & Pacific Coal and Iron, Pioneer Coal, Little and Company, and Lehigh Coal. In 1886 736,000 tons were brought to the

UNLOADING COAL AT SUPERIOR, WIS.

7558. Unloading Coal, Duluth, Minn.

COAL DOCKS, SEEN FROM GREAT NORTHERN ELEVATOR, SUPERIOR, WIS.

Twin Ports for use in homes and businesses in Duluth and Superior—and that doesn't include coal loaded onto rail for other destinations.

As the century turned Duluth received more than 2.5 million tons of coal; ten years later, 8.3 million tons. By 1921 Duluth alone was home to twenty-two docks with the capacity of 11,305,000 tons of coal. Coal shipments hit their peak just two years later, when 12.6 million tons passed through the Duluth-Superior Harbor. At this time the coal industry provided 3,600 full-time jobs, 5,000 during peak periods.

As people and businesses turned to cleaner-burning oil and gas to heat their homes and offices, the demand for coal dropped dramatically. Half as much coal passed through the Twin Ports in 1936 than did in 1923; by 1972 tonnage had dropped below 100,000. Then the market reversed. Montana and Wyoming began mining cleaner-burning low-sulfur coal in the 1970s. Instead of loading it from ships onto trains bound elsewhere, Duluth's coal now arrived on trains from the west and was loaded onto ships bound for the east—and beyond. The first load shipped out of Duluth in 1973, aboard the British ship *Gloxinia*, bound for Scotland.

Shipbuilding

The Twin Ports' shipbuilding industry began in earnest in the winter of 1869–1870 when Lewis Merritt, his son Alfred, and Henry Ely built the *Chaska*, a seventy-two-foot, forty-nine-ton schooner—the largest ship built in Duluth at the time (unfortunately, it was battered to pieces off the coast of Michigan's Upper Peninsula a year later).

The Twin Ports' most famous shipbuilder was of course Alexander McDougall, who created the whaleback (see page 147). Perhaps Duluth's most successful early shipbuilder was a French-Canadian named Napoleon Grignon, who arrived in Duluth in the 1870s and built a shipyard on Minnesota Point at Buchanan Street. In 1880 he incorporated his business as the Marine Iron and Shipbuilding Company; the company would go on to build many ships: fifty-seven of them between 1918 and 1940 alone.

While ships would be built in earnest in Duluth and Superior over the next eighty years, the industry peaked during the two world wars. During World War I, ten tugs launched at the Whitney Brothers Wharf, and nineteen 260-foot ocean freighters were built at the Globe Shipyards. Throughout World War II the Twin Ports' eight shipyards employed over ten thousand men and women, averaging ten ships a month while producing a fleet of 230 vessels. Zenith Dredge Company made eight tankers and thirteen cutters; Butler in Superior built thirteen coastal freighters, twelve frigates, and seven cargo carriers; Globe delivered eight frigates and ten ocean-going tugs; Marine Iron and Shipbuilding supplied the Coast Guard with eighteen cutters; and thirteen plane-rearming boats and four subchasers came out of Inland Waterways. Together Scott-Graff Lumber Company and Industrial Construction Company aided the war effort by building one hundred landing barges.

On May 8, 1943, the Butler Yards became the first shipbuilder to ever launch five vessels in one day from the same shipyard. The launch was turned into a civic event when owner Robert Butler invited Canada's Dionne Quints, the world's first surviving quintuplets and arguably the most famous children in North America at the time, to christen the cargo ships. Over fifteen thousand people showed up to watch the small pack of nine-year-olds, also born in May, take the stage carrying champagne bottles. They entertained the crowd by singing songs in their native Quebecois in honor of their mother's thirty-fourth birthday.

Launching an Ore Boat, Superior Ship Building Yards, Superior, Wis.

9111

LAUNCHING OF A 600 FT FREIGHTER, DULUTH, MINN.

Captain McDougall's Whalebacks

Born on Scotland's Isle of Islay, Alexander McDougall moved to Canada as a boy. In 1861, sixteen-year-old McDougall took his first job as a deckhand on the Great Lakes; by twenty-five he had command of his own ship. For twenty more years he worked the Great Lakes, adopting Duluth as his home.

In 1888 he dove head-first into the shipbuilding industry. He designed and built a steel boat with a flat bottom "designed to carry the greatest cargo on the least water." He rounded the top deck so water would run off and gave the bow a spoon shape to better cut through water; deck turrets allowed passage inside the ship's hull. The design earned the vessels the nickname "Pig Boats," but McDougall gave them a more noble title: whaleback. McDougall's American Steel Barge Company in Superior cranked out thirty of them by the end of 1892. All but the *Christopher Columbus* were built as cargo barges. McDougall had grander plans, including a transatlantic mail carrier and a man-o'-war, but those were never built. Size limitation doomed the future of whalebacks, but many of McDougall's design advances were employed in modern ore boats. The last whaleback, the *Alexander McDougall*, launched in 1898. The American Steel Barge Company would move to Duluth and build ships again during World War I, along the way creating Riverside, a company community on a smaller scale than Morgan Park. The company also turned out many ships during World War II, but McDougall never saw them; he died in 1923.

Whaleback Steamer "Christopher Columbus", Milwaukee, Wis.

A Whaleback.   Duluth, Minn.

The Christopher Columbus (top) was probably the best-known whaleback on the Great Lakes. Unlike other "Pig Boats," the Columbus was a passenger ship outfitted with three upper decks. Built in Superior in 1893, the ship spent most of her life steaming around Chicago and Milwaukee; she was scrapped in 1936.

NO. 37. SKIDDING IN THE NORTHERN WOODS.

ABERING NEAR DULUTH, DULUTH, MINN.

507—Cutting Timber, Duluth, Minn.

Logging

Much of the logging in the western Lake Superior region took place in the Minnesota Arrowhead country along the big lake's North Shore (northern Wisconsin was also thoroughly logged). Minnesota lumberjacks felled enough timber between 1891 and 1924 to produce nearly eight billion board feet of lumber.

The work was hard and the conditions cold; the logging season stretched from November to April as the frozen ground prevented oxen and draft horses from bogging down under their heavy loads. At camp, the foreman oversaw everything, from building construction to tree selection—even where the trees should fall. A logging crew typically consisted of two sawyers, a swamper, a teamster, and a decker. The sawyers notched trees with an axe then worked in pairs with a cross-cut saw to take the tree down; on a good day a team of sawyers could cut up to one hundred white pines. Swampers trimmed limbs off felled trees, cleared brush, kept roadways clear, and removed manure. Teamsters (also called skidders) used horses to pull felled trees from where they were cut to landing areas where they were later

Lumber Camp, Northern Minnesota.

Life in a lumber camp was no stack o' flapjacks. The camp woke at 5 A.M.; breakfast came an hour later. The Jacks had twelve minutes to eat, and the cooks allowed no talking. They then went straight to work until 11:30 A.M., when the chore boy brought them hot lunches packed in large cans. At noon they were back to work and toiled until the sun set. After a leisurely twenty-minute dinner, the loggers occupied themselves by repairing clothes and equipment or playing a few hands of cards. Lights went out at 9 P.M. On Sundays the men were allowed to wash their clothes and themselves, write letters home, and pack their beds with fresh straw. Most camps were small; a camp of forty to fifty men was considered large.

View of Lumber Camp near Duluth, Minn.

loaded and sent to lumber mills. If the tree was less than a mile from the loading area, it was dragged out with chains; when trees were felled further away, logs were stacked on sleighs pulled by teams of oxen or draft horses. Once at the landing area, deckers made parallel stacks of logs so they could more easily be rolled into the river for transport to the mills. In the water men tied the logs into giant rafts which they floated or towed downstream to Lake Superior and the mills. Later trains were used to transport the logs; trucks have been used since the 1930s.

One site of the North Shore's logging heyday has become a stunning spot to view fall colors. Heartbreak Ridge takes its name from its steep grade, which was often too much for even the sturdiest of horses when it was covered with ice and snow. Consequently, loggers could not move logs up and down the rise, and bypassing the ridge created extra work; they spent more time removing fewer trees, thereby making less money, and breaking their hearts.

The success of the logging industry rose and fell with the economy—when Duluth boomed, so did timber production. Logging reached its peak during the first decade of the twentieth century and was thought all but dead

in Duluth by 1920. Still, it hung on through the twenties, but was hit particularly hard during the Great Depression, and never quite recovered. In 1941 the last logging railroad was dismantled.

Some logging still takes place in northern Minnesota, but most of it is done outside the Arrowhead region. Today's loggers use heavy machinery rather than hand tools, and transport logs on flatbed semis. But some things never change: in January 2006 Minnesota logging companies reported that production had been slowed by the unusually warm winter, causing logging trucks—like the teams of oxen and draft horses before them—great difficulty when moving their heavy loads over the soft, unfrozen ground.

Off to the Mills

Henry W. Wheeler built Duluth's first sawmill in 1856, and within a few years mills dotted the North Shore from the Twin Ports to Beaver Bay. Firms such as Culver & Nettleton, Duncan & Brewer, Alger Smith Company, Scott Graff Lumber, Oneota Lumber Company, Hubbard & Vincent, Mitchell & McClure, Merrill & Ring, Huntress & Brown, Clark & Jackson, and many others operated mills wherever log rafts, and later trains, could reach them.

In the 1880s area mills produced an average of 10 million board feet a year; in 1890 they produced 150 million feet. By 1894 thirty-two mills employed 7,700 in Duluth and Superior. The peak year for Twin Ports milling was 1902, when 443 million board feet were produced. During the first ten years of the twentieth century over 3 billion board feet of lumber came out of Duluth's mills, but just over 1 billion feet was cut from 1910 to 1921, the year many declared the industry played out. Indeed, the milling industry had been in decline since at least 1910, when Twin Ports operations dropped to just six major mills; by 1925 only one mill operated out of Duluth.

LUMBERING NEAR DULUTH. (LOGGING TRAIN THAT WALKS ON THE SNOW). DULUTH, MINN.

7454. A LUMBER RAFT, DULUTH, MINN.

DETROIT PUBLISHING CO.

Menominee Saturday 1:25 from Escanaba

Part III

Greetings from Superior

A Very Quick Flyover Look at Superior's Early History

Much of Superior's history parallels Duluth's, but of course Superior has been around longer than the Zenith City. After the Ojibwe had settled in the region and set up a central encampment on what is now Madeline Island, the French started arriving. In 1618 voyageur Etienne Brulé paddled along Lake Superior's south shore where he encountered the Ojibwe and found copper specimens. The copper samples, along with a glowing report of the region, he brought back to Quebec. Not long after that, French traders and missionaries began settling the area, and a Lake Superior tributary was named for Brulé. Among them was Father Claude Jean Allouez, who is often credited for an early map of the region (see page 3; Superior's Allouez neighborhood takes its name from the Catholic missionary). By 1700 the area was crawling with French traders, who had developed a working relationship with the Ojibwe. After the French and Indian War ended in 1763, the area came under British rule, but that ended with the America Revolution and the

Treaty of Peace in 1783. Treaties with the Ojibwe would give more territory to settlers of European descent, and by 1847 the U.S. had taken control of all lands along Lake Superior's south shore.

In 1854 (some say 1853) the first claims were staked at the mouth of the Nemadji River, and that same year the township of Superior became the county seat of the newly formed Douglas County. Just two years later 2,500 people called Superior home. But the town's population stagnated from the financial panic of 1857 through the end of the Civil War, and the building of the Duluth Ship Canal in 1871 was a crushing blow to Superior's economic future. Still, the town did see growth starting in 1887, when Robert Belknap's and General John Henry Hammond's Land and River Improvement Company began building elevators, docks, and industrial railroads. The city boomed between 1887 and 1893. Since then its growth has ebbed and flowed along with Duluth's, but it remains about one fourth the size of its twin across the bay.

BIRD'S-EYE VIEW OF SUPERIOR, WIS.—10

BALLOON VIEW: HARBOR, RIVER AND NATURAL BREAKWATER; DULUTH TO LEFT, SUPERIOR TO RIGHT.
No. 19. V. O. HAMMON PUB. CO., MINNEAPOLIS AND CHICAGO.

Federal Building

1401 TOWER AVENUE • 1908
EARL BARBER, ARCHITECT

Federal Building, Superior, Wis.

The Federal Building has been serving Superior since 1908, when it was built, as most federal buildings were at the time, as a courthouse, customs office, Internal Revenue office, home of U.S. Marshalls, and a post office. Successful lobbying nearly doubled the building's construction budget, and the extra money was spent on extravagances such as marble, mahogany, solid bronze, and opulent furniture.

In 1925 four men the local papers described as "gentleman burglars" broke into the Federal Building, while a fifth trained a gun on the family of Assistant Postmaster C. J. McGill, holding them hostage in their own home. Encountering the night janitor, the burglars bound and gagged him and placed him in the vault, promising him a $10,000 reward for his silence once they were able to convert their booty into cash. They walked out of the Federal Building carrying $71,000 worth of postage stamps.

COURT HOUSE, SUPERIOR, WIS.—8

Douglas County Court House

1315 BELKNAP STREET • 1919
JOSEPH W. ROYER & EDWIN RADCLIFFE, ARCHITECTS

Principal architect Joseph Royer of Urbana, Illinois, beat out thirty other entries in a contest to design the Douglas County Courthouse; he took home a grand prize of $400. Today the Superior building stands as the city's prime example of Classical Revival architecture.

Made of Bedford blue cut stone, the building's inner and outer vestibules are lined with marble wainscotting imported from Italy. Its entrance doors are made of copper, and it includes a leaded glass skylight. For its day, the building featured an unusual number of modern conveniences, including both men's and women's lavatories on each floor, office clocks controlled by a bronze master clock, and frost-proof locks on its exterior doors. Six-hundred pound chandeliers still hang from the building's courtrooms, and the facility even included a "janitor's residence" when first constructed.

City Hall, Superior, Wis.

Superior Public Library

HAMMOND AVENUE & 12TH AVENUE • 1902
CARL WIRTH, ARCHITECT

The Superior Public Library organized in 1888—a year before the city itself was incorporated—but little is written about the early history of the organization. Andrew Carnegie donated funds to have the library built in 1902. Carnegie emigrated from Scotland at thirteen, eventually organized Carnegie Steel Company, and was once considered the richest man in the world. He said that the rich have a moral obligation to give away their wealth, and he exercised that idea by helping fund over 2,500 free public libraries.

The building closed as a library in 1991 when a new facility was opened on Tower Avenue. An investor planned to rehabilitate the building, but it took Superior officials a great deal of time to obtain clearance from the Hammond family—John Hammond (see page 163) had donated the property stating that the city could use it as long as it held the public library. By the time the property was cleared for sale, the building had been compromised by vandalism and neglect. Its windows remain boarded, and the current city administration has investigated whether to have it, along with several other historic Superior buildings, destroyed.

Old City Hall

1409 HAMMOND AVENUE • 1890
CLARENCE JOHNSTON, ARCHITECT

Originally built in 1890 as the Trade and Commerce Building, Superior's old City Hall was the home of local government from 1904 until 1970. Architect Clarence Johnston (who also designed Glensheen, the Congdon estate in Duluth) had the building's façade covered in "a local rock-faced brownstone ashlar" and intentionally rounded the building's corners to dramatize the surfaces' continuity. A police station was built along the north side of the building on Hammond Avenue.

SUPERIOR PUBLIC LIBRARY, SUPERIOR, WIS.

East High School

1814 E. 5TH STREET • 1922
H. E. JOHNSON, ARCHITECT

EAST END HIGH SCHOOL, SUPERIOR, WIS.

Construction on Superior's East High School began in 1922. When its doors opened to students in 1924, the school served students from the city's East End, Central Park, Allouez, and Itasca neighborhoods. With Superior's population on the increase, it became a four-year high school in 1950, its athletic teams competing under the name "Orientals." In 1965 Superior built a new high school and consolidated East and Central, and East was converted to a junior high school and, later, a middle school. The school was demolished in 2004.

High School, Superior, Wis.

The "Summer White House" of 1928. Superior's Central High School library was converted to offices for President Calvin Coolidge, who spent his summer fly fishing on northern Wisconsin's Brule River along the south shore of Lake Superior.

Central High School

1015 BELKNAP STREET • 1909
EARL BARBER, ARCHITECT

Several famous people have graced the history of Superior's Central High School. Richard Bong, top American World War II flying ace, went to school here, as did legendary football star Ernie Nevers and Minnesota Vikings' coach Bud Grant. Herbert Hoover announced his presidential candidacy on its steps, and John F. Kennedy stumped there during his presidential campaign. But the high school is most famous for acting as the "Summer White House" in 1928. President Calvin Coolidge spent his summer at the estate of his friend Henry Clay Pierce, fly fishing on the Brule River. On June 8, officials announced that part of the school library had been "fitted for the use of President Coolidge during his summer stay when the school will be the capitol of the United States." After he returned to Washington, the room Coolidge used became known as the "Coolidge Room" and was the site of senior teas and gatherings of the honor society; later, it became a notorious detention hall. Despite public outcry, the building—perhaps Superior's most historically significant structure—was razed in 2004, the same year the city celebrated its 150-year anniversary.

State Normal School

Faced with white brick lined with red Lake Superior sandstone, Superior's State Normal School, founded in 1893, was built on land donated by the Land and River Improvement Company. A wing was added to the building in 1908, and a second addition was made in 1912 (compare the mis-colored postcard below with the accurate one at the lower right). Crownhart Hall (upper right), a women's dorm, was built in 1910.

Unfortunately the main building burned in 1914; a new building took its place in 1916 (right, center). The school's name had changed from State Normal School to State Teacher's College by 1927. The main building, called "Old Main," survives as part of the University of Wisconsin Superior. The original Crownhart Hall was torn down and replaced by a more modern dorm building in the late 1960s. The school's first class, made up of nine women and three men, graduated in 1897. Perhaps the school's most famous alumnus is famed body builder, movie star, Kennedy in-law, and California governor Arnold Schwarzenegger.

Dormitory at State Normal, Superior, Wis.

W-6 State Teachers' College, Superior, Wis.

STATE NORMAL SCHOOL, SUPERIOR, WIS.

Superior, Wis. State Normal School

St. Mary's Hospital

1001–1003 Clough Avenue • 1894
Bauer & Hill, Architects

ST. MARY'S HOSPITAL, SUPERIOR, WIS.

During the early months of 1893, three nuns serving with the Poor Handmaids of Jesus Christ arrived in West Superior with instructions to open a hospital. In August of the following year, the order opened St. Mary's Hospital along Clough Avenue, to be operated by the nuns and lay people. Seven years later the sisters added an annex to the rear of the building to house themselves, which freed the hospital's third and fourth floors, their former residence, for hospital use, increasing bed capacity from fifty to two hundred. In 1920 the hospital opened a training school for nurses, and in 1929 a facility for student housing was built. In 1969 St. Mary's merged with St. Joseph's to become Holy Family Hospital. The building was used for administrative staff and nuns' quarters until it closed in 1975; it was torn down in 1979, a year after St. Mary's Nursing Home was built in Billings Park.

St. Francis Hospital

2325 E. 3rd Street • 1889
Brother Leonard Darschield, Architect

St. Francis Hospital, Superior, Wisconsin

9A-H1793

When Father Eustace Vollmere approached the mother superior of the Poor Handmaids of Jesus Christ in Donaldson, Indiana, and asked her to send him some nuns to become the nursing staff of a hospital he had opened, she refused until a facility was built to house them. The building went up by 1889, and in November of that year five sisters arrived.

They helped Vollmere care for injured lumberjacks as well as the poor and homeless. Lumberjacks and dockworkers were guaranteed free hospitalization by donating $5 or $10 each per year, solicited by the nuns at lumber camps and on the docks. The building closed as a hospital in 1952; later that year Carmelite nuns converted it to a "home for the aged." The nursing home closed in the late 1970s, and the building was converted to apartments before it was destroyed in 1985.

Hammond Avenue Presbyterian

1401 BELKNAP STREET • 1911
ARCHITECT UNKNOWN

Despite its name, the Hammond Avenue Presbyterian Church address is 1401 Belknap Street. The building stands at the corner of Belknap and Hammond, streets named for Robert Belknap and General John Hammond, officers of the Land and River Improvement Company (which owned most of Superior at the time—and donated the land for the building). In 1998 Hammond Avenue Presbyterian merged with First Presbyterian—which had organized way back in in 1855—to become United Presbyterian. The Hammond Avenue Presbyterian building became the Harrington Arts Center after United Presbyterian built a new church in 2002.

Many other Superior streets are associated with the Land Company. Hammond himself is credited for clearing and grading Tower, Ogden, and John Avenues; Ogden and John are named for his sons, and Tower takes its name from Charlemagne Tower, who developed the Vermilion Iron Range.

Superior Bishop's Residence

1808 E. 2ND STREET (THEN BAY STREET) • C. 1890
ARCHITECT UNKNOWN

This grand Queen Anne home—festooned with towers, dormers, and ornamental details—was built around 1890 as the home of physician W. J. Conan. It became the residence of the Right Reverend Augustine Francis Schinner, bishop of the Superior Diocese (composed of northern Wisconsin's sixteen counties), in 1905 when the diocese first formed. Schinner lived there until 1913, when he resigned; he later took a position as bishop of Spokane, Washington, where he died in 1921. Following Schinner, bishops Joseph Koudelka, Joseph Pinten, Theodore Reverman, William O'Connor, Albert Meyer, Joseph Annebring, and George A. Hammes lived in the house. The building was razed in 1965. The postcard at right dates from between 1905 and 1912.

Board of Trade Building,
Superior, Wis.

Board of Trade

1507 TOWER AVENUE • 1892
C. C. HAIGHT, ARCHITECT

When it first opened its doors in 1892, Superior's Board of Trade build-ing was known as the Minnesota Block—and was yet another Superior building financed by Robert Belknap's and John Hammond's Land and River Improvement Company. Its name changed in 1894 when Superior's Board of Trade moved in. By 1908 the Fair Store, a large dry-goods store operated by brothers P. C. and A. J. Pederson, occupied the lower two floors. The Pedersons sold men's and women's clothing as well as household goods, acting as an early department store. In 1911 local architect John O. Bach drew up plans to remodel the building; they called for an arcade front that would double the display area in the first-floor show windows, but no records state whether the plans were ever put into place.

Masonic Temple,
Superior, Wis.

Masonic Temple

1503 BELKNAP STREET • 1906
ARCHITECT UNKNOWN

Superior's Masons built this Classical Revival hall, complete with four two-story columns topped by Corinthian capitals, in 1906—but left no record of who designed it, or what went on inside. The Masons of Superior (like all Masons, a secretive lot) first organized in 1884 and had built sever-al halls in the city by 1900. In 1982 the Masons left, and the Elks moved in. Today the Superior Masons meet in Billings Park.

Masons who helped shape the Head of the Lakes include John Jacob Astor, who owned the American Fur Post at Fond du Lac; J. P. Morgan, whose U.S. Steel built Morgan Park; and John D. Rockefeller, who bought out the Merritt Brother's mining interests on the Mesabi Iron Range. Many prominent residents of the Twin Ports, including Superior's Martin Pattison (see page 171), were also Masons.

Soo Line Passenger Station, Superior, Wis.

Soo Line Passenger Station

1615 WINTER STREET • 1908
ARCHITECT UNKNOWN

When the Wisconsin Central Railroad had a passenger depot built in Superior in 1908, it included a freight station, store houses, a machine shop, and even a roundhouse. In 1909 the St. Paul, Minneapolis & Sault Ste. Marie Railroad, known as the "Soo Line," purchased Wisconsin Central's outstanding capital stock, essentially taking over the railroad and its assets—and the Superior passenger station along with it. The Soo Line still operates, but it has not offered passenger service through Superior (or Duluth) since 1967. The station was used as a freight depot until it closed in 1989. In 1993 the Soo Line Station was used in the Disney film *Iron Will*, much of which was shot in Duluth; the building has been converted into retail shops.

Webster Chair Factory

2101 N. 57TH STREET • 1891
ARCHITECT UNKNOWN

As early as 1891 A. J. Webster was making chairs in Superior. Stumpage, cut by factory workers, arrived in Superior from all across Wisconsin to be made into chairs. By 1915 the company offered nine hundred different styles of chairs and operated branches across the country. In 1927 the Superior factory alone employed five hundred workers, and by that time they were making other furniture besides chairs. The Great Depression caused the company to close in 1932. It reopened briefly in 1935, but closed for good just two years later. At one time the company had been the largest chair manufacturer in the world. Today, chairs made by the Superior company are highly valued by antique collectors.

Webster Chair Factory, Superior, Wis.

Superior Hotel

1501 TOWER AVENUE • 1889
CARL WIRTH, ARCHITECT

Superior, Wis.

Superior Hotel, Superior, Wis.

Built by—who else?—Robert Belknap's Land and River Improvement Company, the Superior Hotel was outfitted with every luxury available in its day. The hotel played host to a variety of events, from lectures to dances; a dance club named the "8 to 12 Club" called the hotel home during the 1890s, and William Jennings Bryan spoke from its steps during his presidential campaigns. A fire in 1940 destroyed the hotel's north wing, and that portion of the hotel was never rebuilt. The hotel closed in the late 1960s and was later razed. The Superior Public Library now stands in its place. An urban legend once claimed that the hotel included a two-hundred foot tunnel to the Grand Opera House, but the truth is the two building shared a common heating plant, and its pipes ran beneath Belknap Street.

J. Edgar Hoover and six of his FBI agents, along with two shackled prisoners, spent a night in the Androy in 1938.

SUPERIOR'S NEW MILLION DOLLAR HOTEL.

THE ANDROY, SUPERIOR, WIS.   104682

Androy Hotel

1213 TOWER AVENUE • 1925
ROLAND BUCK, ARCHITECT

When it opened in 1925, the Androy sported a jewelry store, barber shop (with an electric face steamer), and ballroom; its Fountain Grill included a soda fountain, coffee shop, and full dining room. The hotel's offices and 140 guest rooms each included a telephone. For safety's sake, the hotel had a fire alarm system (a gong on each floor) and a city fire alarm box at the clerk's desk; the fire escape was enclosed. In 1926, as a scheme to raise money for the local VFW's drum corps, Billie "The Human Fly" O'Brine escaped from a straight jacket while suspended upside down atop the hotel. After that he climbed the hotel's nine stories and shinnied up its flag pole. He pulled in $203 from the crowd and took home half.

Grand Opera House, Superior, Wis.

Grand Opera House

1713–1715 BELKNAP STREET • 1890
CARL WIRTH, ARCHITECT

Superior's Grand Opera House first entertained Superiorites in 1890 after it was built by—yes—the Land and River Development Company, managed by John Hammond. The theatre was made of brownstone and Dreback sandstone and included a dozen private boxes and sat 1,200 audience members. Over the years the Opera House's patrons enjoyed concerts, plays, operas, boxing and wrestling matches, and later, vaudevillians. The players dressed in rooms in the basement and on the second floor of the building, and the rear of the structure was made high enough for the curtains to actually raise rather than being rolled up. The Opera House recovered from fire damage in 1909 and again in 1911, but couldn't survive the burning popularity of motion pictures. It closed in 1924. Fire did finally destroy the building in 1939.

Broadway Theatre

1706 BROADWAY STREET • 1906
CARL WIRTH, ARCHITECT

Built in 1906 as a vaudeville house, by 1916 Superior's Broadway Theatre was also showing movies. A year later it added some rooms and opened a hotel. It closed as a theatre in 1922 and in 1926 the local Eagles Club moved in; in 1940 the hotel changed its name to the Mayeton Hotel. It closed in the 1970s and was later demolished.

During its first year the Broadway hosted the Marx Brothers, the largest vaudeville act at the time. Julius, Leonard, Milton, and Arthur on the harp entertained Superiorites with their music and comedy review under their stage names Groucho, Chico, Gummo, and Harpo. Herbert (Zeppo) was only eleven years old at the time and hadn't yet joined his brothers onstage (he eventually replaced Gummo in the act).

Broadway Theatre, Superior, Wis.

Hammond Avenue

General John Henry Hammond first came to Superior from New York City in 1878. He returned two years later, bought four thousand acres of land in west Superior, and promptly transferred it to the Land and River Improvement Company, which he managed for Robert Belknap. The company went on to develop most of west Superior, building elevators, docks, and railways—essentially, Hammond and Belknap were the Jay Cookes of Superior. Superior's Belknap Street and Hammond Avenue were named for the developers.

With the 1961 construction of the Blatnik Bridge, which connected Duluth to Superior at Hammond Avenue, Superior officials anticipated tens of thousands of people crossing daily, causing traffic congestion along the divided boulevard. Despite opposition, its center islands were removed, but the town never saw the traffic it had imagined.

Hammond's grandson, also named John Henry Hammond, worked in the music business and is credited for discovering such music legends as Billie Holiday, Aretha Franklin, Bruce Springsteen, and Duluth-native Robert Zimmerman, who moved to Hibbing as a child and later changed his name to Bob Dylan.

Hammond Boulevard, Superior, Wis.

TOWER AVENUE "THE WHITE WAY", SUPERIOR, WIS.

The Grand Army Monument

The Grand Army of the Republic consisted of Union veterans of the Civil War, and in 1900 the Wisconsin GAR lobbied the city to build a monument for their upcoming convention in Superior. At the intersection of Tower and Broadway four curved steel shafts rose from each corner and met thirty-five feet above the street. A twenty-foot centerpiece sat atop the arch, and a thirty-six-foot flagpole topped that, creating a monument reaching ninety feet in the air. At one point the arch contained 220 light bulbs, which were lit just four hours a night (it cost $1 an hour to keep them lit). Unfortunately the arch rusted and was scrapped in 1921 (the mayor also wanted it gone…).

Tower Avenue: Superior's "Strip" and Focus of Social Activity

If the old saying is true that Superior has "more bar stools than church pews," then most of them can be found along Tower Avenue. Named for Charlemagne Tower, who developed the Vermilion Iron Range, the street has long been known as Superior's hub of social activity. Theatres once lined its sidewalks, providing entertainment for folks on both sides of the bay. When electricity first came to town, Tower Avenue became Superior's "White Way." During Prohibition, Superior had a reputation as a rough-and-tumble town, and much of the reputed activity took place along Tower. In fact, gangster Al Capone once told a lady friend that Superior "is full of speakeasies and brothels…the law won't give you any trouble there." Today, many of its fine old buildings are home to bars that cater mainly to college students.

Tower Avenue from Thirteenth Street, Looking North, Superior, Wis.

TOWER AVENUE AT 13TH STREET, SUPERIOR, WISCONSIN

Fourteenth and Tower, looking South, Superior, Wis.

Sixteenth and Tower, looking North, Superior, Wis.

The White Way, Tower Ave. at Night, Superior, Wis.

Avenue, Looking North, Superior, Wis.

The Princess Theatre (above) was built in 1913 at 1310 Tower Avenue. Legend has it that Judy Garland's parents, Frank and Ethel Gumm, met at the Princess. They were small-time vaudevillians who would move to Grand Rapids, Minnesota, before taking their daughter west to Hollywood, where she eventually went over the rainbow. The building is currently home to Frankie's Tavern.

Tower Avenue, Superior, Wis.

TOWER AVENUE FROM POST OFFICE. SUPERIOR, WIS.

Billings Park

MUNICIPAL BATHING BEACH, SUPERIOR, WIS.

Boathouse, Billings Park, Superior, Wis.

BILLINGS PARK, SUPERIOR, WIS.

Located at New York Avenue and Eighteenth Street, Superior's Billings Park sits next to the St. Louis River and used to include a swimming beach and boathouse; the waters surrounding it were once the site of various water sports, including sailboat races. Remnants of granite bleachers used by crowds to watch the various competitions on the river can still be found along the riverbank.

The neighborhood that surrounds the park now shares its name, but it hasn't always been called Billings Park. In 1889 James Roosevelt's West Superior Iron & Steel opened along the shores of St. Louis Bay north of Belknap Street. In 1892 the plant turned ore from the Vermilion Range into steel plates used to build Captain McDougall's whalebacks. The area surrounding the plant was first known simply as the Steel Plant; later it became the Ninth Ward and was referred to as the City of Churches after nine denominations built twelve churches for the plant's employees and their families. But the Panic of 1893 closed the plant.

Fortunately, capitalist Frederick Billings owned a great deal of land along the river, much of it considered the most beautiful in the region. He donated a large portion of it for the formation of Billings Drive, which follows the shore to the upper Pokegama River (he also donated the land for Gitchinadji, Superior's first golf course). Later, his heirs donated more land. The city renamed the neighborhood Billings Park, and it included forty acres on a point jutting into the river; there the city established a park. In 1907 Billings' heirs expanded the park by donating another eighteen acres; newspapers reported that they refused to take money for the land.

Today Billings Park is just about the best place for a family picnic in all of the Twin Ports. Its man-made facilities include pavilions, grills, picnic tables, and restrooms (including a facility for people with disabilities) as well as horseshoe pits, swings, a small backstop for softball, and plenty of lawn for volleyball, bocce ball, or croquet. Trails within the park provide hiking access along a gentle, gravel-lined path to the shore—and to a great view of Spirit Mountain across the river. The park is home to a variety of plant life, including lily pads, rushes, cattails, raspberries, and black-eyed susans. Unfortunately, while the St. Louis River has become cleaner over the last few years, the river is currently too polluted for the city to allow swimming at the park.

W-7 Billings Park, Superior, Wis.

Scene at Billings Park, Superior, Wis.

BILLINGS PARK, SUPERIOR

MOONLIGHT ON SUPERIOR BAY,
SUPERIOR, WIS.

Wisconsin Point

While Wisconsin Point and Minnesota Point make up the world's largest sandbar, the points differ greatly from one another. Minnesota Point is highly developed with homes, community buildings, businesses, and even an airport. Wisconsin Point has been left almost completely natural, most likely because it is considerably more narrow than its Minnesota counterpart.

Most of the Point is covered by pine forest and a vast stretch of beach. The Superior Entry Lighthouse stands at the end of a long stone pier. The Point is also home to the site of a traditional Fond du Lac Ojibwe burial ground that dates from the seventeenth century; it contained the graves of an estimated seven generations of Ojibwe, including Chief Joseph Osawgee. The graves were moved to Superior's St. Francis Cemetery in 1918, but the site is well marked and many visitors still leave offerings of respect, such as tobacco, dream catchers, and other less traditional gifts.

Osawgee Beach

Ojibwe chief Joseph Osawgee was born in Michigan in 1802 and came to Wisconsin Point as a young boy. There he established Superior's first shipyard—a canoe-making outfit along the Nemadji River near Wisconsin Point. His birch bark canoes supplied transportation for both Ojibwe trappers and French Voyageurs. Chief Osawgee signed the 1854 Treaty of La Pointe on behalf of the Fond du Lac Ojibwe—and subsequently lost his land. He died in Solon Springs, Wisconsin, in 1876.

Research can't pinpoint the exact location of Osawgee Beach, but the site was most likely on Wisconsin Point. In 1927 the beach was listed as a "forty-acre park at the end of Schafer Drive," but Superior records show no mention of the street. Today the Osaugie Recreation Trail treks five-and-a-half miles along the Nemadji River to Moccasin Mike Road at the base of Wisconsin Point, onward to the point's end, and beyond to Barker's Island.

OSAWGEE BEACH, SUPERIOR, WIS.

107532

Part IV

LAKE SUPERIOR CIRCLE ROUTE

NIPIGON SCHREIBER 120 MARATHON WHITE RIVER

ROSSPORT TERRACE BAY 17 WAWA

PORT ARTHUR FORT WILLIAM 70 17

PIGEON RIVER

GRAND MARAIS

LAKE SUPERIOR

BEAVER BAY 61 110

HANCOCK HOUGHTON

TWO HARBORS 26 SAULT STE MARIE

DULUTH SUPERIOR 28 180 MARQUETTE 50 Big Mac Bridge

ASHLAND 67 WAKEFIELD 312 2

61 23

Around the Shore

Manitou Falls at Pattison Park

Pattison Park's Big Manitou Falls drops the Black River 165 feet, making it the highest waterfall in the state of Wisconsin and the fourth highest in the United States found east of the Rockies (Little Manitou Falls lowers the river 30 feet). The Ojibwe believed the voice of the Great Spirit, *Gitchi Monido*, could be heard in the cascading waters of Big Manitou Falls. They called the rapids found below the falls *Bohiwum Sasigewon*, or "Laughing Waters," and Little Manitou Falls *Cacabeeca Bunghee*, "Little Waterfalls." Big Manitou Falls is the centerpiece of Pattison Park, a 1,436-acre state park that contains Interfalls Lake, nine miles of hiking trails, and, of course, the Black River.

Called *Mucudewa Sebee* ("black river" or "dark river") by the Ojibwe, the Black River gets its name from its brownish color, which comes from decaying vegetation along the river. The waterway begins its journey twenty-two miles from the park, at Black Lake on the Minnesota-Wisconsin border. After passing through the park and over the two falls, the river joins with the Nemadji, which goes on to feed Lake Superior. Interfalls Lake, found between Little Manitou Falls and Big Manitou Falls, is a twenty-seven acre flowage just thirteen feet deep at its deepest point; a three-hundred-foot sand beach lines its shore.

Copper has been mined along the Black River since ancient times. As far back as 5,000 B.C., Native Americans of the Old Copper culture lived in and around what is now Pattison Park, mining copper from rocky outcroppings. Surveyor George Stuntz found a broken stone hammer and other evidence of Native American metalworking and copper mining near Little Manitou Falls. The first European copper outfit mined the park's Copper Creek from 1845 to 1847. When the American Civil War created a demand for copper, prospectors swarmed the area, operating mines across the county. But the mines produced mediocre yields, and after the war copper mining was abandoned. Evidence of mining, including a triangular mine opening at the base of Big Manitou Falls, can still be found throughout the park.

From 1879 to 1882 the park area was logged by an outfit managed by Martin Pattison (see page 171). Portions of Pattison's logging operation can still be found in the park that bears his name.

W-8 Manitou Falls, Pattison State Superior, Wis.

Big Manitou Falls— Wisconsin's highest cascade and the fourth largest east of the Rockies—gets its name from the Ojibwe Great Spirit, or Gitchi Monido; the Ojibwe once thought the spirit's voice could be heard in its waters.

The Black River (Mucudewa Sebee in Ojibwe) gets its name from its dark waters, tinted brown by decaying vegetation.

BLACK RIVER, NEAR SUPERIOR, WIS.

Amnicon Falls State Park

As at Pattison Park, the area that makes up Amnicon Falls State Park along the Amnicon River was first home to people of the Old Copper culture, which gave way to the Woodland peoples. By the time Europeans arrived, the Ojibwe populated the area. Fur trappers ran lines along the Amnicon, and later the river witnessed the same boom and bust copper mining activity the Black River experienced. By the 1880s logging had moved into the region; lumberjacks used the fast-flowing waters of the Amnicon to carry logs to Lake Superior. In 1886 Superior pioneer James Bardon (for whom Spirit Mountain's Bardon's Peak is named) bought 160 acres of land from the Chicago, St. Paul, Minneapolis & Omaha Railroad, much of it along the river and waterfall. Sandstone quarries had been operating on the Apostle Islands and along the south shore for years, and Bardon opened another, Arcadia Brownstone Quarry, on his new property. Some of the stone removed from the Amnicon quarry was used to build Superior's Fairlawn mansion, the stately home of Martin Pattison's family. The quarry shipped over a million cubic feet of sandstone during its twenty years of operation. Amnicon Falls Park still contains evidence of the old sandstone quarry.

AMNICON FALLS, SUPERIOR, WIS.

W-10—Bathing Beach, Pattison State Park, Superior, Wis.

Martin Pattison: the Man Who Saved Big Manitou Falls

In 1879 Martin Pattison moved his Michigan logging company to Superior, and his crews spent three years felling trees along the Black River. When Pattison heard news of Charlemagne Tower's success mining ore on the Vermilion Range, Pattison sold his logging company interests and invested in iron mining, and his prospects paid off. Few people owned more land in Minnesota's Iron Range than did Pattison, making him quite wealthy. In Superior he bought an entire city block and had Fairlawn, a forty-two-room Victorian mansion, built on the site.

In 1917 plans were announced to harness the Black River as a power source; the proposed dam would have destroyed Big Manitou Falls. So Pattison approached James Bardon and other area landowners and paid them for their land along the Black River. His purchase put an end to all talk of a power dam. He donated the land to the state of Wisconsin, which turned it into its sixth state park in 1920.

Pattison said this of his generous gesture: "In being able to grant this site to the public, I have accomplished one of my chief ambitions. For years I have spent much time amid the surrounding of the falls and have received so much enjoyment there that it gradually became part of my life."

GRAND ARCH. LAKE SUPERIOR

Apostle Islands, Wis. Presque Isle or Stockton, Balancing Rock.

Apostle Islands

According to Ojibwe legend, the twenty-three Apostle Islands were formed when the spirit *Winneboujou* went hunting deer near his home on the Brule River. He had exhausted his quiver of arrows pursuing a stag, which he tracked to what is now Bayfield. There, he watched the deer escape by swimming across Lake Superior. The angry spirit began throwing rocks at the deer, and these rocks became the Apostle Islands.

The Ojibwe came here first, setting up camp at what is now the city of La Pointe on Madeline Island (see page 180) as one of the final legs of their great migration. It was most likely early French Jesuits who named the islands the "Apostles"; they had a habit of labeling places with biblical names and were perhaps under the mistaken belief that there were only twelve islands. (The Jesuits called Chequamegon Bay *La Baye du St. Espirit*, "the Bay of the Holy Ghost.") By 1744 "Apostle Islands" was in general use. But when he first encountered the islands in the 1820s, explorer Henry Schoolcraft called them the Federation Islands and named each after a U.S. state or territory.

His idea never quite caught on (even today's Michigan and York Islands had different names in Schoolcraft's plan).

In 1854 the Treaty of La Pointe opened most of the land in the region to European settlement. During the mid-nineteenth century the islands were clear cut for the timber industry, their logs floated across Chequamegon Bay to mills in Bayfield, Washburn, and Ashland. In the 1880s the islands were exploited for their sandstone and quarried on Stockton, Basswood, and Hermit Islands; they closed at the turn of the century when steel and brick became the building materials of choice. Frederick Prentice, called the "father of the Chequamegon brownstone industry," opened a quarry on Hermit Island and operated other quarries on the mainland.

The islands were once the home of at least ten lighthouses; the earliest, on Michigan Island, was built in 1856. Lighthouse expert F. Ross Holland called Apostle Islands lighthouses "the largest and finest single collection of lighthouses in the country."

Madeline Island

Madeline Island is by far the most well-known of the twenty-three Apostle Islands and a very holy place to Ojibwe people. *Midewiwin* ("Grand Medicine Religion") prophecy sent the Ojibwe on a great migration that would end when they reached their final destination, a place where "food grows on water." They first journeyed to *Moneuang* (Montreal) then to *Boweting* (Sault Ste. Marie). Eventually they settled on an island they called *Moningwunakauning* or "home of the golden-breasted woodpecker," known to French traders as La Pointe for the fort they built there in 1693. From *Moningwunakauning* the Ojibwe ventured out and indeed found food growing on the water: *manomin*, known today as wild rice. *Moningwunakauning* became known as Madeline Island to Ojibwe and Europeans alike after Equaysayway, daughter of Chief White Crane, married French explorer and trader Michel Cadotte, who in 1793 established a trading post at La Pointe; she was baptized a Christian and adopted the name Madeleine, and her father renamed the island in her honor (it is unclear how the spelling changed).

In 1850 Benjamin Armstrong, an Alabama native who lived among the Ojibwe, heard that Washington politicians were lobbying to force the Ojibwe to move to Minnesota's prairie country. In fact, President Zachary Taylor issued a proclamation discounting earlier treaties and told the Ojibwe to prepare to leave. Armstrong feared the Ojibwe would sooner go to war than move away from the graves of their ancestors.

Meanwhile Taylor died and Millard Fillmore took his place. In 1852 Armstrong decided to take a small party of Ojibwe, including his father-in-law Kechewaishke (Chief Buffalo), to Washington to plead their case to the new administration. Despite storms of nature and bureaucracy, the group made it to Washington, only to be refused an audience with the commissioner of Indian Affairs. Back at his hotel, a dejected Armstrong found Chief Buffalo and the other Ojibwe in the center of a crowd, which included members of President Fillmore's cabinet. The next afternoon they found themselves in the White House, sharing Chief Buffalo's tobacco with the president in a gesture of friendship. Chief Buffalo's spokesman, Oshaga, spoke for over an hour while Armstrong translated and the president listened carefully. Two days later Fillmore rescinded Taylor's order with a compromise: the land would be opened for European settlement, but the Ojibwe would not be forced from their lands. In 1854 Chief Buffalo was one of the Ojibwe leaders who signed the Treaty of La Pointe, placing Fillmore's decision into action, creating several Ojibwe reservations. Armstrong again translated for his father-in-law, who died the following year at age ninety-six.

LA POINTE, MADELINE ISLAND, LAKE SUPERIOR, NEAR WASHBURN, WIS.

This is where we were on Saturday. It is fine amongst the Islands. Come and I'd show them to you. Love to all. How is school?

Apostle Islands, Wis. Madeline Island, La Pointe, the Shore, Row Cottages, view from Boat Landing

Street Scene, showing Lake Superior in distance, Bayfield, Wis.—2

Bayfield

St. Paul's Henry Rice organized the Bayfield Land Company in 1856, two years after the Treaty of La Pointe opened the region to European settlement. The village of Bayfield was established in 1857. ("Bayfield" comes from British Admiral Henry Bayfield, who had surveyed Lake Superior's south shore in the 1820s; Rice and Bayfield were good friends.) Within a year the town boasted over one hundred homes. Logging and lumber milling dominated Bayfield's economy in the 1880s, with the Pike and Knight mills employing 125 people. As early as 1868 R. D. Pike began opening brownstone quarries near Bayfield, and in the 1870s Frank Boutin opened a fishery that shipped twelve thousand barrels of fish in one season. The Booth fishery opened in 1880, employing up to 500 men when fishing was at its peak.

Further up the shore toward Superior on the Siskiwit Bay, the village of Cornucopia also played a key role in the Lake Superior fishing industry (the Ojibwe called the bay *Siskawekaning* or "where the fish can be caught"). Beyond Cornucopia at the mouth of the Flag River, Port Wing was established in 1891 by Finnish immigrant Axel Johannson; the town also served the fishing, logging, and sandstone industries.

Washburn

The history of Washburn centers around commerce. The Chicago, St. Paul, Minneapolis & Omaha Railroad founded it in 1884, naming it for Cawallader C. Washburn, Wisconsin's governor from 1872 to 1874. Six years later the town was home to coal docks, a grain elevator, and three lumber mills. During the 1890s the town built a grand collection of brownstone buildings, including a courthouse, a Carnegie library (right), an iron works, and a bank (the bank is now home to the Washburn Cultural and Art Museum). In 1891 electricity came to the city, and it took the title of county seat from Bayfield the next year. The era of Washburn's lumber industry, which according to reports cut 100 million feet of lumber annually during the 1890s, ended in 1900 when the area's pine forests were logged out. Brownstone went out of fashion as a building material around the same time. The grain elevator enterprise and its subordinate shipping industry failed when using trains and trucks became more efficient. Washburn now relies on tourism as its main source of employment.

Public Library, Washburn, Wis.

Second Street looking East, Ashland, Wis.—20.

High School, Ashland, Wis.

The Ashland High School (left) and the Washburn Public Library (page 174) were both designed by Henry Waldhagen, a German immigrant who arrived in the U.S. in 1886 and set up an architectural firm in Ashland in 1893. He designed many schools, courthouses, and libraries using locally quarried sandstone. Both the Ashland High School and Washburn Library were faced in Washburn brownstone, which has a light purple tint.

Ashland

In about 1859 French explorers Groseilliers and Radisson built themselves a small log house near the Ojibwe village of *Agamiwikedosubiwishen*, which was protected from Lake Superior's rough weather by a bay the Ojibwe called *Shagawaumikong*, the "place of shallow water." The inlet's name would later evolve to Chequamegon Bay, and Ashland would grow along its shores.

The French explorers soon left for Montreal and would never return, having lost their license to trade in the area (which motivated them to switch loyalties from France to Britain, prompting the English to open the Hudson's Bay Company). Instead, in 1865 French Jesuit Claude Jean Allouez came to Chequamegon Bay and built a chapel of tree bark. Nearby Ojibwe as well as Kickapoo, Fox, and Sauk came to see the French priest's odd chapel, and within ten years of his arrival Chequamegon Bay had become a major trading center.

In 1854 Asaph Whittlesey and George Kilbourne reportedly cleared a small stand of ash trees at the end of the bay and named the clearing, of course, Whittlesey. Six years later the fledgling township was rechristened Ashland. But the financial panic of 1857 and the Civil War stopped the town from growing, and even Whittlesey moved away; at one time just one family lived in the town. Rumors of an impending railway to Chequamegon Bay in 1871 got things moving again, and soon Whittlesey and other early settlers returned. Discovery of iron ore on the nearby Gogebic Range also fueled the population boom, and soon the town thrived, boasting over two hundred buildings. When the Wisconsin Central Railway reached the bay in 1877, Whittlesey drove the final spike. Soon Ashland was shipping out iron ore, including every ton pulled from the Gogebic Range.

Like other towns along the Wisconsin south shore, Ashland benefitted from sandstone quarrying and some fishing. It also became the home to many coal docks and once ranked as the seventh largest coal dispersion center in the country. But for a short time lumber was king. At one point nine mills operated out of Ashland. It has been said that on a calm day, the sawdust from mills in Bayfield, Washburn, and Ashland covered the entire bay. Ashland's early industries suffered the same fate as those in other towns along the South Shore.

Isle Royale

Michigan's Isle Royale, the largest island on Lake Superior, sits fifty-five miles from Michigan's Upper Peninsula and eighteen miles from the Canadian shore. Stretching forty-five miles long and between three and ten miles across, the 850-square-mile island forms the "eye" of Lake Superior's wolf's head shape. Many smaller islands surround it.

Ancient Native Americans called the Old Copper peoples once populated the island, mining its rich copper beds. They extracted the mineral by heating the native rock with fire and then dousing it with cold water, causing the rock to crumble, leaving the copper behind. They then extracted the larger pieces for use as hammers and chisels, but never developed a method for heating the smaller particles. In the early 1920s Pennsylvania newspaper editor William P. F. Ferguson excavated the purported remains of an Old Copper village near the site of ancient copper mines, but the authenticity of his findings were debated. When European settlers tried to revive copper mining on the island in the 1840s (the island was then rumored to be made entirely of copper), they found little activity by natives outside of a seasonal fishing site on Grace Island and a maple sugaring camp at Sugar Mountain. Copper enterprises would come and go again in the 1870s and 1890s.

Some of those miners stayed to try their hands at commercial fishing, which first came to the island in 1800 with the Hudson's Bay Company. Later the American Fur Post fishing fleet would thrive on Isle Royale, particularly between 1837 and 1841, when the company employed thirty fishermen and an untold number of Ojibwe and Metis women, who worked cleaning fish. Other companies operated from the island, but by far the largest was the A. Booth Company, which recruited fisherman from Norway, offering them equipment, housing, and supplies on credit until they had made their money back. By 1915 more than one hundred fishermen worked the waters around Isle Royale.

In 1931 President Herbert Hoover signed a congressional authorization to conserve "a prime example of North Woods Wilderness." Nine years later President Franklin Roosevelt established Isle Royale National Park. This act, along with invasion of exotic fish such as smelt and the sea lamprey, dramatically reduced commercial fishing. As of 1990 only one fisherman dropped his nets near Isle Royale, operating a family fishery over one hundred years old.

Many of Isle Royale's one-time fishermen turned to tourism to earn their keep, some long before the industry died out. John's Hotel, the island's first resort, was built in 1894. Other resorts and lodges soon followed, offering guests such activities as dancing, tennis, bowling, and fishing—they even built a golf course on Belle Isle. Like Park Point, Isle Royale was promoted as a haven for hay fever sufferers. By the 1930s the archipelago's smaller islands were dotted with summer homes. Today much of Isle Royale, despite its long history of human activity, remains an untamed wilderness.

The Shipwrecks of Isle Royale

The Isle Royale archipelago is made up of many smaller islands and dotted with reefs and rocks, making its shipping lanes very dangerous to navigate. At least a dozen ships have wrecked off Isle Royale, including the *Algoma* (1885), the *America* (1928), the *Chester A. Congdon* (1918), the *Chisolm* (1898), the *George M. Cox* (1933), the *Cumberland* (1877), the *Emperor* (1877), the *Glenyon* (1924), the *Kamloops* (1927), and the *Monarch* (1906).

The *America*, owned by the A. Booth Company, was a beloved ship on Lake Superior, serving for most of its life as a transportation link between Isle Royale and settlements along the Minnesota north shore (which also made the *America* an important communication tool). In 1908 a forest fire threatened those very North Shore townships, and the Minnesota governor called on the *America* to evacuate those at Beaver Bay. She rescued about three hundred villagers. On June 6, 1928, the *America* left Grand Marais for Isle Royale to drop off passengers before heading to Port Arthur. In the early morning hours of June 7, she struck a reef near Isle Royale's Washington Harbor, skidding over the rocks four times and ripping a hole in her hull just below the engine room on the starboard side. The ship's pumps couldn't keep up with the water pouring in. The captain ordered the ship to steer for the north gap of Washington Harbor in an attempt to beach her, but it struck more rocks and stopped ninety feet from shore. All thirty-one passengers and crew managed to get off the *America* before she slid off into deep water.

CHIPPEWA HARBOR, ISLE ROYALE, LAKE SUPERIOR—4

WASHINGTON HARBOR, ISLE ROYALE, LAKE SUPERIOR NEAR DULUTH

No. 581. V. O. Hammon Pub. Co., Chicago

TWO EXCURSION BOATS LANDING AT TWO HARBORS, MINN.

Two Harbors

Over the eons Lake Superior's waves carved two natural bays out of the northern coastline roughly twenty miles from Duluth. The Ojibwe called the site *Wasswewining*, "a place to spear by moonlight." In 1856 Thomas Saxon became the first European to settle at what would initially be named Agate Bay. The following year a sawmill sprang up in the adjacent bay, marking the birth of a settlement called Burlington. Outside of a little logging and some fishing, the two bays had no industry to support a population; the financial panic of 1857 also kept settlers away.

That all changed in 1884, when Charlemagne Tower's Duluth & Iron Range Railroad built an ore dock at Agate Bay in order to load ore transported from its Tower-Soudan mine on the newly opened Vermilion Iron Range. The community boomed, but it still wasn't officially a town. When a township was finally platted in 1888, Agate Bay and Burlington Bay together became Two Harbors. Soon it was the busiest port on Lake Superior outside of the Twin Ports, home to some of the world's largest ore docks.

Two Harbors: The First Home of 3M

Two Harbors also gave birth to Minnesota Mining and Manufacturing, better known today as 3M, one of the largest companies in the world. In 1902 Two Harbors attorney John Dwan and a few of his friends organized the company, intending to set up a mining operation along the shore at Crystal Bay near the Baptism River to extract corundum, an abrasive used in grinding wheels—it would have been one of only two such operations in North America. Unfortunately, the mineral they mined at Crystal Bay was not corundum but anorthosite, a much less valuable product. The company nearly collapsed before St. Paul's Lucius P. Ordway bailed them out. They set up a sandpaper factory in an old Duluth flour mill, but the inferiority of the anorthosite and Duluth's humidity almost crushed them again. Ordway then moved the company to St. Paul where it thrived—and continues to do so.

Two Harbors' Lighthouse

The advent of iron mining had turned Two Harbors into somewhat of a boomtown. Not only was the iron ore industry causing increased harbor traffic, but coal carriers, lumber vessels, various commercial boats, and passenger ships added to the congestion. Thirteen hundred ships passed through Agate Bay alone in 1892, just eight years after the first load of Vermilion Iron Range ore left its docks. Breakwaters were built to make the harbor safer, but it needed a lighthouse. In March 1891 the U.S. Government paid Thomas Feigh $1.00 for an acre of land and almost immediately began work on a lighthouse. The lighthouse's fourth-order Fresnel lens was lit for the first time on April 15, 1892.

The twelve-foot square tower stands just shy of fifty feet in the air and includes a watch room, lantern room, cleaning room, and even an extra bedroom for the second assistant keeper.

The light tower connects to the keeper's house, allowing the keeper passage without going outside in the winter. The tower's walls are built in three layers of brick, the house's with two; where they meet the wall is five courses thick, engineered to act as a fire break to keep the keeper's family safe (the lamp oil was highly combustible).

The postcard above celebrates the North Shore's reputation for severe winter weather. Two Harbors' lighthouse is shown in the lower-right panel.

Memorial Engine "3 Spot"

Two Harbors is home to the memorial engine "3 Spot," a steam locomotive built by the Baldwin Locomotive Works of Philadelphia, Pennsylvania, and shipped to Duluth by rail in 1883. A scow and a tugboat then hauled it to Agate Bay, a predecessor of Two Harbors. There the 3 Spot became the first engine of the Duluth & Iron Range Railroad. The locomotive pulled the first load of Vermilion Range iron ore sixty-eight miles from Soudan, Minnesota, to the brand new D&IR dock on July 31, 1884.

The 3 Spot was sold for scrap in 1920, but the D&IR's Thirty Year Veterans Club purchased the engine and put it on display in 1923. It is currently on display with the Duluth, Mesabi & Iron Range Railroad's engine "229" at the depot in Two Harbors.

Two Harbors' Ore Docks

As you have most likely read by now, Charlemagne Tower's Duluth & Iron Range Railroad built an ore dock at Agate Bay in what is now Two Harbors in 1883; a year later the dock accepted its first load of of Vermilion Iron Range ore, ten cars full pulled from Soudan, Minnesota, by the steam locomotive 3 Spot. The railroad became the property of Illinois Steel in 1887, and in 1901 part of U.S. Steel; it merged with U.S. Steel's Duluth, Missabe & Northern Railroad in 1938 to form the Duluth, Missabe & Iron Range Railway. The railroads would eventually build six docks at Two Harbors. During World War II, the DM&IR docks in Duluth and Two Harbors combined to load record-setting shipments of ore in 1944, breaking records three times (see page 139). They reached an all-time high of 49 million tons in 1953. As the iron-rich ore was mined out, the docks slowed down. The Two Harbors docks actually closed from 1963 to 1966, when the mining industry picked up again with the development of taconite. Three docks remain, two of them still in operation.

ORE DOCKS, TWO HARBORS, NEAR DULUTH, MINN.—14

Ore Docks at Two Harbors, near Duluth, Minn.

11292.   Ore Docks, Two Harbors, Minn.

Stewart River

Located three miles north of Two Harbors, the Stewart River takes its name from early pioneer John Stewart, who settled in the area in 1865. Today the mouth of the Stewart is a popular place to catch lake trout.

In 1924, just three years after Minnesota began its trunk highway system, a bridge was built to span the Stewart River. Bridge No. 3589, a reinforced concrete arch adorned with Classical Revival details, stretches nineteen feet across the river. Because the North Shore's Lake Superior tributaries are particularly rocky waterways, it was one of only a few regions in Minnesota provided with the funds to build concrete bridges in the highway system's early years. The Minnesota Highway Department boastfully declared the bridge "the most aesthetically accomplished statement…produced by the state highway program."

STEWART RIVER, NEAR TWO HARBORS ON HIGHWAY No. 1

NORTH SHORE OF LAKE SUPERIOR

107546

Where You Want This Killin' Done?

Out on Highway 61, naturally—at least according to the title song of Duluth-native Bob Dylan's 1965 album *Highway 61 Revisited*. Of course, Dylan's song (and album) had little to do with the actual Highway 61, but mentioning it makes a fun transition to revisiting its North Shore history.

The stretch of highway along the Minnesota north shore of Lake Superior began in 1879 as a simple brushed trail used by sled-dog drivers like John Beargrease to deliver mail in the winter (during summer months, all transportation along the north shore was done on the water). By 1900 a rough stage road was somewhat complete, but only passable in the winter by horse-drawn sleigh. Between 1900 and 1920 local communities along the lake built their own stretches of the road. Only the link between Duluth and Two Harbors was graded adequately for safe motor traffic, but from there to the Canadian border the road was little more than a narrow path, and many of those sections of "road" wandered miles from the shore. (Remnants of some of those roads remain, indicated by "Old North Shore Road" signs.)

In 1921 Minnesota made plans for a trunk highway system that included Highway 1, which would run from Iowa to Canada. The 154-mile stretch from Duluth to the Canadian border was known as the North Shore Drive (later the North Shore Scenic Drive) and was designed to stay as close to Lake Superior's northern coast as nature would allow. The roadway was first fully paved in 1933. It later became part of U.S. Highway 61—and forever memorialized in Dylan's song—which reaches from New Orleans to Minnesota's Pigeon River at the Canadian border. A 1941 advertisement for the North Shore Drive noted that the North Shore, America's "Summer Playground" and "Hay Fever Haven," had no snakes or poison ivy.

HIGHWAY No. 1, NORTH SHORE, LAKE SUPERIOR, NEAR

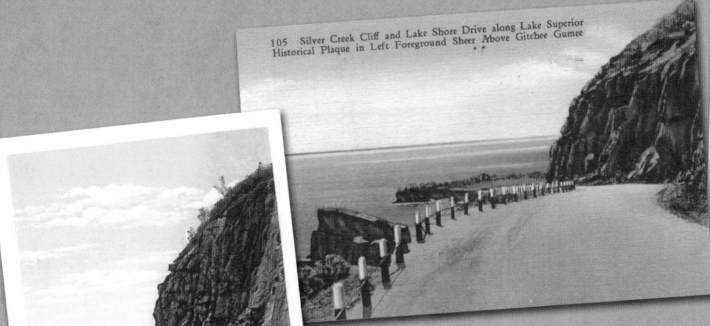

105 Silver Creek Cliff and Lake Shore Drive along Lake Superior
Historical Plaque in Left Foreground Sheer Above Gitchee Gumee

107544

SILVER CREEK CLIFF ON HIGHWAY No. 1, NEAR TWO HARBORS

Silver Creek Cliff

For years the North Shore Drive's most breathtaking moment was driving along the Silver Creek Cliff, formed by volcanic activity more than a million years ago. Before it became part of the trunk highway system in the 1920s, the road actually diverted inland several miles to avoid the cliff. When the trunk highway was built, workers dynamited a section of the cliff and used steam-powered bulldozers to clear the rock (which was then carried off by horse-drawn wagons). This allowed a narrow road to pass along the lake side of the cliff, forming a giant blind corner. Little other than a small barrier separated the road—and travelers—from a significant drop to the rocky shores below. If that wasn't dangerous enough, boulders freed by erosion would often tumble down the side of the creek and onto the roadway.

The excitement ended in 1994, after a tunnel begun in 1991 was finally completed. The initial plan to make passing the Silver Creek Cliff safer

107542

SILVER CREEK CLIFF, LAKE SUPERIOR NORTH SHORE DRIVE,
TWO HARBORS, NEAR DULUTH, MINN.—4

110-D LOOKING NORTH FROM SILVER CREEK CLIFF, LAKE SUPERIOR

NORTH SHORE DRIVE, MINNESOTA ARROWHEAD COUNTRY

involved widening the roadway to keep vehicles further from the edge, but engineers estimated that would have required the removal of 1.5 million cubic yards of rock. The tunnel only required removing 500,000 cubic yards, and it's a stunning piece of engineering: 1,300 feet of roadway with tile-covered walls and continuous lighting, plus entry façades that complement the rocky hillside. The tunnel has made the passage much safer for drivers, particularly for the thousands of tourists, most of them unfamiliar with the highway's twists and turns, who travel the road each year. Of course, there are many North Shore residents who feel the tunnel has stripped the roadway of some of its charms.

During the 1950s a family of billy goats set up home on the cliff after escaping form a nearby farm. They spent four years on the cliff, peacefully grazing for food until a bobcat killed the doe and a kid born earlier in the year. The local sheriff then shot the buck, thinking it the most humane thing to do. Another local legend tells of fisherman Orville Rise being lowered over the cliff by a rope held by his friend Jim Anderson to rescue a newborn goat, but then there are apparently lots of legends about Mr. Rise....

Gooseberry Falls State Park

The Gooseberry River appeared on explorers' maps as early as 1670. The river's name comes from the Ojibwe *Shabonimikanisibi* ("the place of gooseberries river"), although some say it was christened in honor of French explorer Sieur des Groseilliers, who explored the area in the 1660s with Pierre Espirit Radisson (*Groseilliers* is French for "currant bushes"). The river has an estuary at its mouth, which made it an ideal place for voyageurs to stop and camp.

The Nestor Logging Company set up camp at the river's mouth between 1900 and 1909, using two narrow-gauge rail lines to bring logs to the estuary, where the timber was tied into rafts and towed by tugs to mills in Baraga, Michigan, or Ashland, Wisconsin. One such raft contained six million feet of logs and took eight days to reach Baraga.

In the late 1920s the state of Minnesota bought 638 acres of land along the river from the estate of Wisconsin's Henry Vilas. It was intended to be a game preserve and public hunting ground, but in 1934 it became a state park, and the Civil Conservation Corps went to work on it. From 1934 to 1941 the CCC built twenty-seven rustic structures made of stone and wood throughout park, including administration buildings, officers' quarters, barracks, a mess hall, and a latrine. They also created picnic shelters and indoor facilities with kitchens, a sanitation building, and several picnic tables with surrounding fireplaces. Gooseberry's CCC unit included two Italian stone masons, John Berini and Joe Cattaneo, brought in to oversee and execute the intricate stone work still found in the park.

Today the park has been expanded to 1,687 acres and features three of the river's five waterfalls, including Upper Falls, which drops seventy-five feet, and Lower Falls, which cascades three hundred feet. In 1996 the park's facilities received a major makeover: a new bridge over Highway 61 and an award-winning Visitor's Center designed by Duluth architect David Salmela, which features a fireplace made from stone blasted out of the Silver Creek Cliff Tunnel. More than 570,000 people visit the park each year.

GOOSEBERRY FALLS AND RIVER ABOVE U. S. HIGHWAY 61 BRIDGE, NORTH SHORE DRIVE

GOOSEBERRY STATE PARK, MINNESOTA ARROWHEAD COUNTRY

Split Rock Lighthouse

SPLIT ROCK LIGHTHOUSE, NORTH SHORE, LAKE SUPERIOR

The Lake Superior storm of November 28, 1905, that damaged more than twenty-five ships and claimed thirty-three lives (see page 128) also left two ships foundering on the rocky shoreline near the Split Rock River—then considered "the most dangerous piece of water in the world." Soon after, a local delegation went to Washington D.C. to state its case, and in 1907 Congress appropriated $75,000 for a lighthouse and fog signal near the Split Rock.

Immigrant workers built Split Rock Lighthouse, a fifty-four-foot octagonal brick tower, between 1909 and 1910. The lens, a bivalve Third Order Fresnel, was set in motion on July 31, 1910, after the lighthouse's first keeper, Orrin "Pete" Young, lit the incandescent oil vapor lamp for the first time. From its position high atop a North Shore cliff, the lighthouse's lens had a focal plane of 168 feet, the highest of all lights on the Great Lakes. By 1939 it was considered the most visited lighthouse in the U.S.

Little Two Harbors, seen in the postcard at lower left, was once a Norwegian fishing camp kept by herring fishermen. The tiny facility also allowed boats to bring supplies for the lighthouse keeper and his family.

LITTLE TWO HARBORS AND SPLIT ROCK LIGHTHOUSE, NORTH SHORE, LAKE SUPERIOR ON HIGHWAY No. 1

135-D—Palisade Lookout at Castle Rock, Minnesota's Scenic North Shore Drive

Palisade Head

Palisade Head, a cliff that climbs 348 feet above Lake Superior near the mouth of Palisade Creek, stands four miles up the shore from Silver Bay. (Silver Bay was created in 1954 by the Reserve Mining Company for workers at its taconite processing plant.) This eighty-acre precipice, formed by ancient volcanic activity, provides one of the most spectacular views of the lake and its shoreline. On clear days visitors can see the Apostle Islands, thirty miles away off Wisconsin's south shore, as well as the North Shore's Sawtooth Mountains (actually lava deposits) and nearby Shovel Point—sometimes called "Little Palisades"—which rises 180 feet above the big lake. Both Shovel Point and Palisade Head are part of Tettegouche State Park, which takes its name from the old Alger-Smith logging camp established in 1898 by eastern Canadians near Mic Mak Lake (Mic Mak is the name of an Algonquin Indian tribe from New Brunswick, Nova Scotia).

In recent years, Palisade Head and Shovel Point have become magnets for rock climbers looking for a challenge. The sheer face of Palisade—igneous rhyolite overlaying soft basalt that has been undercut by Lake Superior's waves—provides just what they're looking for; kayakers also enjoy the waters off Palisade Head.

Beaver Bay

Beaver Bay, home to legendary mail carrier John Beargrease, is the oldest continuous European settlement along the North Shore. Established in 1856 by a group of German immigrants who moved to the area from Maumee, Ohio, the community's first business was a sawmill set up by the four Weiland brothers (the Weilands later tried to bring an ore dock to Beaver Bay, but the D&IR chose to build theirs at Agate Bay).

The Weilands' sawmill allowed the community to ride out the panic of 1857 and for twenty-five years it remained the town's main source of employment. The mill even hired some Ojibwe people, who came to the area to find work at the bay they called *Gajiikensikag*, "the place of little cedars." The most famous among them was John Beargrease, born in Beaver Bay in 1858, who along with his brothers used a dogsled to deliver mail along the North Shore from 1879 to 1899, sledding on Lake Superior's ice whenever it was frozen enough to allow safe passage. Beaver Bay is home to an Ojibwe cemetery, where Beargrease and other members of his family lay in rest. Today the annual John Beargrease Sled Dog Race commemorates his efforts.

BEAVER RIVER, NEAR TWO HARBORS, HIGHWAY No. 1, LAKE SUPERIOR

107533

Baptism River

Called *Au Bapteme* by French voyageurs, the North Shore's Baptism River drops seven hundred feet before reaching Lake Superior, making it home to several waterfalls. The most spectacular of these is High Falls, a seventy-foot drop—second only to the Pigeon River's 120-foot High Falls in all of the state—located a mile or so from the entry to Tettegouche State Park. The river also contains Two-Step Falls, downstream from High Falls. Though not as tall, Two-Step spills over some spectacular rock formations. Illgen Falls (misidentified in the postcard below as "Elgin Falls") is found upriver from High Falls and drops the river thirty-five feet where it roils into a cauldron on its way downstream.

In 1910 the Alger-Smith Logging Company sold its logged-out land surrounding the Baptism to the "Tettegouche Club," a group of Duluth businessmen, for use as a fishing retreat. The property was later sold to the deLaittres family, who acted as its stewards until the land became a state park.

CROSS RIVER, NORTH SHORE DRIVE, BETWEEN TWO HARBORS AND GRAND MARAIS, NEAR DULUTH, MINN.—43

145-D—Elgin Falls on Baptism River on Scenic North Shore Drive of Lake Superior

Cross River

Missionary Frederic R. Baraga, born in Yugoslavia in 1797, came to the U.S. in 1830 to devote his life to the Native Americans of the Upper Great Lakes and was named Bishop of Upper Michigan in 1853 (Baraga, Michigan, is named for him). But before that, he had a little trouble in a canoe. Crossing thirty miles of open Lake Superior waters from La Pointe on Madeline Island ten years prior to becoming a bishop, he and some Ojibwe guides encountered a storm that almost claimed their lives. They eventually found harbor at the mouth of a gently flowing river, and there Baraga nailed a wooden cross to a stump and wrote upon it, "In commemoration of the goodness of almighty God in granting to the Reverend F. R. Baraga safe passage from La Pointe to this place, August, 1843." The river became Cross River, and the wooden cross has since been replaced by one made of concrete.

Grand Marais

The natural harbor found about halfway between the Temperance River and the Canadian border once contained a large marsh, causing French trappers to name the spot *Grand Marais*, "great marsh." The American Fur Company operated a fishing station at Grand Marais as early as 1834, but no communities were established until the 1854 Treaty of La Pointe opened the North Shore to European settlements. Robert McLean brought a party to the site that same year to prospect for rumored veins of copper, gold, silver, and iron ore, but little materialized. In 1856 John Godfrey set up a trading post and has since been considered the town's first permanent resident (he named Mount Josephine, actually just a rocky peak near grand Portage, after his daughter). But Godfrey became discouraged and returned to his native Detroit just a few years later. The town didn't see significant growth until the fishing industry picked up and regional logging started in 1871 to feed the growth of Duluth. During the 1870s Henry Mayhew, Samuel Howenstein, and Ted Wakelin settled on the bay, purchased most of the surrounding land, and developed warehouses, docks, and a railroad right-of-way. Tourists began arriving as early as 1890, and today Grand Marais remains the North Shore's biggest visitor destination.

130-D—Airplane View of Beautiful Harbor, Grand Marais, Minn. Minnesota's Scenic North Shore Drive

Temperance River & Hidden Falls

A mile up Highway 61 from Cross River the Temperance River, the focal point of Temperance River State Park, plays host to the dangerous beauty of Hidden Falls. A series of cascades brings the river down 162 feet through a rocky gorge within the space of only half a mile. The last cascade drops only one hundred feet from the river's mouth. Along this span, the river's erosive power has carved deep cauldrons into the native rock, thus "hiding" the falls (also called the Temperance River Gorge). Missteps have led to tragedies over the years, as hikers have accidentally dropped into the gorge.

The area surrounding the river became a state park in 1938. The name "Temperance" is actually a play on words: the river's sheer drop allows it to empty into Lake Superior without leaving behind much sediment or vegetation, and therefore the mouth of the Temperance has no "bar."

PIGEON RIVER. TAKEN FROM BRIDGE ON HIGHWAY No. 1

107552

Pigeon River & Grand Portage

Each spring passenger pigeons would arrive near a Lake Superior tributary to breed; the local Ojibwe would snare the birds, which they called *Omimizibi*, in large nets—and so they named the river after the birds. The passenger pigeon went extinct by 1900, but the Pigeon River continues to flow. Outside of the St. Louis River, the Pigeon is the largest river feeding Lake Superior and acts as a border between the United States and Canada. Two miles from its mouth Middle Falls drops the river seventy feet; upstream the highest waterfall in Minnesota, High Falls, cascades 120 feet.

Nine miles west of the Pigeon River lies the town of Grand Portage (*Git-cheonigaming* or "great carrying place" in Ojibwe), the starting point of a path to the river that bypasses twenty miles of river containing the falls and impassable rapids. Before the Voyageurs arrived and gave the site its French name, the Ojibwe used the portage for generations. Pierre La Verendrye arrived at Grand Portage in 1731 along with his sons and fifty French soldiers, after which it became one of the most important fur trading centers in North America.

Spirit Little Cedar Tree

The Spirit Little Cedar Tree (*Minido Geezhigans* in Ojibwe; also known disrespectfully as the "Witch Tree" or "Witch's Tree") is a cedar monarch that sprouted from seemingly barren rock on the Hat Point prominence some four hundred years ago. (Erosion actually wore away the soil in which the tree first took seed, and its roots have grown beyond what has been worn away, giving the appearance of a tree growing from rock.) For generations the Ojibwe left offerings of tobacco at the tree for safe passage on the big lake. When they encountered Grand Portage, French voyageurs respected the tradition and left offerings of their own. Reports conflict as to how it came to be called the "Witch Tree." Some say it was given that name by the voyageurs and other early European explorers; others give credit to Dewey Albinson, one of many artists drawn to draw the tree.

Unfortunately, vandals have caused the local band of Grand Portage Ojibwe, who now own the land near Grand Portage where the tree is found, to close off public access to the Spirit Little Cedar Tree. Over the years, ignorant visitors have carved their initials in the tree or have cut away portions of it for souvenirs. Today those wishing to see the Spirit Little Cedar Tree must arrange a tour with a member of the band. For a distant view, you can take the *MV Wenonah* from Grand Portage to Isle Royale; it passes by Hat Point to give passengers a view of the tree.

The only known post-cards featuring the Spirit Little Cedar Tree are modern "chrome" post-cards made after 1945. The woodcut at right was made by St. Paul artist and letter-press printer Kent Aldrich of the Nomadic Press.

Superior National Forest

Logging activity in the forest along Lake Superior's Minnesota north shore between 1870 and 1900 nearly cut the wilderness clean. Some called for portions of the forest to be left untouched, causing lumber companies to threaten to pull out of the region, which at the time would have substantially damaged the local economy by leaving many immigrants unemployed. Christopher Andrews, who had served as a Union general during the Civil War, took up the cause of those who wanted to save part of the forest, organizing what would become Minnesota's state and national forest systems. As a result, in 1939 thirty-six thousand acres were set aside, creating the Superior National Forest.

Today's Superior National Forest contains the Boundary Waters Canoe Area Wilderness, which connects with Canada's Quetico Provincial Park to create a wilderness of over three million acres. The forest, made up of fir, spruce, aspen, birch, and maple trees, is the largest forest in the United States outside of Alaska. The surface area of the Superior National Forest's more than one thousand lakes and streams alone takes up 445,000 acres and provides 1,200 miles of canoe routes. Over two hundred thousand people visit the B.W.C.A.W. every year to canoe and camp among its waterways, and most of them spend time fishing for smallmouth bass, walleye, northern pike, and lake trout.

The forest is among the largest nesting spots for bald eagles in the lower forty-eight states, and is also home to an abundance of other wildlife, including loons, osprey, eagles, otters, deer, moose, black bears, and the gray wolf. In fact, the International Wolf Center makes its home in the B.W.C.A.W.'s unofficial gateway of Ely, Minnesota. And, of course, the Superior National Forest is also the home of a certain rodent that brought the French (and, subsequently, the industrialized development of the entire region) to western Lake Superior way back in the seventeenth century: this book's hero, the beaver.

"THIS IS THE LIFE"

SUPERIOR NATIONAL FOREST IN ARROW HEAD COUNTY, MINN.

HAPPY DAYS ARE HERE

SUPERIOR NATIONAL FOREST IN ARROW HEAD COUNTY, MINN.

Living the good life and enjoying happy days canoeing and fishing in the Superior National Forest. What a pleasant spot to end a book....

Index of Postcard Topics and Historic Figures and Vessels

References

Books, Articles, and Web sites

"About the Zoo." *Lake Superior Zoo-Duluth Web site.* http://www.lszoo.org/about.htm (accessed Janaury 8, 2006).

Agnew, Michael P. *The Historic Zenith Industrial District.* Duluth, Minn.: City of Duluth Planning Division, 1989.

Alanen, Arnold R. *A Field Guide to the Architecture and Landscapes of Northeastern Minnesota.* Prepared for the Vernacular Architecture Forum, 2000, in Duluth, Minnesota. Madison, Wisc.: Self published by the author, 2000.

Aubut, Sheldon T. and Maryanne C. Norton. *Images of America: Duluth, Minnesota.* Chicago, IL: Arcadia Publishing, 2001.

Barry, James P. *Ships of the Great Lakes.* Berkeley, Cal.: Howell North Books, 1973.

"Beaver Fur Hat." *The White Oak Society Web site.* http://www.whiteoak.org/learning/furhat.htm (accessed October 24, 2005).

Beck, Bill and C. Patrick Labadie. *Pride of the Inland Sea: an Illustrated History of the Port of Duluth-Superior.* Afton, Minn.: Afton Historical Society Press, 2004.

Bell, Mary T. *Cutting Across Time: Logging, Rafting, and Milling the Forests of Lake Superior.* Schroeder, Minn.: Schroeder Area Historical Society, 1999.

Beymer, Robert. "Boundary Waters Canoe Area." *Gorp Away Web site.* http://gorp.away.com/ gorp/resource/us_Wilderness_area/mn_bound.htm (accessed January 17, 2006).

Bishop, Hugh. "The First 100 years of Lake-Superior Born Business." *Lake Superior Magazine Online.* http://www.lakesuperior.com/online/242/2423m.html (accessed January 16, 2006).

Boyle, Pat. "A Minor League Lookback." *Baseball Almanac Web site.* http://www.baseball-almanac.com/minor-league/minor3.shtml (accessed January 2, 2006).

Buchanon, James. *The Twin Ports: A Guide to Duluth and Superior.* Minneapolis, Minn.: Nodin Press, 1992.

Cochran, Michael. "A Historical Study of the Duluth Boat Club." *DRC Web site.* http:// eteamz.active.com/duluthrowing/ (accessed January 2, 2006).

Cochrance, Tim. "Ise Royale: A Good Place to Live." *Michigan History Online.* http://www. michiganhistorymagazine.com/features/discmich/isleroyale.html (accessed January 16, 2006).

Collins, Pat. "The Recent Past: A Legacy of the White Pine Logging Boom." *Lake Superior Habitat Coordination Web site.* http://www.d.umn.edu/~pcollins/gp2-3.htm (accessed January 9, 2006).

Cooley, Jerome Eugene. *Recollections of Early Days in Duluth.* Duluth, Minn.: Published by the Author, 1925.

Diary of Duluth. Transcript of Radio Program. Aired July 15, 1948.

Dierckins, Tony and Kerry Elliott. *True North: Alternative and Off-Beat Destinations In and Around Duluth, Superior, and the Shores of Lake Superior.* Duluth, Minn.: X-communication, 2002.

— — and Jerry Paulson. *Greetings from Duluth, Volumes 1 & 2.* Duluth, Minn.: X-communication, 2003.

Dorland, Dionne and Judith Weir. "Pollution and the St. Louis River." *Cura Reporter.* Vol. XXII, No. 3, October 1992.

Duluth Directories. Livonia, Michigan, Polk City Directories, 1883-2005.

Duluth Properties on the National Register of Historic Places. Collection of nomination forms. Duluth: Duluth Public Library, 2004.

Eichten, Gary, et al. *Minnesota Public Radio Online.* http://www.mpr.org/index_main.shtml (accessed September 28, 2001).

El-Hai, Jack. *Lost Minnesota: Stories of Vanished Places.* Minneapolis, Minn.: University of Minnesota Press, 2000.

Ellis, Charles E. *Iron Ranges of Minnesota.* Publisher and date unknown.

Eubank, Nancy. *The Zenith City of the Unsalted Sea.* Duluth, Minn.: Duluth Heritage Preservation Commission, 1991.

Facts About Minnesota Iron Mining. Virginia, Minn.: Iron Mining Industry of Minnesota, 1958.

Federal Writer's Project of the Works Progress Administration. *Minnesota: A State Guide.* New York: Hastings House, 1938.

— —. *Wisconsin: A Guide to the Badger State.* New York: Duell, Sloan and Pearce, 1941.

Fedo, Michael. *The Lynchings in Duluth.* St. Paul, Minn.: Minnesota Historical Society Press, 2000.

Flower, Frank A. *The Eye of the Northwest.* Milwaukee, Wisc.: King, Fowle and Co., 1890.

Frederick, Chuck. *Duluth: the City and the People.* Helena, Mont.: American & World Geographic Publishing, 1994.

Fritzen, John. *Fond du Lac and Jay Cooke Park.* Duluth, Minn.: St. Louis County Historical Society, 1978.

Gilbert Munger Web site. http://www.d.umn.edu/tma/MungerSite/ChronDetails.html (accessed January 11, 2006).

Great Lakes Vessels Index: Historical Collections of the Great Lakes. http://digin.bgsu.edu/lakes.htm (accessed between November 14 and December 12, 2005).

Greenwood, John D. *The Fleet Historic Series, Volume 7*. Cleveland, Ohio: Freshwater Press, 1999.

Griffith, Becca. "Sieur du Lhut." http://rhet5662.class.umn.edu/heroes/sieur.html#THE (accessed October 3, 2001).

Gruentzel, Robert. *Descendants of Joseph O-Saw-Gee*. Delafield, Wisc.: Publisher and date unknown.

Hacker, Louis M. *The World of Andrew Carnegie, 1865-1901*. Philadelphia and New York: J. B. Lippincott, 1968.

Harnish, Sue, et. al. *Mission Creek Nature Trail*. Duluth, Minn.: Junior League of Duluth, 1975.

History of Buildings and Building Associations of Superior, Wisconsin, 1871-1899. Superior, Wisc.: WPA Project #11068, publication date unknown.

History of Clubs and Lodges of Superior and Douglas County, Dec., 1860-March, 1900. Superior: WPA Project #10117, 1940.

History of the State Normal School of Superior, Wisconsin. Superior, Wisc.: WPA Project #11068, publication date unknown.

Holden, Thomas. *Duluth's Aerial Lift Bridges*. http://www.duluthshippingnews.com/aerialliftbridge.htm. (accessed December 27, 2005).

Hertzel, Laurie, ed. *Boomtown Landmarks*. Duluth, Minn.: Pfeifer-Hamilton Publishers, 1992.

"Islands of History." *Apostle Islands National Lakeshore Web site*. http://www.nps.gov/apis/history.htm (accessed January 16, 2006).

Koop, Michael and Morris, Chris. *Historic Resources of Downtown Duluth, Minnesota, 1872-1933*. Washington, D.C.: U.S. Department of the Interior, 2005.

Kimball, Gerald M., editor. *Duluth's Legacy: Volume 1, Architecture*. Duluth: City of Duluth, 1974.

"Lakewood Pumping Station Nomination" National Register of Historic Places. On file at State Historic Preservation Office, Minnesota Historical Society, St Paul, Minn., 197).

Lamppa, Marvin G. *Minnesota's Iron Country: Rich Ore, Rich Lives*. Duluth, Minn.: Lake Superior Port Cities, 2004.

Lapinski, Patrick. "Saga of the Interstate Bridge." *North Star Port*. Duluth, Minn.: Duluth Seaway Port Authority, 2004.

"Launching the Quint Fleet." Duluth Seaway Port Authority Web site. http://www.duluthport.com/pride/quints.html (accessed January 13, 2006).

Lenihan, Daniel J. *Shipwrecks of Isle Royale National Park*. Duluth, Minn.: Lake Superior Port Cities, 1987.

Lundgren, Paul and Brad Nelson and Heidi Bakk-Hansen, eds. *Ripsaw Online*. http://www.ripsawnews.com (accessed January 7, 2002).

Lydecker, Ryck and Lawrence J. Sommer, eds. *Duluth: Sketches of the Past, a Bicentennial Collection*. Duluth, Minn.: American Revolution Bicentennial Commission, 1976.

MacDonald, Dora Mary. *This is Duluth*. Duluth, Minn.: published by the author, 1950.

Mack, Stanley L. *Ionic Lodge No 186 A F & A F of Duluth, Minnesota*. Duluth, Minn.: Steele-Lounsberry, 1940.

"Mansions on Oregon Creek." http://www.mansionsonoregoncreek.com/duluth-Minn (accessed January 9, 2006).

Meronek, Teddie and Unterberger. "Superior Business Improvement District Historical Walking Tour." First published 1997.

Minnesota Historical Society. *Minnesota Historical Society Web site*. http://www.mnhs.org (accessed periodically from October 2005 to January 2006).

Minnesota Naval Military. Duluth, Minn.: St. Louis County Historical Society, publication date unknown.

Morgan Park/Smithville Community Club 1994 Calendar. Duluth, Minn.: Morgan Park/Smithville Community Club, 1994.

Nash, Anedith and Robert Silberman. *Morgan Park: Continuity and Change in a Company Town*. Publisher unknown, 1992.

Neis, Stefano. "A Brief History of Postcard Types." http://www.geocities.com/Heartland/Meadows/2487/pchistory.htm (accessed November 24, 2005).

"Northern League Teams 1902–present." *National League History Web site*. http://www.snake.net/nl/hist/nlteams.html (accessed January 2, 2006).

"Northland Country Club Story, The." Typed manuscript from the Duluth Public Library archives. Author and publisher unknown.

Ogland, James W. *Picturing Lake Minnetonka: a Postcard History*. Afton, Minn.: Minnesota Historical Society Press, 2001.

Oleszewski, Wes. *Great Lakes Lighthouses: American and Canadian*. Gwinn, Mich.: Avery Color Studios Inc., 1998.

Olsenius, Richard. *Minnesota Travel Companion*. Minneapolis, Minn.: University of Minnesota Press, 1982.

"Once Upon a Time in Lester Park." *St. Louis Historical Society Newsletter*. Summer, 2001.

Pepper, Terry. "North Pier Lighthouse." *Seeing the Light Web site*. http://www.terrypepper.com/lights/superior/duluth-n-pier/duluth-n-pier.htm (accessed December 17, 2005).

Perich, Shawn. *The North Shore: a Four-Season Guide to Minnesota's Favorite Destination*. Pfeifer-Hamilton Publishers, Duluth, Minn.: 1992.

Powell, Mrs. Thomas. *Congdon Creek Park*. Duluth, Minn.: Junior League of Duluth, publication date unknown.

Raff, Willis H. *Pioneers in the Wilderness*. Grand Marais, Minn.: Cook County Historical Society, 1981.

Roberts, Bruce and Jones, Ray. *American Lighthouses: A Comprehensive Guide*. Old Saybrook, Conn.: The Globe Pequot Press, 1998.

Rogg, Christopher. *A Brief History of Duluth From the 1500s to 1870*. http://www.police.ci. duluth.mnus/policesite/duluth.asp (accessed October 4, 2005).

Ruplry, George. "Isle Royale, Enchanted Isle." *Christian Science Monitor*. June 10, 1931.

Ryan, J. C. "Buzz." *Early Loggers in Minnesota, Volume I*. Duluth, Minn.: Minnesota Timber Producer's Association, 1973.

——. *Early Loggers in Minnesota, Volume II*. Duluth, Minn.: Minnesota Timber Producer's Association, 1976.

Ryan, Mark. *The History of Seven Bridges Road*. http://www.amitycreek.com/seven-bridges (accessed January 4, 2006).

——*The History of Skyline Boulevard*. http://www.amitycreek.com/sevenbridges/sky-line1.html (accessed January 4, 2006).

Sanborn Fire Insurance Maps: City of Duluth. Pelham, New York: Sanborn Map Company, 1883-1941.

Sandvick, Glenn N. *Duluth: An Illustrated History of the Zenith City*. Woodland Hills, Calif.: Windsor Publications, 1983.

Scott, James Allen. *Duluth's Legacy: Volume 1, Architecture*. Duluth, Minn.: City of Duluth, 1974.

"Short, Ancient, and Recent History of the Diocese of Superior." *Diocese of Superior Web site*. http://www.catholicdos.org/history.htm (accessed January 15, 2006).

"Silver Cliff Billy Goat." *North Shore Commercial Fishing Web Site*. http://www.commercialfishingmuseum.org/newsletters.htm (accessed January 17, 2006).

Stonehouse, Frederick. *Lighthouse Keepers and Coast Guard Cutters*. Gwinn, Mich.: Avery Color Studios, Inc., 2000.

——. *Haunted Lakes*. Duluth, Minn.: Lake Superior Port Cities, Inc., 1997.

Study of the St. Louis River Basin. Duluth, Minn.: The League of Women Voters, 1958.

Superior East High School History, 1924-1965. Superior, Wisc.: publisher and publication date unknown.

"Superior History." *Superior Memories Web site*. http://hofferstudio.com/superiormemories/id1.html (accessed January 15, 2006).

"That Ride Up the Hillside." *Duluthian*. Vol. 9, No. 1, January–February 1973.

Thomas, Thomas R. "Duluth's Aerial Lift Bridge." *Duluth Shipping News*. http://www.duluthshippingnews.com/aerialliftbridge.htm (accessed December 26, 2005).

Tierney, Carol. *Chester Creek Nature Trail*. Duluth, Minn.: Junior League of Duluth, 1974.

"Timeline History of the Wisconsin Central Railway." *History of the Soo Line Web site*. http://www.kohlin.com/soo/wc-hist.htm (accessed January 15, 2006).

Two Harbors, 100 Years: A Pictorial History of Two Harbors, Minnesota and Surrounding Communities. Two Harbors: Two Harbors Centennial Commission, 1983.

Upham, Warren. *Minnesota Geographic Names (reprint edition)*. Minneapolis: Ross & Haines Company, 1970.

Van Brunt, Walter. *Duluth and St Louis County, Minnesota: Their Story and People, Volumes 1, 2, and 3*. Chicago and New York: The American Historical Society, 1921.

"Wade Stadium, Duluth, Minn." *Minor League Parks Web site*. http://www.minor-leagueballparks.com/wade_mn.html (accessed January 2, 2006).

Weber, C. J. *The Catholic Church in Superior, Wisconsin*. Superior, Wisc.: Telegram Job Dept., 1905.

Wilbur, W. R. *A History of Douglas County Wisconsin*. Superior, Wisc.: Douglas County Historical Society, publication date unknown.

Wilson, Bonnie G. *Minnesota in the Mail*. Afton, Minn.: Minnesota Historical Society Press, 2004.

Wilyterding, John H. *McDougall's Dream: the American Whaleback*. Duluth, Minn.: Lakeside Publications, 1969.

Wisconsin Department of Natural Resources Web site. http://www.dner.state.us/org/land/parks (accessed January 18, 2005).

Woodbridge, Dwight E., and Pardee, John S. *History of Duluth and St Louis County*. Chicago: C. F. Cooper & Company, 1910.

Yukon Beringia Interpretive Center. "Giant Beaver." http://www.beringia.com/02/02main6. html (accessed November 24, 2005).

Newspapers

Duluth Daily News	*Saturday Evening Call*	*Superior Times*
Duluth Herald	*Superior Daily Call*	*Wisconsin Sunday Times*
Duluth News-Tribune	*Superior Daily Leader*	
The Truth	*Superior Evening Telegram*	

Image Credits

Nearly all of the postcard images presented in this book come from cards collected by Jerry Paulson; additional cards were provided by Bob Swanfeld, Tom Kasper, Teddie Meronek, Maryanne Norton, Mildred Nimmo, the Superior Public Library, the Lake Superior Maritime Collection, and the author.

Non-postcard Images:

American Fur Company Trading Post at Fond du Lac (page 5) watercolor by James Otto Lewis, originally appeared in *Sketches of a Tour of the Lakes* by Thomas L. McKenney, published in Baltimore, 1827; courtesy of the American Philosophical Society.

Daniel Greysolon Sieur du Lhut at Little Portage (page iv) painting by Clarence Rozenkranz; courtesy of the Duluth Public Library.

Daniel Greysolon Sieur Du Lhut at Saint-Germain-Laval, France (page 4) painting by David Ericson; courtesy of the Duluth Public Library.

Duluth at the Head of Lake Superior (page 8) etching from the *Harper's Weekly Supplement*, April 29, 1871; courtesy of Maryanne Norton.

Duluth, 1871 (page 9) painting by Albert Bierstadt; courtesy of the Duluth Public Library.

Duluth, 1871 (page 10) painting by Gilbert Munger; courtesy of the Duluth Public Library.

Duluth, 1871 (page 11) bird's-eye map by E. Chrisman; courtesy of the Minnesota Historical Society.

Duluth, Minn. 1883 (page 13) bird's-eye etching by Henry Wellge; from the author's collection.

Duluth, Minn. 1887 (page 14) bird's-eye etching by Henry Wellge; from the author's collection.

Duluth 1909 (pages 16-17) color bird's-eye etching of Duluth and Superior by Henry Wellge; courtesy of the Lake Superior Maritime Collection.

Fitger's Brewing Company (page 79) etching of corporate letterhead c. 19__; courtesy of Scott Vesterstein.

Jay Cooke (page 7) photograph originally appeared in *Jay Cooke: Financier of the Civil War* by Ellis Paxson Oberholter, published in Philadelphia by George W. Jacobs & Co., 1907; courtesy of the Duluth Public Library; sepia toning by the author.

Lac Tracy 1671 (page 2) map by an anonymous Jesuit cartographer (possibly Father Claude Jean Allouez or someone traveling with him); courtesy of the Illinois State Museum. Tinted by the author.

Lacrosse Playing Among Sioux Indians, 1857 (page 1) painting by Seth Eastman; courtesy of the Duluth Public Library.

Ojibwe Maple Syrup Camp (page 2) watercolor, artist unknown; courtesy of the Duluth Public Library.

Ojibwe Women (page 2) painting by Eastman Johnson; courtesy of the Duluth Public Library.

Paris Beau Beaver Fur Hat (page 3) from *Castorologia, Or, The History and Traditions of the Canadian Beaver: An Exhaustive Monograph* by Horace T. Martin, published by W. Drysdale & E. Stanford, London and Montreal, 1892; background added by the author.

Sam Snively (page 18) painting, artist unknown; courtesy of Mark Ryan. The painting has since become part of the collection of the St. Louis County Historical Society.

Superior, Wis. 1883 (page 12) bird's-eye etching by Henry Wellge; from the author's collection.

Treaty of La Pointe, 1856 (page 6) painting, artist unknown; courtesy of the Duluth Public Library.

Whaleback Christopher Columbus (page 15) from *American Steam Vessels* by Samuel Ward, published by Smith & Stanton, New York, 1895.

Greetings from the Zenith City!

If you enjoyed *Zenith: A Postcard Perspective of Historic Duluth*,
then you'll also enjoy both volumes of our *Greetings from Duluth* books,
each of which features twenty reproduction postcards that can be removed for mailing.

We also have forty postcard images available as framed and matted postcard-size prints
as well as four poster-sized art prints of the *Greetings* books' most popular postcards
(and we can make any of the postcards in Zenith available as custom images).

Zenith is also available in a limited-run, slip-cased hard-cover edition sold exclusively through the publisher.

For more information please visit us online at www.x–communication.org
or at our offices in Duluth's historic Garfield News Building.